*Trees of Northern Florida*

Herman Kurz &

with the collaboration of

*Kenneth E. Wagner*

Robert K. Godfrey

# TREES of Northern Florida

**University Press of Florida**

Gainesville  Tallahassee  Tampa  Boca Raton
Pensacola  Orlando  Miami  Jacksonville

00  99  98  97  96  95  94  13  12  11  10  9  8

ISBN 0-8130-0666-X

Library of Congress Catalogue Card No. 62-17479

The University Press of Florida is the scholarly publishing agency for
the State University System of Florida, comprised of Florida A & M
University, Florida Atlantic University, Florida International University,
Florida State University, University of Central Florida, University of
Florida, University of North Florida, University of South Florida, and
University of West Florida.

University Press of Florida
15 Northwest 15th Street
Gainesville, FL 32611

# Foreword

AS DELIMITED by the authors of *Trees of Northern Florida*, Herman Kurz and Robert K. Godfrey, with the collaboration of Kenneth E. Wagner, northern Florida is that portion of the state north and northwest of a line drawn from the Atlantic Ocean through Marion County to the Gulf of Mexico—an area extending from the Atlantic Ocean westward to the Perdido River. Within this area, more than half the tree species native in the state are found. Besides these, a few introduced kinds that have become feral are added. The scenic beauty of the region is enhanced greatly by the abundant tree growth. Trees cover large stretches of level lands, add height to low hills and undulations, trim the margins of ponds and lakes, and beautify the banks of slow-moving streams and rivers. They are the principal component of the rural landscape.

Attention should be called to a number of small trees—dogwood, mountain-laurel, redbud, crab-apple, myrtle-leaved holly, sparkleberry, wax-myrtle, silverbell, and Pinckneya—found in the woodlands of the northern region. They are noteworthy for their beauty of flower or fruit or foliage. They grace the streets and gardens of urban areas in the section and have extended their appeal to many towns far away.

Mention too can be made of others that grow into noble trees—pines, oaks, magnolias, ash, maple, and cypress. Some of these shade and grace the landscapes of towns and cities that would be bare indeed were the trees removed.

In the latter part of the nineteenth century, northern Florida became the location of tremendous lumbering industries. Sawmills, some of them geared to cut thousands of board feet daily, were located at various strategic points within the region. There were great areas of slash and longleaf pine forests. There were forests of hardwoods of many kinds. Highways were built by which to reach them, and railroads were constructed to bring logs to the devouring mills. By the middle of the twentieth century the virgin forests were cut out. But lumber industries still persist. Pulp mills have taken the places of sawmills; crops of poles, pulpwood, ties, and posts have replaced the timber of the earlier period. Many acres are planted annually with millions of pine seedlings. These when sufficiently grown will support the lumbering industries of future years. Northern Florida will always be a great area for the production of tree crops.

*Trees of Northern Florida* opens the door to an understanding of the trees of the region and will increase the beauty and value of them for those who read it.  It is entitled to wide usage as a source of knowledge of the trees of a great section of the state.

H. HAROLD HUME

*Gainesville, Florida*                       *Provost Emeritus for Agriculture*
*October 15, 1962*                          *University of Florida*

# Acknowledgments

MANY PERSONS have rendered assistance to the authors in ways which cannot readily be enumerated. We express here our sincere appreciation to everyone who has helped us. We are especially grateful to the following: the late Mr. Ernest J. Palmer, Arnold Arboretum, Harvard University, retired, for providing the keys and descriptions of *Crataegus* and for critical aid in certain problems with *Tilia, Fraxinus,* and *Quercus;* the late Dr. Carleton Ball, U.S. Department of Agriculture, for help in identification of *Salix;* Professor Cornelius H. Muller, Santa Barbara College, University of California, for suggestions concerning certain species of *Quercus.* The senior author expresses his thanks to Dr. Roland M. Harper, University of Alabama, who did much to help him learn the tree flora during his early years in the north Florida woods.

Helpful suggestions, in conference or by means of correspondence, were given by the following botanists: Miss Lillian E. Arnold, University of Florida, retired; Professor Wilbur H. Duncan, University of Georgia; Professor Clair A. Brown, Louisiana State University; Professor Ellwood S. Harrar, Duke University; Dr. Albert E. Radford, University of North Carolina; Professor Aaron J. Sharp, University of Tennessee; Professor Henry R. Totten, University of North Carolina; and Professor Erdman West, University of Florida. To each of these persons we express our thanks.

Although the aid and suggestions of other investigators is gratefully acknowledged, full responsibility for the final treatment is the authors'.

We are most appreciative of the courtesy of curators of herbaria at the following institutions from which specimens were lent or distributional records were furnished: Arnold Arboretum, Harvard University; Ashe Herbarium, University of North Carolina; University of Georgia; New York Botanical Garden; North Carolina State College; University of Florida; University of Tennessee; United States National Herbarium, Smithsonian Institution.

For much assistance in making field collections and in the preservation of herbarium specimens we are indebted to Mr. William H. Cross, former graduate student, The Florida State University.

Most of the delineations were done by Miss Mary Livingston; those of *Fraxinus* and *Tilia* jointly by Miss Livingston and Mr. William H. Cross; those of *Crataegus* by Mr. Cross. Dr. Robert Kral generously contributed a number of drawings. The title page and cover designs are by Mr. Grady W. Reinert.

We wish particularly to express our gratitude to Professor Erdman West, University of Florida, for critically reading the manuscript and for his excellent advice and suggestions.

It is a pleasure to acknowledge the generous support given by the College of Arts and Sciences, The Florida State University, throughout the preparation of this book. Assistance in the herbarium was made possible by two grants-in-aid by the Research Council of The Florida State University.

During the final years of preparation of this book, Mr. Godfrey was at the same time engaged in field studies of aquatic and marsh plants. For this, funds were provided him by the National Science Foundation (NSF G-4321) and by the Division of General Medical Studies, Public Health Service (RG-6305). Field trips incidental to the aquatic and marsh studies provided further opportunity for us to study trees and to obtain information about their distribution. This is gratefully acknowledged.

H. K. and R. K. G.

*The Florida State University*
*January, 1962*

# *Contents*

# Introduction

## SCOPE

THE NORTH FLORIDA LANDSCAPE is blanketed by an arboreal tapestry of exceeding interest and beauty. The composition and design of the tapestry derive from a great diversity of kinds of trees and shrubs, from their presence in very large numbers, and from their association in recurring vegetational patterns. The fine network of highways and waterways of the region makes it possible for the traveller to gain a panoramic view of the forests and permits of easy access for an opportunity to come into intimate contact with the trees which comprise them. For anyone with an interest in natural history, our woodlands are ideal and fascinating areas in which to explore and study. In a single day's exploration along the Apalachicola River and its adjacent hills and valleys, for example, one may encounter about a hundred different species of trees, to say nothing of the shrubs and herbs associated with them.

The trees included in this book are those kinds which are native to northern Florida and those which have been introduced into cultivation and have become established as wild.

Northern Florida as a geographical area of coverage is, of course, completely arbitrary and delimitation of the range necessitates only the setting of a southern boundary, the other boundaries being fixed. A line roughly from the Atlantic Coast through the Ocala National Forest, Marion County, thence across and through the Gulf Hammock, Levy County, to the Gulf Coast approximates the southern boundary. This is as nearly natural a line of division as can be fixed between the warm temperate areas of which northern Florida is a part and the more subtropical areas of central peninsular and southern Florida.

Although for practical purposes the area of coverage is thus specifically restricted, it is nevertheless true that the trees herein described will include nearly all those which occur in the southern parts of Georgia, Alabama, and Mississippi.

## TREE FLORA

The abundance of arboreal species in our range is in large part due to an interrelationship between a great diversity of topographic features, soils, and moisture conditions, and to the warm temperate climate.

Along both the Atlantic and Gulf coasts, dunes of raw shifting sands and older stabilized dunes exposed to differing concentrations of airborne salt spray constitute habitats in which special vegetation types develop. The exposed, raw shifting sands near the coastal waters and under the impact of the greatest amount of salt spray are clothed with a dense clipped scrub which slants upward and landward. Older, more stabilized, humus-laden sands at greater distance from the water, which are subject to spray with lesser concentration of salt, support hammocks of larger and different trees.

Inland from the coasts and more or less paralleling them are extensive areas of relatively low, flat, sandy terrain. Although this is, in general, somewhat elevated above the drainage pattern, the surface sands are fine and are underlain by hardpan. Thus, they are poorly drained and the water table fluctuates markedly in relation to periods of high or low rainfall. The tree flora of these areas is principally slash pine or longleaf pine and the areas are known as pine flatwoods. Throughout the flatwoods are depressions of various sizes, still more poorly drained, forming cypress ponds and swamps, or pond pine-titi flatwoods or bays. Other large, flat or slightly undulating areas are underlain by deposits of Tampa and Ocala limestone. In general, these support a relatively dense stand of mixed hardwoods, commonly accompanied by scattered cabbage palmetto trees.

In various parts of northern Florida are rolling hills of deep, relatively coarse, well-drained sand or sand-clay. In general, where the surface sand of these hills is white, the arboreal covering is largely a mixture of sand pine and evergreen scrub oaks; where the surface soils are buff-colored sand or sand-clay, the arboreal covering is longleaf pine and summer-green (deciduous) oaks. The ravines and small valleys dissecting the sand hills support a variety of trees and shrubs, mostly evergreens. These are referred to as branch-swamps or branch-bays.

From about Leon County westward, mostly across the northern part of the Panhandle of Florida, are extensive areas where the elevations range from 200 to 300 feet. This is sufficient general elevation for the land to have been dissected into well-defined hills and valleys, especially in the vicinity of major rivers and their tributary streams. The soils have been derived from a variety of geological formations but they are more fertile and loamy than elsewhere. Along the large rivers, such as the Apalachicola and Escambia, there are fairly high and steep bluffs, occasional cliffs, tributary ravines, and the hills between them. The river channels are accompanied by a great variety of sand bars, banks, natural levees, and broad floodplains in which are oxbow depressions and ponds. This diversity of physiographic features, combined with fertile loamy soils or limestone outcrops, provides a range of habitats suitable to the requirements of a large number of the species. For example, the uplands, slopes, ravines, and bluffs of the Apalachicola River in Gadsden and Liberty counties expose several geological formations, differing according to locality and elevation. The rich tree flora of this particular region, including such endemics as the Florida torreya and Florida yew, is probably a result of its present diversity of relief features and the variety of geological formations. The Tallahassee Red Hills, characterized by a great variety of upland hardwoods, have a fertile loamy soil derived from the Hawthorn formation. In the redlands of Jackson County, particularly at the Marianna Caverns State Park, Marianna limestone outcrops abundantly. Here abounds a rich upland hardwoods flora, somewhat dissimilar to that of the Tallahassee Red Hills, and containing numerous shrubs and herbs otherwise absent in Florida but more common in similar areas northward.

In northern Florida ample rainfall and high humidity are factors which favor the presence of many kinds of trees. Moreover, winter temperatures are mild enough, on the one hand, for essentially southern trees such as southern magnolia, live oak, water oak, laurel oak, Florida maple, sweetbay, and cabbage palmetto. Winter temperatures are rigorous enough, on the other hand, so that some northern species flourish—white and black oaks, American elm, black walnut, flowering dogwood, white ash, and yellow-poplar, to name but a few.

## TREE DIMENSIONS

In describing woody plants, it is common practice to distinguish between trees and shrubs. By and large there prevails in the minds of persons who deal even casually with plants a fairly reasonable concept as to what is a tree and what is a shrub. Any attempt, however, to make definite delimiting statements as to one or the other involves considerable difficulty. At best one must be arbitrary; even then variability of growth form is such as to demand some flexibility in the exercise of judgment. Moreover, individuals of a given species may unquestionably reach tree stature in some habitats, not in others. Some species characteristically produce several trunks from near the ground, each of which attains tree dimensions, yet, in general, we use the single-trunk versus several-trunk character to distinguish trees from shrubs.

The criteria by which we reckon a plant as of tree stature are in close agreement with those of other students of trees. A tree is a woody plant with a single erect trunk which branches above the ground to form one more or less definite crown. The following are minimum dimensions: a diameter of 3 inches at breast height (4½ feet from the ground) and an over-all height of 12 feet.

In our general statements concerning size normally reached by any given kind of tree, we refer to them as small, medium, or large. This again is arbitrary and has but limited usefulness in a comparative way. The three size classes are as follows:

Small _____12—50 feet high_____3—12 inches d.b.h.°
Medium___51--80 feet high _____1—3 feet d.b.h.
Large_____81 or more feet high ___more than 3 feet d.b.h.

Such a system of referring to size has its limitations. A live oak tree, for example, may have a very large, short trunk and a low, massive crown. We refer to such trees as large.

## TREE NAMES

Every kind (species) of tree (or other plant) known to plant science has a technical or scientific name. This is a Latin or Latinized name consisting of two words. The first is the name of the genus to which a given species belongs and begins with a capital letter; the second is an adjectival word, the specific epithet, which is not capitalized. The two-word name is, then, the species name or the scientific name and a species cannot correctly be referred to by either the generic name or the specific epithet separately. In addition, in scientific literature the double species name is followed by the name (or names) or a standard abbreviation of the name (or names) of the person (or persons) who originally named the species. For example, the species name of the American elm is *Ulmus americana* Linnaeus. Other kinds (species) of elm also belong to the genus *Ulmus*, but each has a different specific epithet so that the species name of each is a different double name. The Latin species name of winged elm is *Ulmus alata* Michaux. Thus, the generic name shows relationship; the specific epithet in combination with it designates a single kind. No two kinds of plants (by international agreement of botanists) can have the same binary, or double, Latin name. This helps provide for stability and world-wide standardization of nomenclature. Since Latin is universally accepted as the technical language of scholars where international understanding is re-

° d.b.h. is trunk diameter at breast height.

quired (it being an unchanging language), the Latinization of plant names contributes to stability and standardization also.

Common or vernacular names (in English or any other modern language) for a species of plant have a very limited, often very local, usefulness. An English common name, even though standardized, has meaning only to English-speaking people. The same is true for common names in any modern spoken language. Not uncommonly, common names are utterly bewildering. In the range of this book, "ironwood," as a common name, is applied to no less than six different species belonging to five different genera. Similarly, several common names may be used for the same species. In our range, *Magnolia grandiflora* L. has at least six vernacular names: magnolia, southern magnolia, loblolly magnolia, evergreen magnolia, bullbay, and laurel. There are five species of Magnolia in northern Florida. For precision in referring to a species by name, there is no satisfactory substitute for the Latin scientific name.

## SOURCES OF DATA

The data which contributed to the identification, descriptions, illustrations, and ranges of the trees included in this book were largely obtained firsthand by the authors. Field observations and collections were made throughout the area of coverage. In numerous instances this involved a large and detailed sampling, observations over a period of several years, or repeated visits to the same places.

The keys and descriptions are adapted exclusively to the species and species populations as they occur in northern Florida. Graduate students and other interested persons have helped greatly, particularly in obtaining specimens from various parts of large trees, so that ranges of variation on individual specimens could be studied.

In the identification and interpretation of particularly puzzling problems we relied heavily, of course, upon various publications dealing with eastern American trees. The treatment of the species of north Florida trees as here presented represents what we think is the best practical aid that can be devised to help interested persons to know them.

## TREE IDENTIFICATION

The greater the number of kinds of trees included in a manual the more difficult is the preparation of a guide to their identification. There are many relatively simple distinguishing characteristics which can be employed, but with a number of species as large as that in this book, it is necessary to resort to and rely heavily on technical botanical language.

The technical descriptive terms used in the keys and descriptions are defined in the Glossary. Some of those which are used very often, or which lend themselves to ease of portrayal, are illustrated.

In addition to the aids mentioned in the preceding paragraph, there are some particularly helpful distinguishing characteristics, hints, and "crutches" upon which we rely. These are used in the keys and descriptions, but attention is called to them here as a matter of emphasis.

Flowers and fruits are important in yielding characters useful to a thorough knowledge of trees and are often extremely helpful in identification. In many instances, however, they are available but a short time during any season. Fruits, more often than flowers, tend to persist on the plant for longer intervals, sometimes even over winter or into the next season. Commonly, they may be found on the ground under the trees which bore them. In cases where the flowers or fruits are particularly useful they are emphasized in the keys and descriptions.

Leaves are more often present on trees for longer periods than either flowers or fruits and much of the character of a given kind of tree is imparted by foliar characteristics, twig and bark characteristics, leaf arrangement, and branching habit. This has led us, as is true for most authors of tree books, to put much emphasis on vegetative characteristics.

The leaves of many kinds of trees are remarkably uniform for the species. It is true, though, that in numerous species there is a remarkable variability in leaf character from tree to tree or even on different parts of the same tree. Attention is called to this in particular cases and a student must of necessity learn to expect it and to deal with it. In general, it is wise, especially for one just beginning to study trees, to collect specimens or make observations from leaves of fertile branches (those mature enough to bear flowers and fruit). Leaves of saplings, or of especially vigorous shoots, or of sucker shoots often vary enormously in size and form from those of fertile branches. Cognizance of such variation is, of course, necessary to a complete understanding of a species in which it occurs, but such variation, poorly understood, may be confusing or misleading to the novice.

The senses of smell, taste, or even touch, in combination with other relatively simple characters, offer means of learning the identity of certain trees. Sassafras, sweetbay, camphor, and others exude distinctive fragrances from the crushed leaves. Leaves of the sweetleaf tree taste sweet, especially the tissues around the larger veins; those of sourwood have a distinctly sour taste; and those of prickly-ash are unpleasantly astringent. With respect to the touch sense, closely related species sometimes have leaves which are markedly different to touch. The American elm, for example, has leaves whose upper surfaces are essentially smooth; those of the red elm are notably rough-sandpapery.

CAUTION: DO NOT RESORT TO THE CONTACT METHOD TO IDENTIFY SMALL TREES WITH HICKORY-LIKE, ALTERNATE, PINNATELY COMPOUND LEAVES. THIS COULD BE THE DANGEROUS POISON SUMAC, WHICH IS MORE SAFELY IDENTIFIED AT A DISTANCE.

In a few kinds of trees, where internodes are short and leaves close together, it is difficult to ascertain whether the leaf arrangement is opposite or alternate. The branching pattern reflects leaf arrangement since branch buds occur in leaf axils. Therefore, trees with alternately arranged leaves display an alternate branching pattern; those with oppositely arranged leaves and whorled leaves display an opposite or whorled branch pattern, respectively. Exceptions to the latter two would occur where branch buds failed to develop though the leaf scars help to ascertain leaf arrangement.

Bark pattern, texture, and form are not so easily described as leaves or flowers. For some trees, bark is strikingly characteristic for a species and can readily be described. The bark of most trees has a specific character which, taken together with other features, can be of great diagnostic value. This comes largely with experience and has much more significance as one gains more general familiarity with trees.

The evergreen versus the deciduous habit is of great significance in tree description. To one who knows trees well throughout the seasons, it is a great temptation to use these two terms as key characters. However, it is nearly impossible to express in simple language any pat phrases which will enable an inexperienced person to distinguish between evergreen and deciduous trees during the growing season. We have, therefore, sparingly used the terms evergreen and deciduous in the keys.

A student of trees ordinarily learns quickly to develop an awareness of the general surroundings in which a given kind of tree normally occurs. What is the general nature of the habitat? What are the tree associates? Answers to questions such as these eventually teach one much about trees other than what they look like. For example, river birch, water hickory, and sycamore are to be sought in floodplain woodlands, sand live oak and sand pine in dune or scrub, cypress and water tupelo in swamps.

## PLATE I

LEAF SHAPES:

1. subulate
2. linear
3. lanceolate
4. oblanceolate
5. oblong
6. elliptical
7. ovate
8. obovate
9. deltoid
10. rhombic
11. cuneate
12. suborbicular

LEAF APICES:

13. acuminate
14. acute
15. obtuse
16. rounded
17. truncate
18. cuspidate
19. mucronate

LEAF BASES:

20. acute
21. obtuse
22. rounded
23. oblique
24. auriculate
25. truncate
26. cordate

# PLATE I

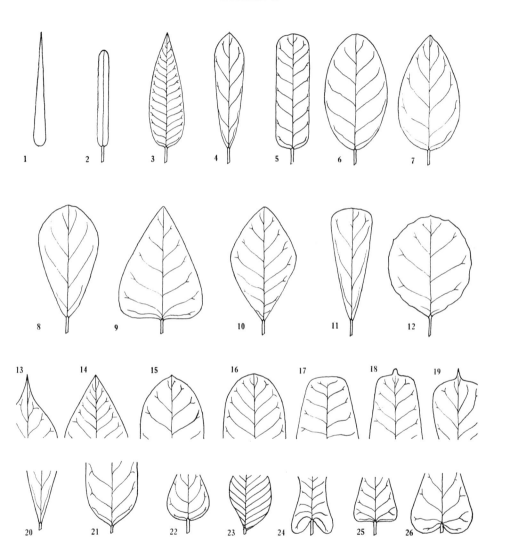

# PLATE II

LEAF MARGINS:

    1. entire
    2. undulate
    3. crenate
    4. dentate
    5. serrate
    6. double-serrate
    7. crenulate

LEAF FORMS:

    8. simple, palmately-veined and lobed
    9. simple, pinnately-veined and parted
   10. simple, pinnately-veined and lobed
   11. palmately compound, the leaflets pinnately-veined
   12. pinnately compound, the leaflets pinnately-veined

INFLORESCENCE TYPES:

   13. globular head
   14. catkin
   15. spike
   16. raceme
   17. panicle
   18. cyme
   19. corymb
   20. umbel

PLATE II

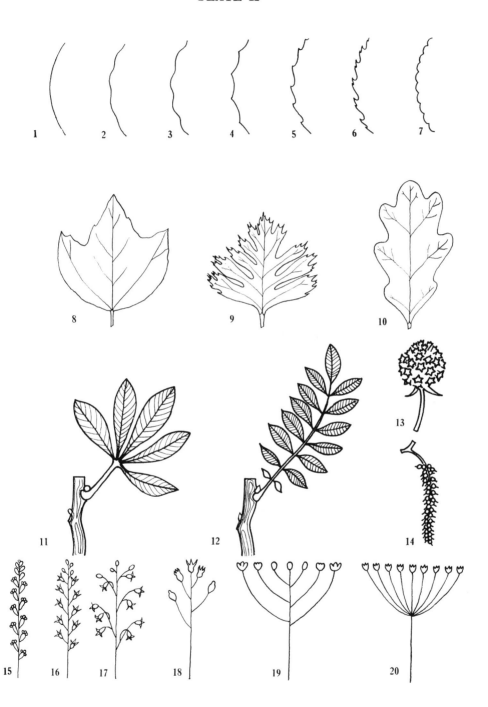

## PLATE III

PORTIONS OF TWIG WITH

    1. axillary thorns
    2. stipules at petiolar bases
    3. stipular ring scars
    4. accessory bud on either side of axillary bud
    5. superimposed buds

ILLUSTRATING

    6. bristle-tipped lobes of oak leaf
    7. female flower of oak
    8. cross-sectional diagram of acorn with pubescent inner surface
    9. leafy twig with epigynous fruits, the withered calyx remains at their summits
   10. conspicuous bract of *Tilia* bearing immature fruiting inflorescence

SAMARAS OF

   11. *Fraxinus*
   12. *Acer*
   13. *Halesia*

# PLATE III

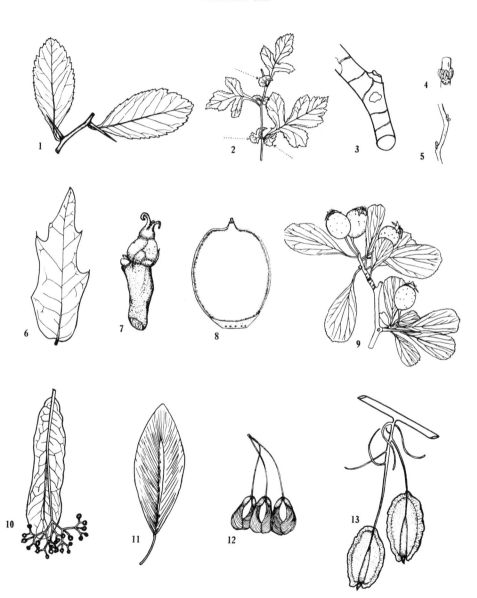

# Key to the Genera

A. GYMNOSPERMS: Leaves needle-like, scale-like, or awl-shaped.

  1. Leaves long needle-like, borne 2, 3, or 4 in a cluster with a sheath at the base................................................................*PINUS* (p. 4)

  1. Leaves linear, linear-lanceolate, scale-like, or awl-shaped, not borne in sheathed clusters.

    2. Branchlets bearing opposite or whorled, closely appressed, tiny scale-like or awl-shaped leaves.

      3. Twigs flattened as viewed in cross-section...................... .........................................................*CHAMAECYPARIS* (p. 20)

      3. Twigs quadrangular as viewed in cross-section.......... ....................................................................*JUNIPERUS* (p. 21)

    2. Branchlets bearing alternate, linear, linear-lanceolate, or awl-shaped leaves, the leaf stalks often twisted so that the leaves are borne more or less in one plane.

      4. Leaves ½ inch long or less, light green; trees of swamps or other wet habitats .................................*TAXODIUM* (p. 16)

      4. Leaves ¾ inch long or more, dark green; trees of mesic woodlands of bluffs or ravines.

        5. The leaves with pungent, resinous odor, stiff, the tips sharp, stiff-pointed, and piercing to touch.............. ............................................................*TORREYA* (p. 2)

        5. The leaves scarcely odorous, soft and flexible, the tips pointed but not sharp....................................*TAXUS* (p. 1)

A. ANGIOSPERMS: Leaves with expanded blades, not needle-like, or scale-like.

  B. MONOCOTYLEDON: Leaves very large, the petioles 6—7 feet long, the blades 4—7 feet long, parallel-veined; stem unbranched ......................................................................*SABAL* (p. 23)

  B. DICOTYLEDONS: Leaves various, but not as above, netted-veined; stems branched.

## KEY TO GROUPS OF DICOTYLEDONS

1. Leaves simple.

  2. The leaves arranged oppositely, 2 at a node, or in whorls of 3 - 4 at a node..............................................GROUP I (p. xxvi)

  2. The leaves alternately arranged.....................GROUP II (p. xxvii)

1. Leaves compound............................................GROUP III (p. xxxii)

GROUP I. Trees with simple leaves arranged oppositely or in whorls.
1. Leaves lobed.
  2. Blades of the leaves on any given plant variable, some unlobed, some 2-, 3-, 4-, or 5-lobed; sap viscid or milky............................. ...................................................................................*BROUSSONETIA* (p. 115)
  2. Blades of the leaves uniformly 3–5-lobed; sap not viscid or milky...........................................................................*ACER* (p. 217)
1. Leaves unlobed.
  3. The opposite petioles connected by stipules or stipular line-scars.
    4. Flowers and fruits individually small, borne in dense, long-peduncled globose heads; sepals minute and remaining so ........................................................................*CEPHALANTHUS* (p. 285)
    4. Flowers and fruits borne in terminal cymose clusters; some of the sepals forming greatly enlarged, conspicuous, creamy to pink petal-like structures so that the inflorescence is markedly showy; individual fruits globose to ovoid capsules about ¾ inch in diameter....................................*PINCKNEYA* (p. 286)
  3. The opposite petioles without connecting stipules or stipular line-scars.
    5. Leaves whorled or both opposite and whorled, broadly ovate, both surfaces velvety-pubescent...................*CATALPA* (p. 283)
    5. Leaves all opposite, not broadly ovate, neither surface velvety-pubescent.
      6. Buds, petioles, and twigs more or less scurfy-pubescent ...................................................................*VIBURNUM* (p. 288)
      6. Buds, petioles, and twigs glabrous, or pubescent but not scurfy.
        7. Leaves thick-leathery, persistent..*OSMANTHUS* (p. 282)
        7. Leaves membranous, deciduous.
          8. Lateral veins of the leaves prominent and strongly curved upward; flowers and fruits borne in terminal cymes or tight, involucrate heads; torn leaves exposing cobweb-like vascular strands................... ......................................................*CORNUS* (p. 246)
          8. Lateral veins curving very gradually; flowers and fruits in terminal panicles, or short lateral clusters; torn leaves not exposing cobweb-like vascular strands.
            9. Leaves entire, oblong-lanceolate or oval, mostly 4–6 inches long and 2–3 inches broad, their apices rounded to acute; flowers and fruits in large terminal panicles...............*CHIONANTHUS* (p. 272)
            9. Leaves serrate from the middle upwards, ovate or rhombic-ovate, 1½–3 inches long and up to 1 inch broad, their apices strongly acuminate; flowers and fruits in short lateral clusters........... ......................................................*FORESTIERA* (p. 274)

GROUP II.  Trees with simple leaves alternately arranged.

1. Leaves as broad as long, very nearly so, or even broader than long.
   2. Petioles with a pair of conspicuous red glands on the upper side at their summits and just below the bases of the leaf blades ...................................................................................*ALEURITES* (p. 188)
   2. Petioles not having glands as above.
      3. Sap viscid or milky.
         4. Leaves velvety below...................*BROUSSONETIA* (p. 115)
         4. Leaves not velvety below.........................*MORUS* (p. 118)
      3. Sap not viscid or milky.
         5. The petioles swollen (with pulvini) at their bases and at their summits..................................................*CERCIS* (p. 176)
         5. The petioles not swollen (without pulvini) at their summits or at their bases.
            6. Leaves uniformly 5-lobed, the 5 acute lobes giving the blade much the effect of a star...................................
            ...................................................*LIQUIDAMBAR* (p. 143)
            6. Leaves unlobed, or if lobed not at all star-like.
               7. Leaves 2-ranked on the stems; flowers and fruits borne in cymes attached to elongate, membranous wing-like bracts.............................*TILIA* (p. 229)
               7. Leaves not 2-ranked; flowers and fruits not in cymes attached to membranous wings.
                  8. Stipular line-scars present as rings all the way around the stem at the nodes of the younger branchlets.
                     9. Leaves 4–6-lobed, the margins otherwise entire, the leaf apices truncate or broadly V-notched; fruits terminately winged; samaras borne in erect cones...................................
                     ...................................*LIRIODENDRON* (p. 121)
                     9. Leaves coarsely and irregularly toothed and commonly 3–5-lobed, the apices of the lobes pointed; fruits small nutlets borne in large numbers in dangling globular balls........
                     .............................................*PLATANUS* (p. 144)
                  8. Stipular scars present but these not continuous as a ring all the way around the stem at the nodes of the younger branchlets.
                    10. Leaves pinnately-veined, never lobed; buds gummy or viscid-varnished.....................
                    .............................................*POPULUS* (p. 24)
                    10. Leaves palmately-veined and 3–5-lobed; buds brown-velvety.................*FIRMIANA* (p. 240)
1. Leaves markedly longer than broad.

11. Buds conspicuously clustered at or near the ends of the twigs; fruit a nut (acorn) borne in a cup of imbricated scales....*QUERCUS* (p. 62)
11. Buds not clustered at or near the ends of the twigs; fruit not an acorn borne in a cup.
  12. Stipular scars present as a line all the way around the stem of younger branchlets.
    13. Buds clothed by numerous overlapping scales; leaves 2-ranked; principal lateral veins of the leaf running straight and parallel to the leaf margin.....................*FAGUS* (p. 60)
    13. Buds covered by spathe-like structures (stipules); leaves more than 2-ranked; principal lateral veins of the leaf not running straight and parallel to the leaf margin...........
      ..............................................................*MAGNOLIA* (p. 123)
  12. Stipular scars, if present, not as a line all the way around the stem.
    14. Foliage and/or twigs notably aromatic when crushed or broken.
      15. Leaves with yellowish callus-like growths in the principal vein angles on the upper leaf surfaces.........
        ...........................................*CINNAMOMUM* (p. 134)
      15. Leaves without callosities in the vein angles.
        16. Leaves irregularly serrate on their upper margins, the blades punctate with resinous dots...........
          ...........................................*MYRICA* (p. 32)
        16. Leaves entire, or if lobed the margins otherwise entire.
          17. Midribs and principal lateral veins of the leaves prominent.
            18. Leaves all unlobed.
              19. The leaves persistent, leathery, broadest at or below their middles, pith not diaphragmed....*PERSEA* (p. 136)
              19. The leaves deciduous, membranous, broadest above their middles, pith diaphragmed.......*ASIMINA* (p. 132)
            18. Leaves variable on a given plant, some unlobed, others 2-lobed and mitten-like, or 3-lobed.................*SASSAFRAS* (p. 140)
          17. Midribs of the leaves prominent but the lateral veins not or scarcely evident............
            ...........................................*ILLICIUM* (p. 131)
    14. Foliage and/or twigs not markedly aromatic.
      20. Trees with thorns or spines.
        21. Sap of leaves and twigs milky.
          22. Spur-shoots present; some thorns naked, others leafy.................*BUMELIA* (p. 257)

22. Spur-shoots absent; all thorns naked....*MACLURA* (p. 117)
21. Sap of leaves and twigs not milky.
    23. Thorns naked.............................*CRATAEGUS* (p. 148)
    23. Thorns bearing leaves, bracts, or leaf scars.
        24. Leaves evenly serrate; spur-shoots absent; stipule scars present on the twigs, the stipules, before being shed, attached to the twigs; fruit a 1-seeded drupe, with no remnants of the calyx or stamens persisting.................................*PRUNUS* (p. 166)
        24. Leaves unevenly serrate; spur-shoots present; stipule scars absent on the twigs, the stipules, before being shed, borne on the petiole bases; fruit a pome with seeds surrounded by papery tissue and with remnants of sepals and stamens persisting at the summit of the fruit......*MALUS* (p. 164)
20. Trees not thorny or spiny.
    25. Sap milky or viscid.
        26. Leaves velvety below................*BROUSSONETIA* (p. 115)
        26. Leaves not velvety below.............................*MORUS* (p. 118)
    25. Sap not milky or viscid.
        27. Leaves 2-3-ranked.
            28. The leaves 2-ranked.
                29. Margins of the leaves double-serrate, sometimes unequally so.
                    30. Bark exfoliating in large papery-curled scales.................................................*BETULA* (p. 52)
                    30. Bark smoothish to ridged and grooved, or exfoliating in irregular scales or shreds but not in large papery-curled scales.
                        31. Fruits (usually present throughout the summer) subtended by foliaceous bracts or enclosed in sac-like bracts.
                            32. Bark blue-gray, tight and smoothish, trunks fluted or ridged; fruit subtended by a foliaceous bract......
                            ............................*CARPINUS* (p. 54)
                            32. Bark brownish or tan, shreddy; trunk not fluted or ridged; fruit enclosed by sac-like bracts.............
                            ............................*OSTRYA* (p. 54)
                        31. Fruits not usually present by the time the leaves are fully developed.
                            33. Leaf blades mostly asymmetrical, lanceolate to oblong, or if ovate neither rhombic or deltoid........
                            ............................*ULMUS* (p. 109)

      33. Leaf blades symmetrical, rhombic-ovate to del-
toid-ovate................................*PLANERA* (p. 107)
  29. Leaf margins entire or toothed but not double-serrate.
    34. Pith of twigs chambered at nodes......*CELTIS* (p. 105)
    34. Pith of the twigs not chambered at the nodes.
      35. Lateral veins of the leaf blades nearly straight,
parallel, extending to blade margin.
        36. Leaves very asymmetric, their margins wavy
or coarsely crenate-undulate with broad
rounded teeth; buds stalked, mitten-like
............................*HAMAMELIS* (p. 142)
        36. Leaves symmetric or nearly so, their margins
almost entire to finely crenate-dentate or crenate-serrate; buds scaly, slender, symmetrical
..................................*FAGUS* (p. 60)
      35. Lateral veins of the leaf blades arching-ascend-
ing, not reaching the leaf margins...............
.....................................*STEWARTIA* (p. 243)
  28. The leaves 3-ranked...............................*ALNUS* (p. 52)
27. Leaves more than 3-ranked.
  37. Lateral veins of the leaves uniform, running conspicuously
parallel toward the leaf margins and ending at the margin or
in the marginal teeth.
    38. Leaves prominently toothed, the teeth tipped by a mucro,
the lateral veins ending in the teeth; fruit a nut enclosed by
a bristly bur...............................*CASTANEA* (p. 57)
    38. Leaves entire or obscurely toothed, the teeth, if any, not
tipped by a mucro; fruit a berry-like drupe...............
............................................*RHAMNUS* (p. 228)
  37. Lateral veins of the leaves, even if prominent, not running conspicuously parallel from the mid-ribs to the leaf margins.
    39. Lateral buds superimposed; stipules or stipule scars absent.
      40. The lateral superimposed buds contiguous, the upper-
most triangular in outline; fruit 2-4 winged, indehiscent.............................*HALESIA* (p. 262)
      40. The upper two lateral superimposed buds spaced apart,
the uppermost thumb-like; fruit globose, about half
enclosed by the floral tube, not winged, dehiscent by
2-4 valves............................*STYRAX* (p. 267)
    39. Lateral buds borne singly, or if superimposed, then stipules
or stipule scars present.
      41. The lateral veins of the leaf (as seen with a 10× lens)
appressed to the midribs for a short distance......
.......................................*AMELANCHIER* (p. 146)
      41. The lateral veins not appressed to the midribs.
        42. Stipules or stipule scars present.

43. Leaves elongate-lanceolate, very long tapering from near their bases *or* broadly oval or oblong, whitish and hairy below; buds covered by a single scale............*SALIX* (p. 26)
43. Leaves variously shaped but not as above; buds with several scales.
    44. Leaves broadly deltoid-ovate or cordate-ovate; twigs roughened by large 3-lobed leaf scars......................
    --------------------------------------------------------*POPULUS* (p. 24)
    44. Leaves not broadly ovate; twigs not roughened by large, 3-lobed leaf scars.
        45. Vascular bundle scar 1 in each leaf scar.........
        ----------------------------------------------*ILEX* (p. 200)
        45. Vascular bundle scars 3 in each leaf scar.
            46. Spur shoots present; stipule scars absent on the twigs, the stipules, before being shed, borne on the petiole bases; fruit a pome with seeds surrounded by papery tissue and with remnants of the sepals and stamens persisting at its summit...............................*MALUS* (p. 164)
            46. Spur shoots absent; stipule scars present on the twigs, the stipules, before being shed, attached to the twigs; fruit a 1-seeded drupe with no remnants of sepals and stamens persisting...............................*PRUNUS* (p. 166)
42. Stipules or stipule scars not present.
    47. Lateral veins of the leaves conspicuously curved-ascending from the midribs; leaves when torn exposing cobweb-like vascular strands...............................*CORNUS* (p. 246)
    47. Lateral veins of the leaves not as above; leaves when torn not exposing cobweb-like vascular strands.
        48. Leaves scaly pubescent, markedly so below...........
        ------------------------------------------------*LYONIA* (p. 252)
        48. Leaves not scaly pubescent.
            49. Leaves entire *or* with few and irregularly spaced teeth.
                50. The leaves thickish, leathery, and evidently persistent.
                    51. Leaf surfaces, or at least the lower, pubescent.................*SYMPLOCOS* (p. 270)
                    51. Leaf surfaces glabrous.
                        52. Leaves short-elliptical, short-oval, or sub-orbicular, not exceeding 1½-1¾ inches long....*VACCINIUM* (p. 255)
                        52. Leaves oval *or* elliptical and mostly exceeding 2 inches in length, or oblanceolate.

53. Surfaces of the leaves glandular-punctate......
.................................................................*MYRICA* (p. 32)
53. Surfaces of the leaves not glandular-punctate.
    54. Flowers and fruits (one or the other can usu-
        ally be seen at nearly all times) in panicled
        corymbs, the flower or fruit stalks about 1
        inch long....................................*KALMIA* (p. 251)
    54. Flowers and fruits in racemes, the flower or
        fruit stalks not exceeding ¼ inch long.
        55. The network of lateral veins of the leaves
            quite evident.............*CYRILLA* (p. 197)
        55. The network of lateral veins of the leaves
            not evident.............*CLIFTONIA* (p. 195)
50. The leaves membranous and evidently deciduous.
    56. Leaves commonly marked by *black* spots or blemishes,
    glabrous and whitish below; growth in length of stems from
    axillary buds owing to abortion of the terminal buds
    ........................................................*DIOSPYROS* (p. 260)
    56. Leaves not blemished or sometimes spotted with *dark-
    maroon* spots, whitish and hairy *or* pale-green *or* hairy and
    conspicuously net-veined below; growth in length of stems
    from terminal buds.
        57. Leaf venation very conspicuous, the principal lateral
        veins prominent and with a fine but conspicuous vein
        network between them, this visible from either surface
        ..........................................................*LEITNERIA* (p. 35)
        57. Leaf venation not markedly conspicuous, the principal
        lateral veins, if prominent, not having a conspicuous
        vein network between them.................*NYSSA* (p. 233)
49. Leaves regularly toothed.
    58. Leaves leathery, persistent, not sour to taste, their margins ap-
    pressed-serrate....................................*GORDONIA* (p. 242)
    58. Leaves membranous, deciduous, sour to taste, their margins
    serrulate....................................*OXYDENDRUM* (p. 254)

GROUP III.   Trees with compound leaves.
1. The leaves digitately 3-foliolate, or palmately compound.
    2. Leaves mostly alternate, digitately 3-foliolate, musky-aromatic
    when crushed; fruit winged, nearly orbicular.....*PTELEA* (p. 182)
    2. Leaves opposite, palmately 5-7-foliolate, not aromatic; fruit a
    leathery 3-valved capsule...............................*AESCULUS* (p. 225)
1. The leaves 1-several times pinnately compound.
    3. Leaves once-pinnately compound.
        4. The leaves opposite.
            5. Buds enclosed by the bases of the petioles; leaf scars en-
            circling the stems....................................*ACER* (p. 217)

   5. Buds in the axils of the petioles; leaf scars not encircling
      the stems...................................................*FRAXINUS* (p. 275)
4. The leaves alternate.
   6. Stems bearing thorns or spines.
      7. Leaves even-pinnate (with a pair of terminal leaflets);
         stems bearing simple or branched, elongate thorns........
         ................................................................*GLEDITSIA* (p. 177)
      7. Leaves odd-pinnate (with one terminal leaflet); stem bear-
         ing short spines or prickles.
         8. Leaflets asymmetrical, with acute or acuminate apices,
            the stems and often the leaf rachi bearing short, sharp
            spines or prickles...................*ZANTHOXYLUM* (p. 183)
         8. Leaflets symmetrical, rounded, obtuse or emarginate
            and with a short mucro at their apices; rachi of the
            leaves spineless; stipular spines commonly present on
            either side of the petiole bases or leaf scars...........
            ........................................................*ROBINIA* (p. 181)
   6. Stems not bearing thorns or spines.
      9. Margins of the leaflets entire.
         10. Lateral buds superimposed........*SAPINDUS* (p. 227)
         10. Lateral buds solitary in the leaf axils or axils of the
            leaf scars (Beware the poison sumac!)....*RHUS* (p. 190)
      9. Margins of the leaflets toothed.
         11. Foliage aromatic when bruised.
            12. Aroma of bruised foliage unpleasant, musky; leaflet
               margins glandular-toothed....*AILANTHUS* (p. 184)
            12. Aroma of bruised foliage pungent, not unpleasant.
               13. Terminal leaflets much reduced or aborted
                  so that most leaves appear even-pinnate; pith
                  transversely partitioned; husk of fruit inde-
                  hiscent, nut rough corrugated........
                  ................................................*JUGLANS* (p. 36)
               13. Terminal leaflet well-developed, the leaves all
                  odd-pinnate; pith not partitioned; husk of
                  fruit dehiscent; surface of the nut smooth....
                  ................................................*CARYA* (p. 38)
         11. Foliage not aromatic when bruised........*RHUS* (p. 190)
3. Leaves 2–several times compound.
   14. Stems bearing thorns or prickles.
      15. Leaves even-pinnate (the terminal leaflets paired), spineless;
         stem bearing simple or branched elongate thorns...........
         ................................................................*GLEDITSIA* (p. 177)
      15. Leaves odd-pinnate (the terminal leaflets solitary), bearing
         spines on petioles and rachi; stem bearing short, stout, sharp
         prickles................................................*ARALIA* (p. 245)
   14. Stems not bearing thorns or prickles.

16. Leaves even-pinnate (the terminal leaflets paired); ultimate leaflets tiny, entire, asymmetrical (each leaflet seemingly a half-leaflet); fruit a legume.................................................._ALBIZZIA_ (p. 174)
16. Leaves odd-pinnate (the terminal leaflets solitary); ultimate leaflets relatively large, prominently toothed and/or lobed, symmetrical; fruit a globular berry........................... .................._MELIA_ (p. 186)

# Taxonomic Treatment

## TAXACEAE.  YEW FAMILY

1. Leaves scarcely odorous, soft and flexible, the tips pointed but not stiff or piercing to the touch; seed partially surrounded by a red fleshy cup, the seed and cup about ¾ inch long and ⅓ inch in diameter..................................................................Taxus
1. Leaves with a pungent, resinous odor, stiff, the tips very sharp, stiff-pointed and piercing to touch; seed olive-like, completely enclosed in a fleshy tissue, about 1 inch long and ¾ inch in diameter...........................................................Torreya

### Taxus

#### 1.  Taxus floridana Nutt.  Florida yew

This is an evergreen, bushy shrub or small tree, not usually exceeding 25 feet in height.  The bark is purplish-brown, sloughing in thin plates, the twigs green and flexible.

The leaves are glabrous, flat, linear, somewhat falcate, flexible, their tips pointed but not sharp to the touch, mostly ¾ - 1 inch long and ⅟₁₂ - ⅟₁₆ inch broad.  They are spirally arranged but the petioles twist so that the leaves appear in one plane or form a V-shaped trough on either side of the twigs.  Leaves are dark green above, the lower surfaces light green and with a grayish longitudinal stripe on either side of the midribs.  The twigs and foliage are faintly aromatic when crushed.

The plants are mostly dioecious.  Male cones are globular, having 4 - 8 scales and bearing 5 - 8 anther sacs per scale.  The female cone consists of an axis with several small sterile scales below and an uppermost cuplike aril which grows up around the ovule at the tip of the axis.  The mature cone, which ripens in September or early October, consists of a single seed virtually surrounded by a fleshy, translucent, red, cuplike aril.

The Florida yew is of very limited distribution, occurring only in Gadsden and Liberty counties, Florida.  It inhabits shady, moist, wooded slopes and ravines along the eastern side of the Apalachicola River and a boggy *Chamaecyparis* swamp about 8 miles southeast of Bristol, Liberty County (Kurz, 1927).  This and the Florida torreya or gopher-wood tree (*Torreya taxifolia*) are endemic in the same general area, but the Florida yew is much rarer.

*Taxus floridana* and *Torreya taxifolia* are similar.  The former is much less aromatic and its leaves are relatively soft and flexible, the tips

1

pointed but not sharp and piercing to the touch.   The latter has a strongly pungent, resinous odor, particularly when crushed, and its leaves are stiff, their tips sharp-pointed and piercing to the touch.

x ¾

Fig. 1.   *Taxus floridana*

## TORREYA

### 1. **Torreya taxifolia** Arn.   Florida torreya; gopherwood-tree; stinking-cedar

This is a small tree with whorled branches and a conical crown.   The bark is thin, shallowly fissured, sloughing in shreds, the twigs green and stiff.

The leaves are glabrous, narrowly linear-lanceolate, somewhat scythe-shaped, stiff, their tips sharp and piercing to the touch, mostly 1 - 1½ inches long and ⅛ inch broad.   They are spirally arranged but the petioles twist so that the leaves spread in one plane on either side of the twigs. Leaves are bright glossy-green above, their lower surfaces lighter green and with grayish longitudinal stripes paralleling the midribs on each side. The leaves and twigs have a strongly pungent, resinous odor, particularly when crushed. The odor tends to become disagreeable to one exposed to it for very long.

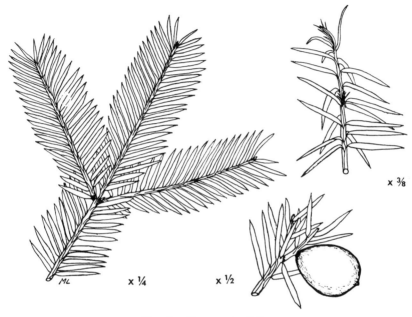

Fig. 2.  *Torreya taxifolia*

The plants are dioecious. The staminate cones are small, globular-ovate, each scale bearing 4 pollen sacs. The female cone is much reduced and matures into a single, fleshy, drupelike seed about 1 - 1¼ inches long and ¾ - 1 inch in diameter. At maturity, the seeds are dark green with purple stripes and are coated with a whitish bloom. They mature in summer.

The Florida torreya is of a very limited distribution, occurring on wooded slopes and in wooded ravines of the hill country along the east side of the Apalachicola River in Gadsden and Liberty counties, Florida, and in closely adjacent Georgia. In addition, there is one small colony at Dog Pond in Jackson County, Florida, west of the Apalachicola River (Chapman, 1885; Kurz, 1938).

*Torreya taxifolia* is unlikely to be mistaken for any tree other than *Taxus floridana*. (See the latter for comparative features.)

# PINACEAE. PINE FAMILY

## Pinus. Pines

The pines are evergreen, cone-bearing trees with resinous wood and needle-like foliage leaves. Young trees, or older trees growing widely spaced, tend to develop symmetrically conical crowns with one vertical leading shoot. The lateral branches are quite secondary and more or less horizontal, ascending, or the lowermost drooping. As the trees of a stand grow, the crowns close forming a canopy and the lower branches slough off, the cleared trunks becoming correspondingly longer and the individual crowns smaller. Eventually, in most of our species, the uppermost branches develop at random intervals, the leading shoot losing its identity and the various crown branches growing crookedly. Thus, an old pine usually has a long, clear trunk and an irregularly rounded or variously lobed crown.

The twigs bear leaves of two kinds: appressed, persistent, spirally arranged scales that quickly become brown, and elongate needle-like foliage leaves. The needles are borne in fascicles, terminally attached to dwarf branches (spurs) and are enveloped at their bases by papery or leathery sheaths. The spurs arise in the axils of the scalelike leaves. In our species, the needles occur 2 - 4 in a fascicle. The needles, and the spur on which they are borne, are eventually shed together. In cross-section, the needles are round, semicircular, or angular, the latter having 2 plane faces and 1 rounded face.

The plants are monoecious. Male cones are borne in late winter or early spring in clusters at the tips of the preceding year's branches. They are elongate-cylindric, mostly dangling, and consist of numerous spirally arranged stamens. The staminate cones wither after the pollen is shed. Female cones are borne on newly emerging shoots just forward of the cluster of staminate cones. They consist of closely imbricate, soft, spirally arranged scales, each scale bearing 2 ovules. After pollination, the ovulate cones become hard and woody. They mature by autumn of the second growing season at which time the scales may separate, releasing winged seeds. The opened cones persist on the trees for varying lengths of time. In some species, the ovulate cones may persist for many years, even unopened.

The several species of pine have ovulate cones of different sizes and shapes. It is to be borne in mind that shapes or measurements for any given species will differ according to whether the cones are open or closed. After having once opened, they tend to remain so during dry weather, but may close during periods of rainy weather.

1. Needles in fascicles of 3, or sometimes in *P. serotina* 3 *and* 4.
    2. Terminal buds silvery white; cones mostly over 6 inches long................
    ..........................................................................................................5. *P. palustris*
    2. Terminal buds rusty-brown to chestnut-brown; cones mostly less than 6 inches long.
        3. Ovulate cones elongated, conic-ovoid, rarely remaining closed; needles 4 - 10 (mostly 7 - 9) inches long................................................7. *P. taeda*
        3. Ovulate cones subglobose to short-ovoid, frequently remaining closed; needles 4 - 8 (mostly 5½ - 6½) inches long..............................6. *P. serotina*
1. Needles in fascicles of 2, or in *P. elliottii* and *P. echinata* 2 *and* 3.
    4. Branchlets, below the needles, rough-scaly or flaky.
        5. Needles 5 - 11 (mostly 8 - 10) inches long; ovulate cones 3 - 6 (mostly 6) inches long................................................................3. *P. elliottii*
        5. Needles 2 - 5 inches long; ovulate cones 1½ - 3 inches long....2. *P. echinata*
    4. Branchlets below the needles smooth, rarely scaly.
        6. Scales of young flowering ovulate cones ovate-acute thence narrowed into slender, straight, slightly spreading tips; anthers dark orange-colored; scale faces of mature cones thickened and conspicuously transversely keeled, each bearing a dark umbo with a short, stout, straight or incurved spine; mature cones frequently remaining closed several years; trees of white sand ridges or hills, associated with evergreen scrub oaks...............
        .........................................................................................1. *P. clausa*
        6. Scales of young flowering ovulate cones broadly ovate thence narrowed into short, straight, slightly spreading tips; anthers yellow-colored; scale faces of mature cones slightly thickened and inconspicuously transversely keeled, each bearing a dark, flattened umbo with a small straight or incurved spine; mature cones seldom if ever remaining closed; trees of fertile soils, associated with mixed hardwoods..............................4. *P. glabra*

## 1. **Pinus clausa** (Chapm.) Vasey. Sand pine

The sand pine is a small to medium-sized tree. It usually grows in relatively open stands and the crowns tend to remain symmetrically conical, lateral branches persisting low on the trunks. The bark of small trunks is tan or brownish and smooth. Even the bark of large trunks is relatively smooth.

The needles are 2 - 4½ inches long and are borne in fascicles of two. The fascicle sheaths are ⅛ to ³⁄₁₆ inch long. The twigs are smooth and slender and much branched.

The anthers of the staminate flowers are dark orange-colored. The scales of the young flowering ovulate cones are ovate-acute thence narrowed into slender, straight, slightly spreading tips. The mature cones are 2 - 4 inches long and usually persist on the tree for many years, open and/or unopened. The cones are stalked but as the branches grow in diameter, they grow around the stalks and bases of the cones; thus on older branches, the cones appear sessile. Unopened cones are elongate-ovoid and the open cones are broad-ovoid. The faces of the cone scales are thickened and conspicuously transversely keeled, each one bearing a dark umbo with a short, stout, straight or incurved spine.

In northern Florida, the sand pine is common near the Atlantic and

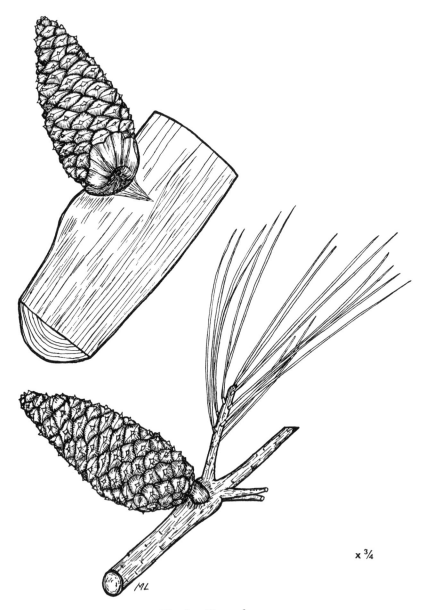

x ¾

Fig. 3. *Pinus clausa*

Gulf coasts on hills and ridges of white sand and in the interior wherever there are white sand ridges and hills. In these places it is associated with the evergreen oaks.

*Pinus clausa* and *P. glabra* are similar in that each has needles in bundles of two. Both differ from our other pines in having smooth bark on their smaller trunks and branches.

The ovulate cones of *P. clausa* remain on the trees so long that the cones bases become embedded in the branches and sometimes in the trunk tissue. This situation does not occur in *P. glabra*. The scales of the ovulate cones of *P. clausa* have stout, sharp spines; those of *P. glabra* have weak spines or none at all. The latter species occurs in mixed hardwood forests on fertile, moist sites; *P. clausa* occurs on white sandy hills and ridges together with evergreen scrub oaks. For a comparison to pond pine, see *P. serotina*.

## 2. **Pinus echinata** Mill. Shortleaf pine

Perhaps the most notable feature of older trees of shortleaf pine is the bark of the trunks. It forms distinctive flat, broad, heavy reddish-brown plates of fairly uniform, more or less rectangular shape. The bark of the twigs is rough and scaly.

The needles are 2 - 5 inches long and occur in fascicles of 2 and 3. The fascicle sheaths are ⅔₆ - ⅗₆ inch long. The twigs are rough-scaly or rough-flaky. A given tree has needles which are fairly uniform in length but there is a marked range of length of needles from tree to tree, more so than in any other species of pine in our area.

The ovulate cones are 1½ - 3 inches long and usually remain on the tree for at least 2 or 3 years. The unopened cones are ovoid-oblong, narrowly conic, or subcylindric while open cones are ovoid. The faces of the cone scales are only slightly thickened and transversely keeled, each with a small oblong, elongated umbo with a short, straight, slightly recurved, frequently deciduous spine.

From about the Aucilla River westward to Okaloosa County in northern Florida, the shortleaf pine invades fertile, upland old fields (often together with the loblolly pine) where even-aged stands are eventually produced. These are ultimately invaded and overtaken by hardwoods (and commonly some *Pinus glabra*) so that old trees may persist, if uncut, as relic trees in mixed hardwood stands on fertile uplands.

Trees of *Pinus echinata* and *P. glabra* are superficially somewhat similar and may occur in the same mixed hardwood forest. In such cases, trees of the former species, at least, are old and exhibit the distinctive bark character mentioned above—that is, the trunk bark breaks up into large, more or less rectangular, broad, reddish-brown plates. More-over, the bark of branches and twigs is reddish-brown and rough-scaly or flaky. The trunk bark of *P. glabra* becomes dull dark gray, is closely ridged and furrowed, or has small, thin, flat plates. The bark of its smaller trunks and branches is dark gray and smooth. *P. echinata* has needles in fascicles of 2 and 3, whereas *P. glabra* has its needles always in clusters of 2. For a comparison to loblolly pine, see *P. taeda*.

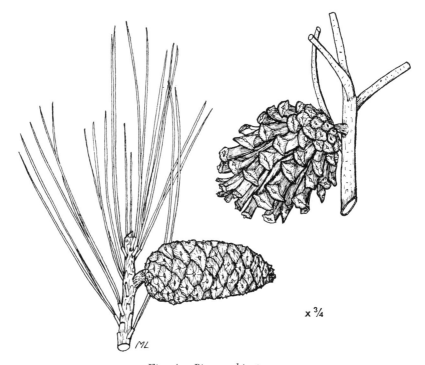

x ¾

Fig. 4. *Pinus echinata*

### 3. **Pinus elliottii** Engelm.    Slash pine

The slash pine is a medium-sized tree with bark that breaks up into fairly large, flat plates. Its twigs are roughened with spreading scales and bear large "brooms" of ascending needles.

The needles are 5 - 11 (mostly 8 - 10) inches long and are borne in fascicles of 2 and 3. The fascicle sheaths are ⅜ - ⅝ inch long. The twigs are rough and stout, usually about ¼ - ½ inch in diameter, ex-clusive of the scale leaves.

The ovulate cones are 3 - 6 (mostly 6) inches long and usually fall from the tree by the end of the second year. When unopen, the cones

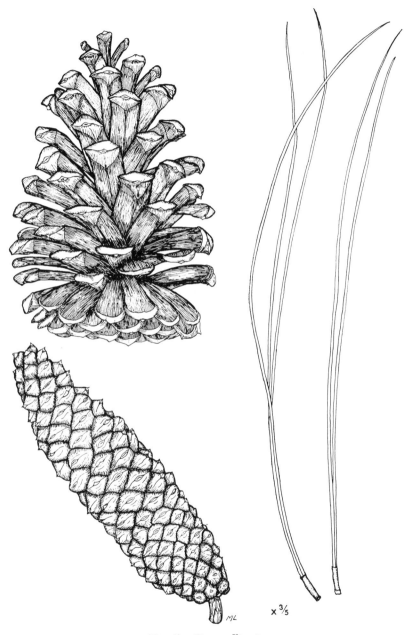

Fig. 5. *Pinus elliottii*

x ³/₅

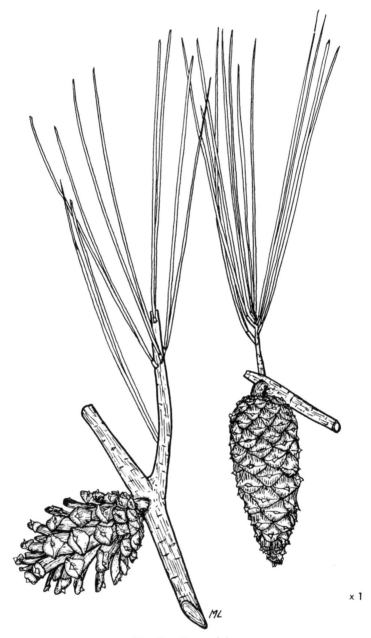

x 1

Fig. 6. *Pinus glabra*

are elongate, ovoid-conic and when open, ovoid-conic. The faces of the cone scales are lustrous tan, transversely keeled, and each has an elongated umbo bearing a small recurved spine (incurved on basal scales).

In our area, the slash pine is the pine most frequently planted in reforestation. Aside from its wide occurrence in plantations, it occurs naturally in wet flatwoods, branch-swamps, areas bordering shallow ponds, and along lagoons and bays near the coasts.

*Pinus elliottii* and *P. taeda* occasionally occur together. They may be easily distinguished in that *P. taeda* has needles in threes and sessile ovulate cones 2 - 5 (mostly 4 - 5) inches long. *P. elliottii* has needles in twos *and* threes and stalked ovulate cones 3 - 6 (mostly 6) inches long. For a comparison to longleaf pine, see *P. palustris*.

### 4. **Pinus glabra** Walt. Spruce pine

This pine has relatively short needles and the leafy twigs are commonly short. The bark on young trunks or small branches is smooth and dark gray. On older trunks, the bark is closely ridged and furrowed, producing small, thin, flat plates. These characteristics are suggestive of spruce, hence the popular name, spruce pine.

The needles are 2 - 4 inches long and occur in fascicles of 2. The fascicle sheaths are ⁹⁄₁₆ - ⁴⁄₁₆ inch long. The twigs are smooth, usually ashy-grey and slender.

The anthers of the staminate flowers are yellow. The scales of young flowering ovulate cones are broadly ovate thence narrowed into short, straight, slightly spreading tips. The mature cones are 2 - 4 inches long and remain on the tree for 3 - 4 years. The unopen cones are ovoid and the open cones are conic-ovoid. The faces of the cone scales are slightly thickened and inconspicuously transversely keeled, each bearing a dark, flattened umbo with a small straight or incurved spine.

The spruce pine occurs mostly as scattered individuals amongst mixed hardwoods of rich woodlands and hammocks, or bottomland woods, from Alachua County northward and westward in northern Florida. It is the most shade-tolerant of our pines and is associated with *Carya glabra, Liquidambar styraciflua, Nyssa sylvatica, Fagus grandifolia,* and *Magnolia grandiflora.*

For comparative features, see *Pinus clausa* and *P. echinata.*

### 5. **Pinus palustris** Mill. Longleaf pine

*P. australis* Michx. f.

The longleaf pine is a large tree having grayish-brown or reddish-brown bark that breaks up into large, thin, irregular scales. Its terminal buds are silvery-white in contrast to the brownish buds of the other pines of our area.

The needles are 8 - 18 inches long and are borne in fascicles of three.

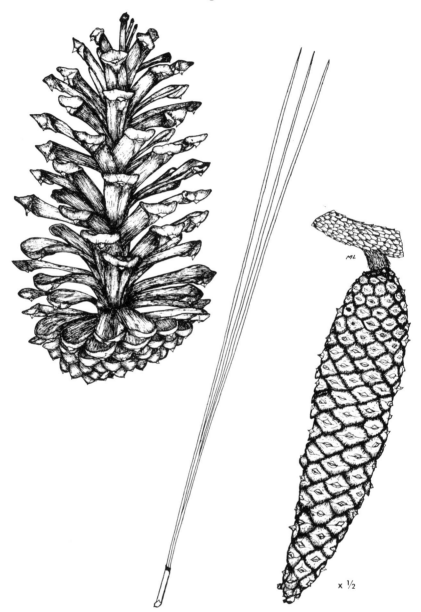

Fig. 7.   *Pinus palustris*

The fascicle sheaths are usually over ½ inch long. The twigs are rough and very stout, usually ½ inch or more in diameter, exclusive of the spirally crowded and spreading scale-leaves. Large spreading tufts of long needles fan out at the ends of the branches.

The ovulate cones are 5 - 10 inches long and usually fall by the end of the second year. When unopen, the cones are long and narrowly cylindric-conic and when open, they are long ovoid. The faces of the cone scales are prominently transversely keeled, each with a dark umbo bearing a small reflexed spine.

The longleaf pine is of common occurrence in northern Florida in flatwoods and in company with the deciduous scrub oaks on sand ridges.

*Pinus palustris* and *P. elliottii* may occur together. They may be easily distinguished, though, for *P. palustris* has needles in threes, silvery-white terminal buds, and ovulate cones 5 - 10 inches long. *P. elliottii* has needles in twos *and* threes, rusty-silver terminal buds, and ovulate cones 3 - 6 inches long. For a comparison to the loblolly pine, see *P. taeda.*

### 6. **Pinus serotina** Michx.    Pond pine

The pond pine is a medium-sized tree with dark gray or reddish-brown bark that forms narrow, irregular, thin, vertical plates. Its crown branches tend to be irregular, crooked, and gnarly, often conspicuously so. A characteristic and distinctive feature of the pond pine is the formation of tufts of twigs and foliage from the trunks, principal branches, or bases of trunks, particularly after fire injury.

The needles are 4 - 8 (mostly 5½ - 6½) inches long, and occur in fascicles of 3 or sometimes 3 *and* 4. The fascicle sheaths are ¼ - ⅜ inch long. The twigs are rough-scaly and somewhat slender.

The ovulate cones are 2 - 3 inches long and usually remain on the tree for several years, sometimes as long as twelve years, at least. The cones are stalked but as the branches increase in diameter, the bases of the cones become imbedded in the tissue and thus give an appearance of being sessile. Unopen cones are subglobose to short-ovoid and frequently remain unopen for several years (a condition that also occurs with the sand pine, *P. clausa*), while open cones are short, conic-ovoid. The faces of the cone scales are transversely keeled and each has a slightly darkened, elongated umbo bearing a sharp incurved, often deciduous spine.

The pond pine inhabits poorly drained sites that have a markedly fluctuating water table and that are subject to frequent fires.

*Pinus serotina* and *P. clausa* both commonly bear persistent and closed cones. They may be readily distinguished, however, in that *P.*

*serotina* has needles in threes or threes *and* fours, rough-scaly branchlets, and subglobose or short ovoid cones.   P. *clausa* has needles in twos,
smooth to very moderately scaly branchlets and elongate-ovoid cones.

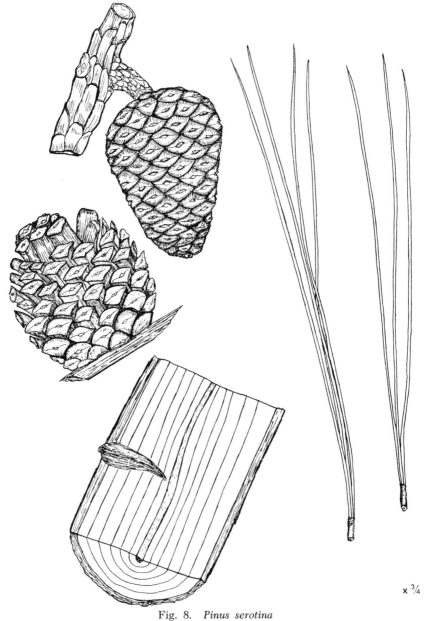

x ¾

Fig. 8.   *Pinus serotina*

Moreover, *P. serotina* inhabits poorly drained flatwoods, whereas *P. clausa* occurs on well-drained, white-sandy, hilly sites together with evergreen scrub oaks.

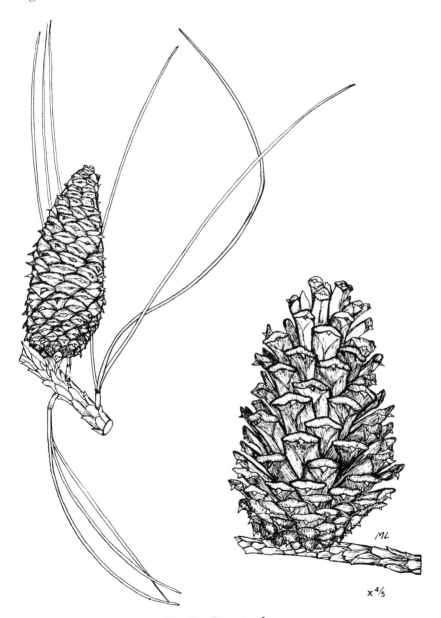

Fig. 9.  *Pinus taeda*

### 7. Pinus taeda L.   Loblolly pine

The loblolly pine is a large tree with bark that breaks up into irregular, elongate, broad, roughish plates.

The needles are 4 - 10 (mostly 7 - 9) inches long and are borne in fascicles of three.  The fascicle sheaths are ¼ - ½ inch long.  The twigs are rough, scaly and somewhat stout.

The sessile ovulate cones are 2 - 5 (mostly 4 - 5) inches long and usually remain on the tree to the end of the third year.  When unopen, the cones are elongate-ovoid and ovoid-conic.  When open, the faces of the cone scales are swollen and transversely keeled, each with a prominent umbo bearing a stout straight or recurved spine.

Throughout northern Florida, the loblolly pine (often together with the shortleaf pine, *P. echinata*) invades fertile upland old fields where, under favorable conditions, closed stands are eventually produced.  See *P. echinata*.

*Pinus taeda* and *P. echinata,* frequently grow intermixed.  They may be readily distinguished, though, for *P. taeda* has needles in threes, mostly 7 - 8 inches long, and cones mostly 4 - 5 inches long.  *P. echinata* has needles in twos or twos *and* threes, 2 - 5 inches long, and cones 1½ - 3 inches long.  For a comparison to the slash pine, see *P. elliottii*.

## TAXODIACEAE.  BALD-CYPRESS OR REDWOOD FAMILY

### TAXODIUM.   BALD-CYPRESSES

The bald-cypresses are deciduous coniferous trees with linear-subulate leaves.  Some of the leaves are borne directly on older twigs, are semi-persistent, and have buds in their axils.  Other leaves are borne on deciduous branchlets and these have no buds in their axils.  The bald-cypresses grow naturally in areas with water tables which fluctuate markedly over considerable periods of time and may be inundated much of the time.  Characteristic growth features are buttressed bases of the trunks and aerial, erect-conical structures ("knees") from the roots.

The plants are monoecious.  Young male and female cones are evident in summer and develop fully in winter before the leaves emerge.  Fully developed staminate cones are short-oval or obovate and are arranged in dangling panicled spikes.  Each cone bears 6 - 8 stamens.  The ovulate cones are globose or subglobose, resinous, fleshy, the scales peltate, spirally arranged, closely adhering, and each bearing 2 ovules.  The mature ovulate cones are about one inch or a little more in diameter, green-glaucous, then brown, the peltate scales becoming more or less woody and separated from each other, the seeds 2 - 3-angled or thick-winged.

1. Deciduous, budless branchlets rigid-ascending, their leaves acicular or awl-shaped, keeled, spirally distributed on and appressed to the branchlets (spreading in one plane on either side of the branchlets only on sprouts or saplings, if at all); knees rounded or blunt-tipped..................................................1. *T. ascendens*
1. Deciduous, budless branchlets spreading laterally from the woody twigs and feather-like, their leaves linear, flat, mostly spreading in one plane on either side of the branchlets (appressed only on drooping branchlets at the summit of the crown, if at all); knees sharp-pointed............................................2. *T. distichum*

### 1. **Taxodium ascendens** Brongn.   Pond-cypress

*T. distichum* (L.) Rich., var. *nutans* (Ait.) Sweet

The pond-cypress is a small to medium-sized tree, commonly with buttressed bases, and with rounded or blunt-tipped "knees." The crowns of the young trees are more or less cylindrical, becoming irregular and flat-topped in age, the crown branches tending to be markedly crooked. The bark is grayish to reddish-brown, prominently ridged and deeply furrowed.

Some leaves are linear-awl-shaped, borne on woody twigs with buds in their axils; other leaves are borne on stiffly ascending deciduous

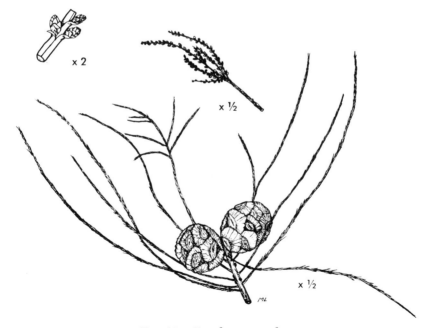

Fig. 10.   *Taxodium ascendens*

branchlets. These are linear-awl-shaped, prominently keeled, sessile, spirally arranged and appressed to the branchlets. Sprouts or some saplings may have flat leaves which spread in one plane on either side of the deciduous branchlets.

The pond-cypress occurs throughout northern Florida in wet sandy

Fig. 11. *Taxodium distichum*

depressions, ponds in flatwoods, on pond or lake margins, or on sandy floodplains. It is frequently associated with the swamp tupelo (*Nyssa biflora*), slash pine (*Pinus elliottii*), sweetbay (*Magnolia virginiana*), the littleleaf titi (*Cyrilla parvifolia*), and myrtle dahoon (*Ilex myrtifolia*). For comparative features, see *Taxodium distichum*.

### 2. **Taxodium distichum** (L.) Rich.  Bald-cypress

The bald-cypress is a large tree, commonly with buttressed bases, and with sharp-pointed, conical "knees." The crowns of the young trees are symmetrically pyramidal, becoming in age irregularly wide-spreading, flat-topped, and with a feathery foliage system. The bark is grayish to reddish-brown, shallowly furrowed and ridged on older trunks, sloughing in flaky thin scales.

The leaves are borne on deciduous branchlets, sessile, spirally arranged but twisted so that they appear feather-like in one plane on either side of the branchlets. The leaves are linear or very narrowly linear-lanceolate, ¼ - ½ inch long, flat, the tips pointed. Occasional branches near the summits of the crowns may have branchlets the leaves of which are spirally arranged, not spread in one plane, and these branchlets tend to droop.

The bald-cypress occurs in clayey, mucky, silty, or limestone soils of swamps, floodplains, or on river banks throughout northern Florida. A tree with which it is commonly associated is the water tupelo, *Nyssa aquatica*.

The feather-like, leafy branchlets, simulating compound leaves, are distinctive for this cone-bearing tree. It is readily distinguishable from the pond-cypress in that the leafy branchlets of the latter, in the main, are rigid-ascending, the leaves mostly keeled, spirally arranged and appressed, not borne in one plane. In bald-cypress the ridges of the buttresses are thin-edged and more or less sharp and planklike; those of the pond-cypress are round-edged. The "knees" of the bald-cypress are sharp at their tips; those of the pond-cypress are rounded and blunt at their tips. Usually the bark of the bald-cypress is thin-flaky while that of the pond-cypress is rough-ridged and deeply-furrowed.

## CUPRESSACEAE.  CYPRESS OR CEDAR FAMILY

1. Plants monoecious; twigs flattened as viewed in cross-section; ovulate cones opening at maturity, shedding winged seeds, the scales woody, brown.....................................CHAMAECYPARIS
1. Plants dioecious; twigs quadrangular as viewed in cross-section; ovulate cones soft, berry-like, bluish.....................................JUNIPERUS

CHAMAECYPARIS

1.  **Chamaecyparis thyoides** (L.) B.S.P.   Atlantic white-cedar

The Atlantic white-cedar is a strong-scented, evergreen, coniferous tree reaching about 80 feet in height and up to 3 feet in diameter.   Its

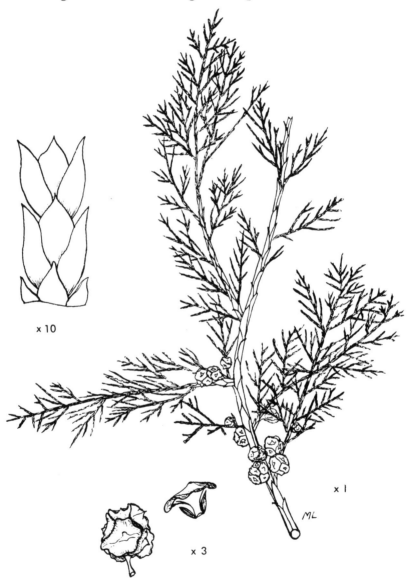

× 10

× 3

× 1

ML

Fig. 12.   *Chamaecyparis thyoides*

crown is narrow and cone-shaped and in dense stands of trees the trunks may be long, straight, and clear of branches to the forest canopy. The bark is thin, grayish to reddish-brown, and exfoliates in long fibrous strips.

The leaves are very small, ⅟₁₆ - ⅛ inch long, sessile, scalelike and ovate-acuminate, often with a gland on the back which appears as a pore on persistent dead leaves. They are borne oppositely on the twigs, are imbricated and closely appressed, the opposite pairs in two rows, thus 4-ranked. The leaves of two of the opposite ranks are keeled, those of the other two flat, giving the twigs a flattened appearance. These flattened, leafy twigs branch considerably, the result being a spray effect.

The plants are monoecious, the staminate and ovulate cones borne on different branchlets. The staminate cones are short-cylindrical. The ovulate cones, at or near maturity, are globular, ⅛ - ¼ inch in diameter. Before opening, they are tough-leathery, green, and glaucous. Six to 12 winged seeds are borne in each cone. After opening, the cones appear woody, the scales are thick, peltate, and bossed.

This tree occurs locally in swamps, or more generally in woods bordering clear or brown cool-water streams, from Liberty County westward in northern Florida. West and Arnold (1946) report its occurrence in Putnam County, eastern Florida.

In our area, the Atlantic white-cedar is unlikely to be mistaken for any native tree except the southern red-cedar. The twigs of the former are flattened as viewed in cross-section, and its seed cones open at maturity shedding their winged seeds, subsequently are woody-scaly. The twigs of southern red-cedar are quadrangular as viewed in cross-section. Its seed cones are berry-like, have fleshy coalescing scales, and do not dehisce.

## JUNIPERUS

### 1. **Juniperus silicicola** (Small) Bailey.   Southern red-cedar

An evergreen, aromatic, coniferous tree, the southern red-cedar has a dense crown of broadly conical form. Typically the trunks are short; often the lowermost branches reach nearly to the ground. The bark is thin, reddish-brown, and exfoliates in thin shreds.

The leaves of the adult branchlets are very small, ⅟₃₂ - ³⁄₁₆ inch long, sessile, triangular and sharp-pointed. The backs of the leaves are marked by a translucent patch or gland. They are borne oppositely on the twigs and in 2 ranks (or occasionally in whorls of 3 and are 6-ranked). Leaves overlap closely and are appressed to the twigs, making the twigs appear quadrangular in cross-section. The leaves of vigorous sprouts

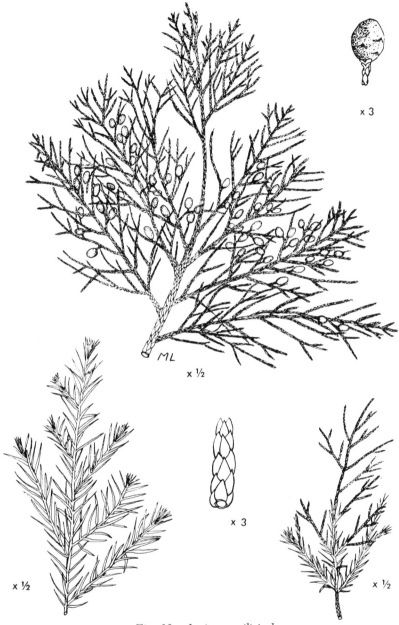

Fig. 13.  *Juniperus silicicola*

or of small saplings are more elongate, awl-shaped, and needle-like, and are not appressed to the twigs.

The plants are dioecious. Male plants produce short-cylindric staminate cones in great abundance during the winter. These are small, ¼ inch long, are yellowish, and owing to their great numbers give the male trees a suffused green and gold color during the latter part of the winter. Female trees bear subglobose or ellipsoid-ovoid, soft, berry-like, resinous cones ("juniper berries") the scales of which are fleshy and coalesced, not dehiscing at maturity. The berry-like cones are ¼ - ⅜ inch long and ¼ inch in diameter. They are virtually full-grown by autumn but persist through much of the winter. At maturity, they are blue (occasional ones brown) and have a waxy coating. Some trees bear only a relatively small number, others a great profusion, so that the latter trees during winter are a suffused blue-green color, seen at a little distance.

In early spring, during humid weather, the red-cedar may bear on its branches conspicuous, globular, gelatinous, orange balls, popularly known as "cedar apples." These are spore-producing bodies of a fungal parasite.

The southern red-cedar is tolerant of a wide range of moisture conditions. In northern Florida, it occurs in upland old fields and open woods where the topsoil is underlain by limestone, in moist to wet hammocks and along streams where limestone is near the surface, on barrier beaches and shell mounds, and often along roadsides near the coast.

This tree and the Atlantic white-cedar are superficially similar. For comparative features, see *Chamaecyparis thyoides*.

## PALMAE. PALM FAMILY

### SABAL

1. **Sabal palmetto** (Walt.) Lodd. Cabbage palmetto

A branchless tree, reaching a height of 75 feet, the cabbage palmetto has a globose or hemispheric crown of large fanlike leaves. The trunks are essentially uniform in diameter from base to summit.

The leaves are persistent, the blades fanlike, 4 - 7 feet long, with a prominent, downwardly curving midrib on either side of which are parallel-veined segments. These segments are free at their tips as narrow drooping lacerations. The petioles are smooth, and are as long as or longer than the blades. The bases of the leaf stalks are persistent for an indefinite period, each stub splitting so that the upper trunk is

sheathed by spirals of "shoes." Below this collar, the "bark" is roughened by the leaf scars.

The flowers are small, creamy-white, and are borne in profusion on
very large, arching, or drooping panicles from the leaf axils. The fruits
are drupelike, blackish, about ⅓ inch in diameter.

This tree occurs on dunes and in moist hammocks or flatwoods, usually
where limestone is near the surface. In northern Florida, it occurs along
the Atlantic Coast, in the interior of northeastern Florida, westward
more or less near the Gulf Coast to about Port St. Joe. It is widely
cultivated.

The cabbage palmetto is the only native palm regularly attaining tree
stature in our range. The introduced Washington palm, *Washingtonia
robusta* Parish, is frequently planted, often together with the cabbage
palmetto. It, too, has fanlike leaves and may be mistaken for the cabbage palmetto. Leaves of the Washington palm have no midribs, and
the petioles are armed with hooked spines. This is in marked contrast
to those of the cabbage palmetto, the leaves of which have prominent
arching midribs and whose petioles are not spiny.

## SALICACEAE.   WILLOW FAMILY

1. Leafbuds covered by several scales; leaves broadly ovate, triangular-ovate, or
   cordate-ovate, nearly as broad as long, or broader than long _____POPULUS
1. Leafbuds covered by a single scale; leaves lanceolate or oval to oblong or ovate-
   oblong, much longer than broad_____SALIX

### POPULUS.   COTTONWOODS; POPLARS

The poplars are fast-growing trees with bitter-astringent bark and
light wood. The buds are several-scaled and gummy. The leaves are
simple, alternate, deciduous, and leave prominent leaf scars which
markedly roughen the twigs. They are long-petioled, ovate, triangular
ovate, or cordate-ovate, often as broad as long or broader than long.
The flowers are individually small and have no perianths. They are
unisexual, the plants dioecious. Flowers are borne in drooping catkins
before the leaves emerge. The staminate flower consists of 5 - many
stamens borne on a scale; the pistillate consists of a single 1-loculed
ovulary with 2 - 4 stigmas. The fruit is a short capsule which bears
numerous silky or cottony seeds ( hence the name, cottonwoods ).

1. Petioles flattened toward their summits; leaf tips acute to acuminate_____
   _____1. *P. deltoides*
1. Petioles not flattened; leaf tips blunt_____2. *P. heterophylla*

1. **Populus deltoides** Bartr. ex Marsh.   Eastern cottonwood

A large tree, the eastern cottonwood has grayish bark which is roughly and irregularly fissured and ridged. The twigs are stout, yellowish-green, and glabrous; the older branchlets are angular and are roughened by large 3-lobed leaf scars. The pith is irregularly 5-angled.

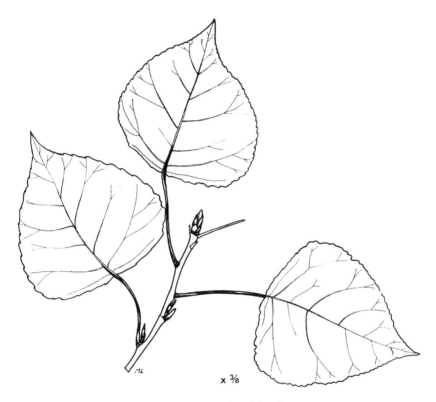

x ⅜

Fig. 14. *Populus deltoides*

The leaf blades are thick and stiff, the principal veins prominent, mostly diverging more or less at right angles from the midribs. They range from 5 - 9 inches long and are commonly equally as broad as long, or broader than long. They are mostly triangular-ovate with truncate, or more rarely subcordate, bases, and short-acuminate or acute apices. The leaf margins are coarsely crenate-dentate, the surfaces green and glabrous, or sometimes the lower surfaces whitish. The long petioles are flattened toward their summits at right angles to the blades. The broad, stiff, long-petioled leaves are readily oscillated by wind currents causing a characteristic rattling of the foliage when breezes are prevalent. In our range, the eastern cottonwood occurs principally in the floodplain woodlands of the Apalachicola and other rivers of western Florida. Isolated trees occur in lowland areas elsewhere.

Distinguishing characteristics of *Populus deltoides* are its yellowish-green, glabrous twigs, its broad, triangular-ovate, thick, stiff, crenate-dentate leaves with acuminate tips, and elongate petioles flattened at their summits.

### 2. **Populus heterophylla** L.   Swamp cottonwood

A large tree, the swamp cottonwood has brownish bark, tinged with red, which is irregularly fissured and ridged. On old trunks, the bark sloughs in long, narrow plates. The twigs are stout and reddish, the younger ones bearing a whitish tomentum; eventually the twigs become glabrous and angular, and are roughened by prominent 3-lobed leaf scars. The pith is 5-angled.

The leaf blades are thick and stiff, the principal veins prominent, mostly ascending from the midribs. They range from 4 to 8 inches long and usually are not more than ¾ as broad as long at their broadest places. They are mostly ovate, sometimes subrhombic, their bases cordate, broadly rounded, or truncate, the apices mostly tapering to a blunt tip. The leaf margins are crenate-serrate or crenate-dentate. The leaf surfaces are somewhat cottony upon expanding, the upper surfaces becoming dark green and glabrous, the lower grayish or whitish and commonly hairy in the vein angles. The long petioles are not flattened.

The swamp cottonwood occurs in floodplain woodlands along the Apalachicola River and in lowland woods in the vicinity of Tallahassee.

*Populus heterophylla* can be distinguished by its reddish twigs with a gray tomentum, its broad, ovate, stiff, thick leaves with cordate or rounded bases and blunt tips, and its long petioles which are oval in cross-section.

### SALIX.   WILLOWS

The willows are fast-growing shrubs or trees, commonly with short trunks, or with several trunks from the base, and with soft, light wood. The bark is bitter-astringent and aromatic. The buds are covered by a single scale. The leaves are simple, alternate, and deciduous. The flowers are individually small and have no perianths. They are unisexual, the plants dioecious. The staminate flowers bear 2-several stamens and are borne in cylindrical, erect catkins. The pistillate flow-

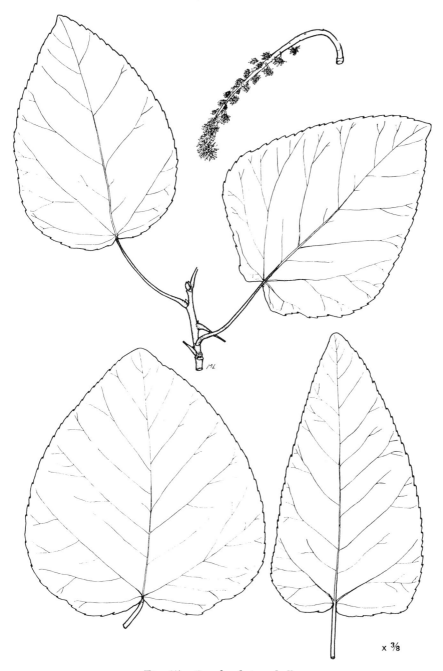

Fig. 15. *Populus heterophylla*

x ⅜

ers have a 2-locular ovulary and two 2-parted stigmas.  Pistillate flowers are borne in drooping, cylindrical catkins.  The fruit is a flasklike, 2-valved capsule bearing numerous silky seeds.

1. Mature leaves lanceolate, glabrous or glaucous below at maturity.
  2. Leaves green below................................................................3. S. *nigra*
  2. Leaves whitish or glaucous below...........................1. S. *caroliniana*
1. Mature leaves broadly oval or oblong, pubescent below, especially along the principal veins....................................................2. S. *floridana*

## 1.  **Salix caroliniana** Michx.  Coastal plain willow; Carolina willow

### S. *longipes* Shuttlw.

This is a small tree or a shrub, often with leaning trunks, and with brown, or nearly black, ridged and furrowed bark.  The twigs are short-pubescent or glabrate, brown or reddish-brown, becoming gray after a year or two.

Fig. 16.  *Salix caroliniana*

The young leaves are commonly elliptical, varying to lanceolate; they may be white-felty-pubescent on both surfaces, or with varying degrees of whitish hairiness on both surfaces, or green and glabrous above and glabrous and glaucous below. The mature leaves are lance-olate, variable in size up to 6 - 8 inches long and about 1 inch broad at their broadest places. The upper surfaces are green, the lower glau-cous, both surfaces glabrous. The bases of the blades are usually rounded, less frequently cuneate, and the blades are long-tapering from their widest points near their bases. The margins are finely serrate, the teeth commonly tipped with yellowish glands, less frequently with reddish glands.

Flowering occurs in early spring as the leaves emerge. The fruits mature in spring before the leaves are fully grown.

The coastal plain willow occurs in swamps, along small streams and rivers, in marshy places, and on pond and lake margins. It is common in northern Florida from the east coast westward to Leon and Wakulla counties, less common westward from there to Walton County.

*Salix caroliniana* and *Salix nigra* are much alike, and in our region (specifically where their ranges overlap) they seem to intergrade. In general, the mature leaves of the former are whitish-glaucous below, have rounded bases, and yellowish glands on the tips of the teeth or in the angles of the teeth. The leaves of the latter are usually green, only occasionally glaucous below. Their bases are more commonly cuneate, and the teeth are tipped with reddish glands or have reddish glands in their angles.

## 2. **Salix floridana** Chapm. Florida willow

The Florida willow is a shrub, or, at most, a very small tree.

The leaves are mostly oval, broadly elliptic, oblong, or ovate-oblong, up to 5 - 6 inches long and 2 inches broad, mostly broadest at about their middles. Their upper surfaces are dark green and glabrous, the lower whitish and soft-pubescent, more densely so on the veins. The bases of the blades are broadly rounded, the apices acute. The leaf margins are irregularly, shallowly dentate, the teeth glandular.

Flowering occurs in spring as the leaves emerge.

This is a rare willow, known to occur in Lake and Levy counties of peninsular Florida, and in Columbia County in northern Florida. It was originally described from specimens collected by Chapman at Marianna in Jackson County, but we have been unable to locate it there. Aside from these stations, it has been collected in Pulaski and Early counties, Georgia. It occurs along small streams and in wet woodlands in calcareous areas.

*Salix floridana* is readily distinguishable from our other willows by its large, broad leaves which at maturity are whitish and pubescent below and shallowly and irregularly glandular-dentate on their margins.

x ½

Kral

x 1

Fig. 17.　*Salix floridana*

### 3. **Salix nigra** Marsh.　Black willow

This is a small tree or a shrub, often with leaning trunks, and having dark brown, ridged and furrowed bark. The twigs are glabrous, brown or reddish-brown, becoming grayish-brown.

The leaves are lanceolate, glabrous and green on both surfaces (except occasionally glaucous below and sparsely pubescent when young). The blades are variable in size, up to 6 - 8 inches long and commonly not

over ¾ inch broad at their broadest places.  The bases of the blades
are mostly cuneate, occasionally rounded, and the blades long-tapering
from their widest points near the bases.  Their margins are finely serrate, the teeth mostly tipped with reddish glands, or with reddish glands
in the angles of the teeth.

x ½

x 8

x ½

x ½                                                    x ⅝

Fig. 18.  *Salix nigra*

Flowering occurs in early spring as the leaves emerge. The fruits mature in spring before the leaves are fully grown.

The black willow occupies the same range of habitats as the coastal plain willow. It occurs in northern Florida from Taylor County westward. In the area in which the ranges of these two willows overlap, they commonly grow intermixed. In these places, they appear to intergrade so that it is virtually impossible to distinguish certain specimen trees.

For features which distinguish *Salix nigra* and *S. caroliniana*, see the latter.

## MYRICACEAE. BAYBERRY FAMILY

### MYRICA. BAYBERRY; WAX-MYRTLE

Our bayberries are evergreen shrubs or small trees with simple, alternate, resinous-dotted leaves. The flowers are unisexual, the plants dioecious. Both kinds of flowers are without perianths, and occur in short-ovoid or short-cylindric scaly catkins which arise on the branchlets of previous seasons. The fruits are globose or ovoid, at maturity heavily coated with wax.

1. Leaf blades thin, flat, or somewhat twisted or ruffled, irregularly and remotely serrate on their upper margins; leaves conspicuously reduced in size toward the ends of the twigs; crushed foliage aromatic; fruits about ⅛ inch in diameter ..................................................................................................1. *M. cerifera*
1. Leaf blades leathery, revolute, and the sides cupped, entire or rarely slightly wavy or with a few irregular teeth; leaves not conspicuously reduced in size toward the ends of the twigs; crushed foliage nonaromatic; fruits about ¼ inch in diameter..................................................................................................2. *M. inodora*

### 1. **Myrica cerifera** L. Southern bayberry; wax-myrtle

This is a small, aromatic, evergreen shrub or small tree. Commonly there are several trunks from near the base. Several characteristics combine to render it a popular ornamental: it is a fast grower, is heavily clothed with attractive evergreen foliage, and responds well to pruning.

The leaves are oblanceolate, more or less twisted or ruffled, 2 - 4 inches long, becoming reduced in size towards the tips of the branches. Their bases are cuneate, the apices acute, and the margins irregularly and remotely serrate from about their middles upward. Both surfaces are punctate with yellowish or brownish glandular dots, the lower surfaces somewhat pubescent. The bruised foliage is pleasantly aromatic. The twigs are hairy, the bark light gray and commonly heavily coated with lichens.

The fruits are globose, about ⅛ inch in diameter, sessile and crowded on the spikes. They ripen in autumn or winter and at maturity are heavily coated with bluish-white wax.

This plant is common throughout our range in a wide variety of habitats: fresh to slightly brackish banks and shores, swamps, hammocks, flatwoods, and upland deciduous woods.

*Myrica cerifera* is readily distinguished by its alternate, persistent, irregularly serrate, glandular-punctate aromatic leaves. In autumn or winter, these characteristics, together with the waxy fruits on the twigs, make the female plants particularly distinctive.

x ⅞

Fig. 19. *Myrica cerifera*

2. **Myrica inodora** Bartr. Odorless bayberry; odorless wax-myrtle

The odorless bayberry is an evergreen shrub or small tree with smooth, light gray bark. Specimens 20 feet tall and 1 foot in diameter are known to us.

The leaves are leathery, elliptic, oblanceolate, or narrowly obovate, and 2 - 4 inches long.  Their bases are tapering, the apices rounded, or occasionally retuse or apiculate.  The margins are generally entire and revolute, the sides cupping; sometimes they appear slightly wavy or have a few irregular teeth.  The surfaces are glabrous, but finely glandular-dotted.  The crushed foliage is not aromatic.

The fruits are globose, about ¼ inch in diameter.  They are olive-

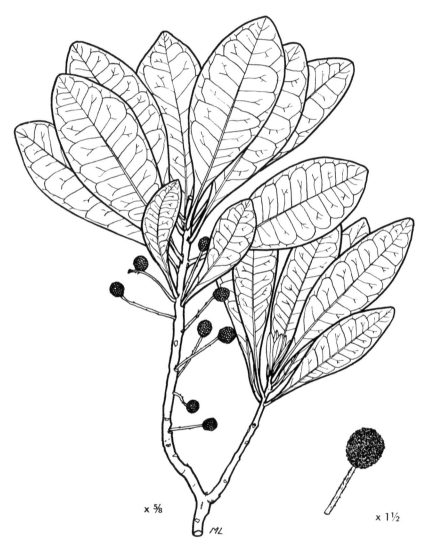

x ⅝

x 1½

Fig. 20.  *Myrica inodora*

brown, with rough-papillose surfaces, the interstices between the papillae waxy.

This plant inhabits bays, branch-bays, and nonalluvial river swamps
from Leon County to western Florida.  It is not common.

The odorless, glabrous foliage, the mostly entire, revolute, cupped
leaves (which are not conspicuously reduced in size towards the ends
of the twigs) distinguish *Myrica inodora* from *M. cerifera.*

## LEITNERIACEAE.  CORKWOOD FAMILY

### LEITNERIA

#### 1.  **Leitneria floridana** Chapm.   Corkwood

The corkwood, a rare plant of peculiar distribution, is a little-branched,
treelike shrub with very soft and light wood.   The bark is reddish-
brown, smooth, and with prominent buff-colored lenticels.   The twigs
of the season are at first densely hairy, becoming glabrate.

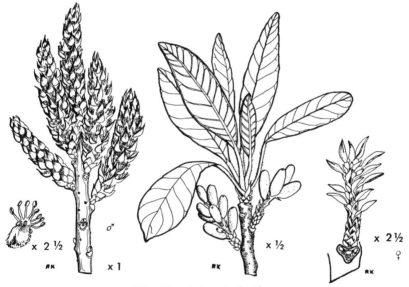

Fig. 21.   *Leitneria floridana*

The leaves are simple, alternate, and deciduous, the blades 4 - 5
inches long and 1 - 1½ inches broad.  They are elliptic or lanceolate-
elliptic, mostly tapering from about the middle to acute bases and
apices.  Their upper surfaces are glabrous, the lower soft-pubescent,

the margins entire.  The principal lateral veins are prominent, irregularly spaced, and between them is a conspicuous, fine, vein network
visible from either surface.

The flowers are unisexual, the plants dioecious.  Both staminate and
pistillate flowers are borne in ascending scaly catkins before or during
leaf emergence.

The fruit is an elliptic or oblong drupe about ¾ inch long and ¼
inch in diameter.

In northern Florida, the corkwood occurs in sawgrass marshes along
the banks of the Apalachicola River and its tributary streams and bayous,
upriver from the city of Apalachicola.  It is known to occur in similar
habitats of Gulf Hammock, Levy County, Florida, and locally in Georgia, Texas, Arkansas, and Missouri.

*Leitneria floridana* may be recognized by its habit which is that of a
small treelike shrub with little branching, and by its elliptical rugose-
veiny leaves.

## JUGLANDACEAE.  WALNUT FAMILY

1. Terminal leaflet mostly reduced or aborted, the leaves thus appearing even-
   pinnate; pith transversely partitioned; staminate catkins borne singly; husk of
   the fruit indehiscent, the shell of the nut rough-corrugated.................JUGLANS
1. Terminal leaflet well developed, all leaves odd-pinnate; pith not partitioned;
   staminate catkins borne in clusters of 3; husk of the fruit splitting by 4 valves,
   the shell of the nut with essentially smooth surfaces.........................CARYA

### JUGLANS

#### Juglans nigra L.   Black walnut

The black walnut is potentially a large tree.  No known large trees
have survived commercial exploitation in our region, nor do any reach
sizable proportions before succumbing to the ax.  The bark of the trunk
is dark brown, roughened by deep furrows interlacing between narrow
ridges.  The twigs usually bear a larger axillary bud superimposed
over against a smaller one.  The pith of the branchlets is chambered by
cross-partitions.

The flowers are greenish, unisexual, the plants monoecious.  Male
flowers are borne in elongate, cylindrical catkins hanging singly from
twig growth of the previous year.  The female flowers are solitary, or
more often 2 to 5 in a cluster on a short, inconspicuous stalked spike
near the tip of the present season's developing branchlets.  The pistils
are fuzzy, ovoid, and have a short style and 2 feathery stigmas.

Fruits are globose, up to 2 inches in diameter, and have a soft, juicy,
pungent, indehiscent husk enclosing a hard, dark brown "nut" or stone.
The husk is green at maturity; after the fruits are shed from the tree,

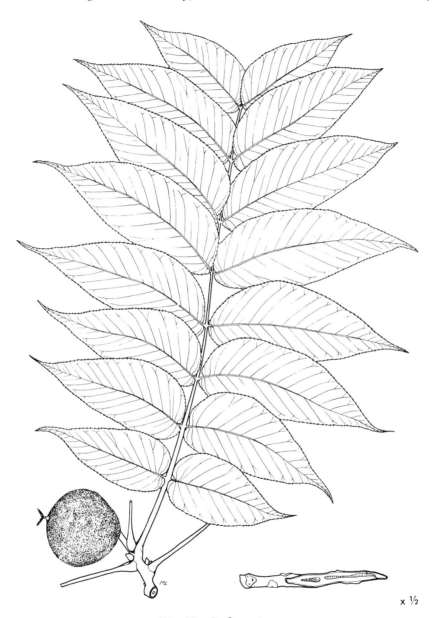

x ½

Fig. 22.  *Juglans nigra*

the husk turns black and disintegrates.    The nuts enclose a single, large seed which is oily and sweet.

This tree is now of limited occurrence in north Florida, being restricted to floodplains of the Apalachicola River in Gadsden and Liberty counties, wooded areas of the Marianna limestone region, and sporadically in the Tallahassee Red Hills region.

Distinctive characteristics of the black walnut are the chambered pith of the twigs, the pungently aromatic once-pinnately compound leaves, and large, globose, indehiscent fruits.    Although the leaves are normally odd-pinnate, the terminal leaflet usually aborts so that the leaves appear even-pinnate.    The leaves usually can be distinguished from those of the hickories because the median leaflets of the walnut leaf are the largest whereas the terminal leaflet of a hickory leaf is largest (the pecan and water hickory are exceptions to this).

## CARYA.   HICKORIES

Our hickories, with one exception, are large trees with hard, tough wood.    The pith of the branchlets is not chambered.    They have alternate, deciduous, once-pinnately compound leaves, 7 - 15 inches long, which commonly have glandular surface scales or dots.    The leaflets are mostly asymmetrical at base, their margins serrate.    Bruised foliage has a characteristic pungent odor.    The flowers are unisexual, the plants monoecious.    Male flowers are borne in elongate, cylindrical catkins, 3 in a cluster, on twigs of the previous season.    Female flowers are solitary, or 2 - 10 in a cluster, and are borne on short stalked spikes on the tips of developing branchlets of the present season.    The fruits are roundish, egg-shaped, or pear-shaped, and have an indurated dehiscent husk which splits by 4 valves.    This encloses a smooth-faced, bony, 1-seeded nut.

The fruit with its 4-valved husk enclosing a smooth-faced nut, together with the pungent, alternately arranged, once-pinnate leaves, are distinctive hickory characteristics.    Ashes have similar compound leaves, but they are oppositely arranged and lack the pungent odor.

1.  Leaflets 9 - 17; fruits winged along the sutures from base to apex, the areas between the wings strongly flattened.
    2.  Petioles, rachi, and lower surfaces of the leaflets pubescent; nuts angled; kernels bitter................................................................................................1. *C. aquatica*
    2.  Petioles, rachi, and both surfaces of the leaflets glabrous; nuts round in cross-section; kernels sweet................................................................5. *C. illinoensis*
1.  Leaflets 5 - 9; fruits not winged along the sutures, or winged only above their middles, the areas between the wings not strongly flattened.
    3.  Petioles, rachi, and lower surfaces of the mature leaflets pubescent.

4. Pubescence of the leaf parts evenly distributed; husks of the fruits and
shells of the nuts thin, less than 1/12 inch thick; kernel bitter.........................
...............................................................................................................2. *C. cordiformis*

4. Pubescence of the leaf parts in tufts; husks of the fruits and shells of the
nuts thick, 1/12 - 1/4 inch thick; kernel sweet.

 5. Leafy twig segments thin, about 1/8 inch or less in diameter; resinous
 scales of the leaflets disklike...................................................7. *C. pallida*

 5. Leafy twig segments stout, about 1/4 inch in diameter; resinous scales
 of the leaflets granular.................................................8. *C. tomentosa*

3. Petioles, rachi, and lower surfaces of the mature leaflets glabrous, or essentially so at maturity.

 6. Bark of young trees (6 - 10 inches in diameter) shaggy, that of older trees
 (24 or more inches in diameter) low-ridged and furrowed with a blocky
 pattern; husks of the fruits freely splitting at maturity...............6. *C. ovalis*

 6. Bark close but with interlacing, shallow ridges and fissures giving a diamond pattern; husks of the fruits tardily splitting at maturity.

  7. Lower surfaces of mature leaflets not resinous-scaly; trees of rich
  woods or hammocks...............................................................4. *C. glabra*

  7. Lower surfaces of mature leaflets heavily clothed with amber-colored
  resinous scales; trees of evergreen scrub oak-sand pine ridges or hills
  ...............................................................................................3. *C. floridana*

### 1. **Carya aquatica** (Michx. f.) Nutt.   Water hickory

The water hickory is a medium to large tree.   Authors have described
it as being a small tree but this, no doubt, reflects a meagre field knowledge of the tree.   Moreover, its name implies that it inhabits areas which
are periodically inundated, as is true for bald-cypress and tupelos; authors have included deep swamps as one of its habitats, and at least
one author has stated that its bases are often inundated.   To our knowledge, it is not a tree of deep swamps, but of low, drained river hammocks, drained floodplains, or of drained, natural levees along rivers,
not in sites where its base would be inundated, except temporarily.
It may grow in close proximity to cypress and tupelo, but the latter are
actually in local depressions.

The bark is at first smoothish, becoming markedly scaly and flaky,
and shredding in long, loose plates.

The leaves have 7 - 15 leaflets which are lanceolate, ovate-lanceolate,
or elliptic, inequilateral, and more or less scythe-shaped.   Their bases
are cuneate to rounded, the apices acuminate.   The petioles, rachi, and
lower surfaces of the leaflets are rusty-pubescent, the leaflets glabrous
above.   The lower and median leaflets may be as large as or larger than
the terminal one.

The fruits are angled, decidedly flattened on the faces, the angles
somewhat winged.   The husks, 1/16 inch thick, split along their entire
length.   The nuts are angled, brown or tan, tinged with red, slightly
wrinkled, their shells thinner than the husk.   The kernel is bitter.

This tree occurs mainly in drained river hammocks, floodplains, and natural levees, occasionally in small stream valleys, from the St. Johns to the Escambia rivers.

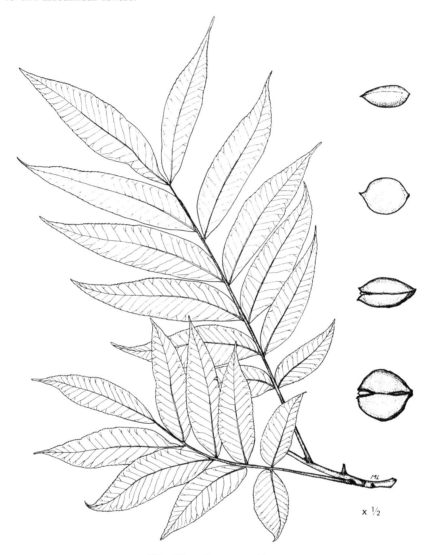

Fig. 23.  *Carya aquatica*

*Carya aquatica* has a greater number of leaflets than other native hickories of our area.  The numerous scythe-shaped leaflets and the angled, flattened fruit distinguish it.  It is most nearly like the cultivated pecan (*C. illinoensis*) in leaf characters. The latter, however, has essentially glabrous leaf parts while those of *C. aquatica* are usually pubescent, and the nut is round in cross-section in the pecan. Pecans which have become naturalized occur along roadsides and in waste ground, whereas the water hickory is in natural forests along rivers and streams.

2. **Carya cordiformis** (Wang.) K. Koch. Bitternut hickory

This is a medium-sized tree having brownish bark which is scaly or peels in small, flaky ridges.

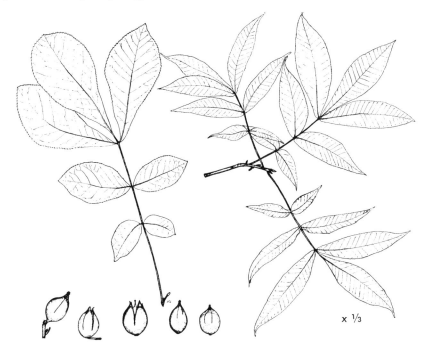

Fig. 24. *Carya cordiformis*

The leaves, including the petioles, are 6 - 8 (or up to 12) inches long; the leaflets number 7 to 9. The leaflets are sharply serrate, lanceolate to ovate-lanceolate, the upper pairs varying from lanceolate to oblanceolate or obovate, sometimes falcate, 3 - 5 (sometimes 2 - 6) inches long. Their bases are rounded to cuneate, symmetrical or asymmetrical, the apices acute to acuminate. The petioles, leaf rachi, and lower surfaces of the leaflets are finely and evenly pubescent, or the lower leaf surfaces may be glabrous except on the veins; the surfaces are clothed with disk-shaped, resinous scales, also.  The terminal leaflets are short-stalked, the lateral sessile or short-stalked.

The fruits are subglobose or ovoid, prominently beaked, sometimes slightly compressed laterally, ¾ - 1½ inches long (including the beak). They are winged on the valves from the middle upward.  The husks are thin, about ¹⁄₁₆ inch thick or less, the shell of the nut thinner.  The kernel is bitter.

The bitternut hickory is of limited occurrence in northern Florida. It is known to us from drained floodplains along the Apalachicola River in Liberty County, shores of Lake Iamonia in Leon County, and limestone uplands in the vicinity of Marianna, Jackson County.

*Carya cordiformis* is distinguished from *C. pallida* in that its fruits are thin-husked and its petioles, rachi, and leaflet lower surfaces have evenly distributed pubescence whereas those of *C. pallida* have the pubescence in tufts.  It is separated from *C. aquatica* by its fruits which are round or only slightly flattened and winged only from about the midpoints upward.  Those of the latter species are distinctly flattened and winged from their bases upward.

### 3.  **Carya floridana** Sarg.   Scrub hickory

This is a small tree or shrub.  The leaves, including the petioles, are 4 - 8 inches long; the leaflets number 3 to 7.  The leaflets are lanceolate, oblanceolate, or ovate-lanceolate, their bases rounded or cuneate, symmetrical or asymmetrical, the apices acuminate.  The upper pairs are 2 - 4 inches long.  Their margins are serrate, the teeth frequently remote; the teeth are tipped with cartilaginous, clublike points, or are reduced to clublike tips.  The petioles, rachi, and leaflet surfaces are glabrous at maturity, but the lower surfaces of the leaflets are yellowish- or rusty-green, thickly dotted by disklike or granular, amber-colored resinous scales.

The fruits are ovoid, subglobose, or somewhat pear-shaped.  They are not winged.

The scrub hickory is confined to the scrub of dry sand ridges from Marion County southward.  Sargent (1933) reports its occurrence on the shores of Pensacola Bay.

Inland from Jacksonville Beach, Duval County, the scrub vegetation of old dunes grades into sandy hammock.  In the scrub is a small hickory that is identifiable with *C. floridana*.  In the hammocks are larger trees identifiable with *C. glabra*.  In the transition zones between the scrub and hammock, the hickories are intermediate in size and other characters between the two.  For convenience we refer the small scrubby hickory associated with the evergreen scrub oaks (sand-live

oak, myrtle oak, and Chapman oak) and the sand pine to *Carya floridana.*
We think, however, that the validity of this species is questionable.

Fig. 25.   *Carya floridana*

## 4. **Carya glabra** (Mill.) Sweet.   Pignut hickory

Including *C. glabra* var. *megacarpa* Sarg.

This common hickory has close bark which is shallowly furrowed
and has low, interlacing ridges forming a diamond pattern.   It is one
of our most shade-tolerant trees.

The leaves, including the petioles, are 6 - 17 inches long; the leaflets
number 5 to 7 (or rarely 3).   The leaflets are lanceolate, oblanceolate, or
elliptical.   The bases are asymmetrical, those of the upper leaflets mostly
cuneate, those of the lower leaflets cuneate to rounded; the apices are

acuminate.   The upper pairs of leaflets are 2½ - 5 inches long.   The leaflet margins are serrate, the teeth slender and incurved.   The petioles, rachi, and upper leaflet surfaces are glabrous, the lower leaflet surfaces glabrous except sometimes the midribs.   The lateral leaflets are sessile, the terminal one short-stalked and tapering to both ends.

The fruits are pear-shaped or globular, 1¼ - 2½ inches long, and smooth or only slightly ribbed at the sutures.   The husks are ½₁₂ - ⅛ inch thick, the shell of the nut about ½₁₂ inch thick.   The husks usually split only part way into 2 - 5 parts, commonly 3 - 4, or in some cases

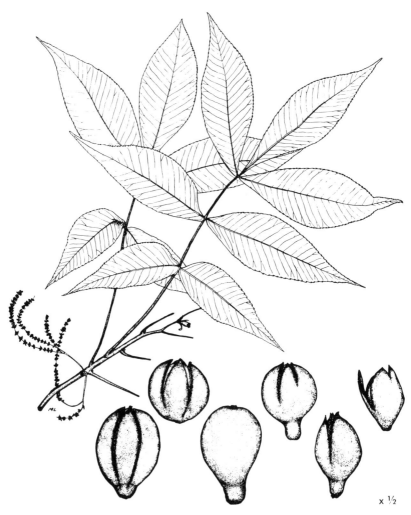

x ½

Fig. 26.   *Carya glabra*

they do not split until long after they have dropped. The kernels are sweet.

The pignut hickory inhabits hammocks and rich woods with fertile, sandy, clayey, or limestone soils, from old dunes along the Atlantic Coast inland and westward throughout our area.

As a hardwood forest hickory with glabrous twigs and leaves, and mostly pear-shaped fruits, this one is distinctive. (For a rare exception see *C. ovalis.*)

### 5. **Carya illinoensis** (Wang.) K. Koch. Pecan

This tree is cultivated in our area but is not native here. The naturalized "seedlings" of cultivated varieties occur in vacant lots, fields, road-

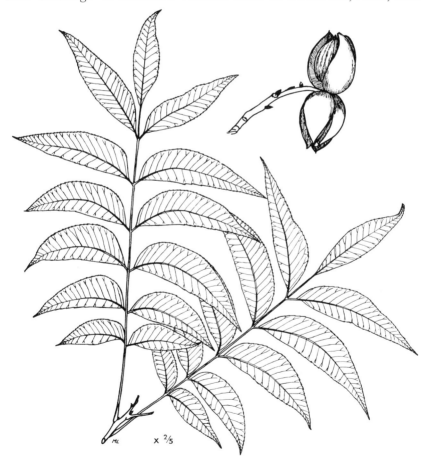

Fig. 27. *Carya illinoensis*

sides, and in margins of woods. It will not be found deep in the forests. The seedling trees are variable, but to aid observers who may encounter them, the following description, based on a few, randomly selected, naturalized trees, is given.

The leaflets are numerous, 9 to 17 in number. They are falcate-lanceolate, rounded or cuneate at their inequilateral bases, the apices long-acuminate. Like *Carya aquatica,* the lower or median leaflets in this species may be larger than the terminal one. This is in contrast to the other native hickories in which the terminal leaflets tend to be as large as, or larger than, the lower or median ones. The leaflet margins are serrate to shallowly crenate. The petioles and rachi are glabrous or sparsely pubescent, the leaflet surfaces glabrous, but their margins ciliate. The bark is rough-scaly or flaky.

The fruits are ovoid or ellipsoid, about 1½ inches long, the sutures of the husks more or less winged, splitting readily, and about ⅕ inch thick. The nut is ovoid, oval, or ellipsoid, round in cross-section, tawny, and with mahogany-colored stripes or patches, its shell about ¹⁄₁₆ inch thick. (See also *C. aquatica.*)

### 6. **Carya ovalis** (Wang.) Sarg. False shagbark

This tree, which becomes large, has shaggy bark when fairly young (6 - 10 inches in diameter), but the bark of older trees (24 inches or more in diameter) loses the shaggy nature, becomes dark and low-ridged and furrowed or blocky; the bark resembles that of old live oaks and sweetgums.

The leaves, including the petioles, are 7 - 11 (rarely up to 17) inches long, and the leaflet number is 5 to 7, commonly 7. The leaflets are serrate, lanceolate, oblanceolate, ovate, or obovate, 2½ - 7 inches long, their bases asymmetric and rounded or cuneate, the apices acuminate. The lateral leaflets are sessile or nearly so, the terminal one stalked and tapering to both ends. The twigs, petioles, and rachi are glabrous, the leaflets glabrous, except sometimes on the veins below.

The fruits are globular, up to 1 inch in diameter, and they split freely into 4 - 5 valves. The husk is thin, about ¹⁄₁₂ inch thick. The nuts are thin-shelled, the kernels sweet.

This hickory is known in our area only at one rich hardwoods station where there are four trees. This is on the northern edge of Tallahassee (at Glenwood Drive and Meridian Road, northwest corner). Home construction taking place there is altering the site; we can but hope one or more of the trees will be preserved. The first record of this species for Florida, made by Kurz, was a single tree about a mile west of the above-mentioned station. This discovery was credited to Kurz by Coker and Totten (1937); unfortunately, that tree has since been destroyed.

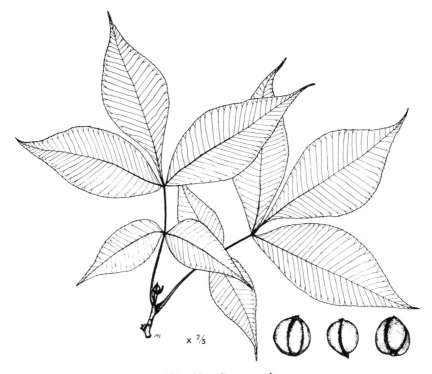

Fig. 28. *Carya ovalis*

*Carya ovalis* differs from *C. glabra* by the freely splitting fruiting husks, and by the shaggy bark of the young tree, as well as the blocky bark of the older tree. Little (1953) treats *C. ovalis* as identical with *C. glabra*. On the basis of the several trees of *C. ovalis* observed at Tallahassee, compared to those of the much more common *C. glabra*, and in view of the fact that several recent authors—Coker and Totten (1945), Fernald (1950), and Gleason (1952)—recognize their distinct identities, we feel justified in doing so.

### 7. **Carya pallida** (Ashe) Engl. & Graebn.   Sand hickory

This tree of medium to large dimensions has roughish, ridged and furrowed bark with a more or less diamond-like pattern.

The leaves, including the petioles, are commonly 6 - 8 inches long (rarely up to 12); the leaflet number is 5 to 9. The leaflets are serrate or serrulate, lanceolate or oblanceolate, the upper pair 2½ - 4 inches long, their bases rounded or cuneate, asymmetrical, the apices acuminate. The lateral leaflets are sessile or nearly so, the terminal one short-stalked, tapering to both ends. The petioles, rachi, and principal veins beneath are clothed with tufts of hairs. The areas between the veins below are glabrous, or sparsely hairy, and are silvery or yellowish with disklike, peltate, whitish or amber scales.

The leaf-bearing twig segments are thin and switchlike, usually less than ⅛ inch in diameter.

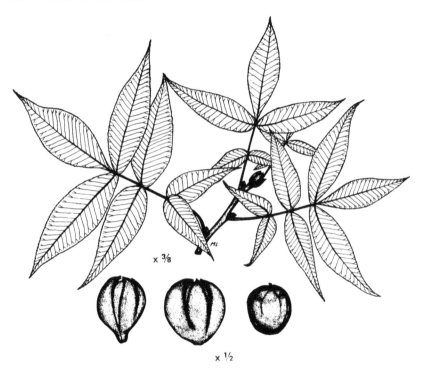

x ⅜

x ½

Fig. 29.  *Carya pallida*

The fruits are globose or obovoid, 1 - 1½ inches long. The husks usually have 4 slightly ridged sutures which split to their bases, one segment often being twice the size of the other 3; occasionally it splits into 2 equal valves. The husk and shell of the nut each are about ¹⁄₁₂ inch thick. The kernel is sweet.

This is a rare hickory in our range. It is known to occur on the slopes of a steephead, Hickory Head, in Okaloosa County, and in sandy, upland woods above the Apalachicola River at Rock Bluff in Liberty County,

Fig. 30. *Carya tomentosa*

x ⅜

and on the perimeter of a sinkhole (public dump on Spring Hill Road) in turkey oak, longleaf pine area south of Tallahassee in Leon County.

*Carya pallida* and *C. tomentosa* are our two upland hickories with tomentose-hairy leaves. The former has disklike scales on the lower surfaces of the leaflets, the leaf-bearing twig segments are ⅛ inch or less in diameter, and the husks of the fruits are about 1⁄12 inch thick. The latter has granular scales on the lower surfaces of the leaflets, the leaf-bearing twig segments are about ¼ inch in diameter, and the husks of the fruits are ¼ - ⅓ inch thick.

### 8.  Carya tomentosa Nutt.   Mockernut hickory

This is a medium-sized tree with close bark which is shallowly ridged and furrowed into a diamond-like pattern.

The leaves, including the petioles, are 8 - 16 inches long (on suckers they are up to 24 inches long), the leaflet number 5 to 9, commonly 7. The leaflets are serrate, crenate, or nearly entire, oblong-lanceolate, broadly elliptic, ovate, or lance-obovate, the upper pair 4 - 8 inches long, their bases rounded or cuneate, symmetrical or nearly so, the apices acute or acuminate. The leaf-bearing twigs, petioles, and rachi are tomentose with tufted hairs. The upper surfaces of the leaflets are covered with granular scales. The lateral leaflets are sessile or short-stalked, the terminal one short-stalked.

The leaf-bearing twig segments are relatively stout, about ¼ inch in diameter.

The fruits are nearly globose to obovoid, large, up to 2¼ inches long. The husks of the fruits are very hard and thick, up to ¼ - ⅓ inch thick, and split readily to their bases. The shells of the nuts are hard and ¼ - ⅓ inch thick. The kernel is sweet but difficult to obtain because of the thick, hard shell.

This is a common hickory in our range. It is characteristically associated with red oak, post oak, and shortleaf or loblolly pine, in woods on well-drained, fertile soils.

The mockernut has the largest and the hairiest leaves, its fruits the thickest husks and nutshells, of all our hickories. These characteristics serve to make its recognition easy. (See also *Carya pallida*.)

## BETULACEAE.  BIRCH  FAMILY

In our area, the birch family is represented by one species in each of four genera. The following key is presented as a means of identifying these:

1. Leaves in 3 ranks; buds stalked; female cones of season becoming woody, persistent through the winter and into the next season...................*Alnus serrulata*
1. Leaves in 2 ranks; buds not stalked; female cones or catkins not persistent overwinter.
    2. Outer bark coppery, curling off in large, thin patches; leaves ovate or rhombic-ovate, acute, densely pubescent below when young and along the veins when old; female cone woolly, deciduous soon after maturity...........*Betula nigra*
    2. Outer bark grayish or brownish, smooth or finely shredding; leaves ovate-oblong, oblong, or oblong-elliptical (not rhombic), acute, or some, at least, acuminate; lower surfaces of the mature leaves with tufts of hairs in the vein angles; or finely downy-pubescent; female cones leafy-bracted, or of inflated sacs, which persist well into the summer.
        3. Outer bark smooth or granular, grayish, the trunks fluted with muscle-like ridges; mature leaves glabrous above, with tufts of hairs in the vein angles below; female cones leafy-bracted...................*Carpinus caroliniana*
        3. Outer bark shredding, brown; mature leaves with few, scattered, straight hairs above, finely downy-pubescent below; female cones with individual fruits enclosed in thin, inflated, papery sacs...................*Ostrya virginiana*

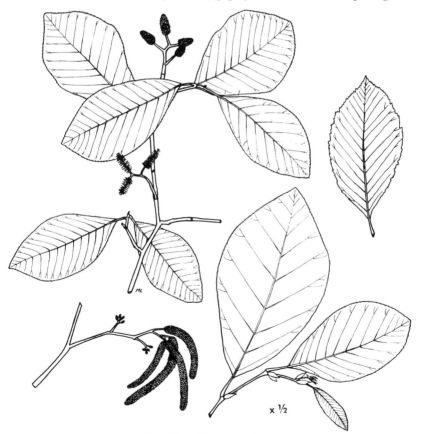

Fig. 31. *Alnus serrulata*

## ALNUS. ALDERS

### 1. Alnus serrulata (Ait.) Willd.  Hazel alder

The hazel alder is usually a shrub: occasionally it attains the dimensions of a small tree.

The leaves are simple, alternate, deciduous, and are borne in 3 ranks. Their blades are elliptic, oblong, or obovate, 3 - 5 inches long, their margins wavy-serrate, mostly with fine serrulations between the principal teeth. Their lower surfaces are glabrous or sparingly pubescent. The leaf bases are obtuse to cuneate, the tips obtuse to rounded. The buds are conspicuously stalked.

The flowers are unisexual, the plants monoecious. The male flowers are borne in long, slender, drooping catkins, the female in short-ovoid, erect spikes, both evident in autumn. The inflorescences develop to maturity in winter or early spring, mostly before the leaves emerge.

Individual fruits are small, slightly winged nutlets borne in a cone which becomes hard and woody and persists through a second year or longer. The flowering or fruiting branches form a zigzag pattern.

The hazel alder occurs locally in wet sites along stream banks, or in swamps associated with streams, throughout northern Florida. It is not common in our area.

Prominent distinguishing characters for this plant are the long-persisting, woody, fruiting cones, stalked buds, and 3-ranked leaves.

## BETULA. BIRCHES

### 1. Betula nigra L.  River birch

The river birch is a medium to large tree, often with a short main trunk from which 2 - 3 ascending, secondary trunks arise. The bark on older trunks exfoliates in large, curly, thin patches of dark, coppery-brown, exposing yellowish- to salmon-red close bark beneath.

The leaves are simple, deciduous, triangular-ovate to rhombic, 2 - 4 inches long, broadly truncate or wide-angled cuneate, the apices acute. Their margins are conspicuously doubly-serrate with 2 - 10 small teeth between the primary teeth. The lower surfaces are densely pubescent when young, and with hairs only along the veins when mature. The petioles are woolly.

The flowers are unisexual, the plants monoecious. The male flowers are borne in slender, drooping catkins, 1 - 3 in a cluster, the female in short, thick-cylindric, conelike, woolly catkins which are not usually clustered. Partially developed male catkins appear in autumn and mature in late winter or spring. Female catkins develop from buds in late winter or early spring.

The fruits are membranous-winged nutlets, each subtended by 3-lobed bracts which drop from the axis of the cone soon after maturation.

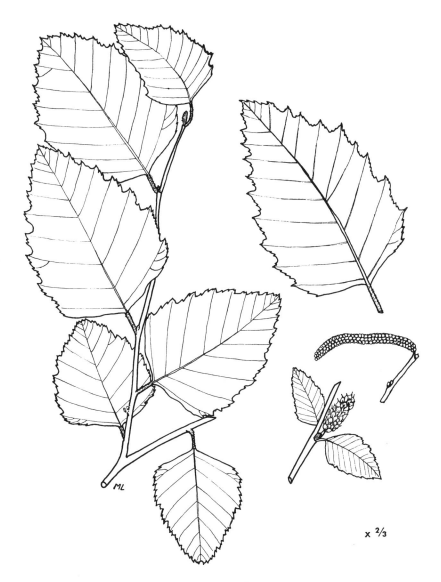

x ²/₃

Fig. 32. *Betula nigra*

The river birch is common along river or stream banks, and on flood-plains, from the Santa Fe and Suwannee rivers westward in Florida. This tree, growing almost exclusively along rivers, is easily identified by its coppery, scaly, curled patches of exfoliating bark and by its rhombic doubly-serrate leaves.

## CARPINUS

1. **Carpinus caroliniana** Walt.   American hornbeam; blue-beech

This is a small understory tree with smoothish, short-beaded or granular grayish bark, and with fluted, more or less twisted-appearing trunks. The crowns are composed of a great many slender leafy twigs, the ultimate twigs and their leaves arranged in one plane, thus forming excellent examples of leaf mosaics.

The leaves are simple, alternate, deciduous, 2-ranked, oblong to ovate-oblong, sometimes somewhat falcate, 1½ - 3½ inches long.   The blades are mostly rounded at their bases, often slightly asymmetrical, the apices acute to acuminate, glabrous above, and with tufts of hairs in the vein angles below.   Their margins are sharply and doubly-serrate. The twigs zigzag as a consequence of the 2-ranked leaves being arranged in one plane.

The flowers are unisexual, the plants monoecious.   The male flowers are borne in long, slender, drooping catkins, the female in inconspicuous, short catkins.   Both develop as the leaves unfurl.

The fruits are small, ovoid, ribbed nutlets, each being subtended by 3-lobed leaflike bracts.   The leafy-bracted fruiting clusters are 2 inches or more in length and they persist through most of the summer.

The blue-beech is of common occurrence throughout the area on river floodplains, in low hammocks, and in low, wet woods.

This tree may be recognized by the smooth, elongate fluting of the trunks which suggests the drawn muscles of a horse.   Its leaves resemble somewhat those of *Ostrya*.   They are glabrous above and hard-to-the-touch; those of *Ostrya* are somewhat hairy above, finely hairy below, more membranous, and soft-to-the-touch.

## OSTRYA

1. **Ostrya virginiana** (Mill.) K. Koch.   Eastern hophornbeam

This, too, is a small understory tree.   Its bark is brown and exfoliates in shreds.   The dead, brown foliage tends to persist on the tree into winter.

x ⅚

Fig. 33. *Carpinus caroliniana*

The leaves are simple, alternate, deciduous, 2-ranked, the blades oblong, ovate-oblong, or elliptical, 2 - 5 inches long, their bases mostly rounded to slightly subcordate, occasionally somewhat unequal, the apices acute to acuminate. The upper surfaces bear scattered, straight hairs, the lower surfaces are finely downy-pubescent. Their margins are sharply serrate, or sharply double-serrate.

The flowers are unisexual, the plants monoecious. The male flowers are borne in slender, drooping catkins, the female in very inconspicuous catkins. Both appear in early spring as the leaves unfurl.

x 1½

x ¾

Fig. 34. *Ostrya virginiana*

Fruits are small, flattened-ovoid nutlets which are enclosed by membranous, inflated sacs; the mature fruiting catkins are 1 - 3 inches long and they persist through most of the summer.

The eastern hophornbeam is of frequent occurrence in rich-wooded high hammocks and on well-drained floodplains from middle Florida westward. It often occurs in proximity to the blue-beech, but tends to be on drier sites.

Aside from the leaf characters mentioned under *Carpinus*, the bark differences are such as to make distinguishing *Carpinus* from *Ostrya* easy. The bark of the former is smoothish to granular and gray; that of the latter is shreddy-flaking and brown.

## FAGACEAE. BEECH AND OAK FAMILY

1. Buds not clustered at or near the ends of the twigs; fruit a nut borne in a spiny, dehiscent involucre.
    2. Marginal teeth of the leaves tipped by a mucro; staminate flowers borne in elongate, erect or ascending catkins; nuts circular in cross-section, enclosed in dehiscent involucres whose surfaces bear clusters of long, stiff spines ....................................................................................................CASTANEA
    2. Marginal teeth of the leaves not tipped by a mucro; staminate flowers borne in pendulant globular catkins; nuts triangular, the angles somewhat winged, borne in dehiscent involucres whose surfaces bear individual short spines ...........................................................................................................FAGUS
1. Buds clustered at or near the tips of the twigs; fruit a nut (acorn) borne in a cup-like involucre composed of many overlapping scales.............................QUERCUS

### CASTANEA. CHINQUAPIN; CHINKAPIN

The chinquapins are small trees or shrubs with simple, alternate, deciduous, straight-pinnately-veined leaves. The flowers, appearing after the leaves, are unisexual, the plants monoecious. Staminate flowers are cream-colored, odoriferous, and are produced in profusion on elongate-cylindrical, erect or ascending catkins. The pistillate flowers are greenish, and are borne in inconspicuous, interrupted, few-flowered catkins (nearer the tips of the developing branchlets than the staminate). Sometimes female flowers are born at the bases of principally male-flowered catkins, particularly on those nearer the tips of the branchlets. Female flowers occur, usually 3 together, in ovoid, soft-spiny involucres, which in fruit become stiff-spiny and enclose 2 - 3 (1) nuts.

The chinquapins comprise a group of very variable trees and shrubs whose identities have been variously interpreted by authors. There appear to be two reasonably clear-cut forms of tree stature in our area. We choose to treat them as *Castanea ashei* and *C. floridana*, which is the best we can do in the light of the wide diversity of opinion as to interpretation of the group.

1. Lower surfaces of the leaves grayish-white, velvety-tomentose to glabrous; staminate catkins crowned with a profusion of flowers, the catkins thickish, about ⅜ inch broad at full anthesis...........................................................................1. *C. ashei*

1. Lower surfaces of leaves pale green, finely subtomentose to glabrous; staminate aments somewhat interrupted, the clusters of flowers with short spaces between them, the catkins slender, about ⅛ inch broad at full anthesis............2. *C. floridana*

### 1. Castanea ashei Sudw.   Ashe chinquapin; coastal chinquapin

This is a small tree or shrub which, when in bloom in early summer, is conspicuous because of its showy sprays of ascending, staminate spikes.

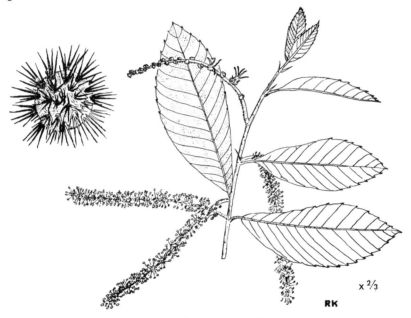

Fig. 35.   *Castanea ashei*

The leaves are oblong, oblong-ovate, or elliptic, averaging 2½ - 3 inches long by 1 - 1¼ inches broad.  They are green and smooth above, whitish-tomentose to whitish-glabrate below.  The lateral veins extend straight and parallel from the midribs and terminate in the sharp teeth of the serrate margins.

The male flowers are borne in crowded profusion on numerous erect or ascending cream-colored catkins about ⅜ inch broad.  The flowers are very fragrant.  The female flowers are inconspicuous, mostly borne on separate, interrupted catkins nearer the tips of the branchlets; sometimes there are a few at the bases of catkins bearing chiefly male flowers.

The fruiting involucres (burs) are nearly an inch broad at maturity, occur 1 - 7 per stalk, and split into 2 - 4 valves. Their faces are tawny- or brown-tomentose, and bear numerous clusters (scales) of branched, stiff and sharp bristles or spines. These spine-bearing scales are set apart so that there are open areas between them on the faces of the burs. One to three nuts are enclosed in each involucre. The nuts are ovoid, pointed, round in cross-section, and are about ½ inch in diameter.

The Ashe chinquapin occurs in open sandy woods, edges of hammocks, on sandy roadsides, and along fence rows in sandy fields, nearly throughout northern Florida.

Chinquapins may be identified as such by the spiny burs which enclose 1 - 3 ovoid, acorn-like nuts. The burs may be found, if not on the trees at any given time, on the ground beneath the trees. The Ashe or coastal chinquapin is distinguished from the Florida chinquapin by its markedly whitish lower leaf surfaces. When in flower, the staminate catkins bear a greater profusion of crowded flowers, and the catkins are thicker, about ⅜ inch broad, as against more interrupted, more slender catkins, about ⅛ inch broad, in *C. floridana*.

2. **Castanea floridana** (Sarg.) Ashe. Florida chinquapin

This is a small tree of fertile, upland, deciduous woods and flatwoods hammocks.

The leaves are oblong-obovate, elliptic-obovate, to long-elliptical, averaging 3 - 4 inches long by 1¼ - 2 inches broad. Their margins are serrate, the venation as in *Castanea ashei*. The blades are green and smooth above, paler green (but not definitely whitish) below; the lower leaf surfaces vary from finely subtomentose and pale to glabrate and green.

The male flowers are borne in interrupted clusters on erect-ascending, slender, greenish-yellow catkins, the catkins about ⅛ inch broad. The flowers are moderately fragrant. The sprays of staminate catkins are much less conspicuous from a distance than are those of *Castanea ashei*. The female flowers are as in the preceding.

The fruiting involucres (burs) are similar to those of *C. ashei*.

This tree is considered by some authors as a larger form of *Castanea alnifolia* Nutt., a low, clonal shrub. What its true status may be we are unprepared to stay, but from the Tallahassee Red Hills region to Bay and Escambia counties, it is definitely a tree and it is not associated with the low clonal shrub.

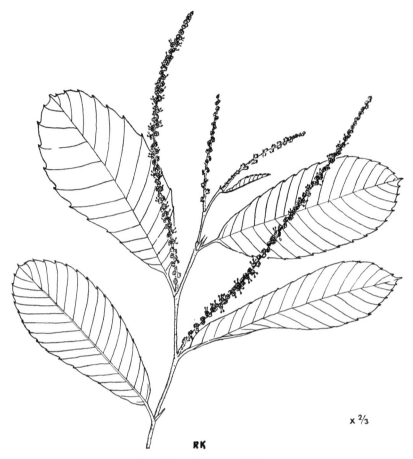

x ⅔

RK

Fig. 36.   *Castanea floridana*

## Fagus.  Beeches

### 1.  **Fagus grandifolia** Ehrh.   American beech

A large, hardwood forest tree, this is one of eastern North America's handsomest.  Its smooth, ash-gray bark, which never exhibits the corky outgrowths as does that of the sugarberry, is striking although it is commonly mottled by lichens, liverworts, and mosses which grow upon it. Not infrequently, the bark, because it is smooth and does not slough off, bears the mark of the romantic adolescent initial or "heart" carver. Although the sugar hackberry falls victim to the same practice, injury to its bark stimulates corky development so that the carvings become raised or tend to be obliterated by corky warts.

The leaves are simple, alternate, 2-ranked, deciduous, glossy above, and stiff-papery. The blades are oblong, broadly elliptic, oval, or more rarely ovate, 2½ - 6 inches long and mostly up to 2 inches broad. The leaf bases are broadly cuneate, rounded, or very slightly cordate, often slightly inequilateral, the apices mostly acuminate. The principal lateral veins are prominent, running straight and parallel with each other from the midrib and terminating in the teeth or at the margin. The leaf margins are shallowly crenate-serrate, crenate-dentate, or nearly entire. The upper leaf surfaces are smooth at maturity and dark green, the lower somewhat paler, with soft short hairs only on the veins, or sparsely beset with short, soft pubescence throughout.

x ½

Fig. 37. *Fagus grandifolia*

The unfolding leaves in spring have abundant long, silky white hairs on the veins below, making the lower surfaces prominently white-lined, and the surfaces between the veins are pubescent with short, soft hairs.

By midsummer or late summer, thence throughout the winter, the terminal buds are distinctive. They are elongate, lance-awl-shaped, about ¾ inch long, the overlapping scales chestnut-brown and with buff-colored, hairy tips. The twigs are marked by stipule scars which nearly encircle them.

The flowers, appearing with the leaves, are unisexual, the plants monoecious. The staminate flowers are individually small and are borne in dangling globular balls. They are apetalous, but the calyx of each is bell-shaped, 5 - 7-cleft, and bears long silky hairs. The pistillate flowers occur in pairs or clusters at the end of short peduncles in the leaf axils. The peduncle is densely clothed with long silky white hairs.

The fruits are triangular, 3-winged or 3-edged nuts, 1 - 3 (usually 2) invested by an involucre whose surface is clothed with hooked, but not sharp, prickles. The involucre splits into 4 parts at maturity.

The American beech occurs mainly in hammocks and on rich hardwoods slopes from the Tallahassee Red Hills area westward in northern Florida. West and Arnold (1956) report that its southernmost occurrence is an isolated colony near Santa Fe in Alachua County. Also there are specimens in the University of Florida Herbarium from Lake City, Columbia County.

Distinguishing characteristics of this tree are its tight, smooth, ash-gray bark, its stiff-papery, bright green leaves whose lateral veins are prominent, paralleling each other and ending in the teeth or at the leaf margin (which is usually remotely crenate-serrate or dentate). In winter, the characteristic bark, together with the long awl-shaped buds and twigs with stipular ring-scars, serve to distinguish it. Although the chinquapins have leaves with similar venation, the marginal teeth of the leaves abruptly contract into an extended point, whereas those of the beech are blunt. Moreover, the nuts of the chinquapin are invested in an involucre clothed in stiff, sharp, straight prickles.

## QUERCUS. OAKS

The oaks are trees with heavy and hard wood and as a group exhibit distinctive characteristics of flowers and fruits. The flowers are individually small and unisexual (the plants monoecious), appearing in mid-spring. The staminate are borne in slim, drooping catkins which appear singly or in clusters from the axils of the developing leaves. Each flower consists of 3 - 12 stamens seated in a 2 - 8-lobed calyx. The pistillate are borne in inconspicuous solitar᾽ spikes of one or few flowers, in the axils of the developing leaves of the season, and usually nearer the tips of the twigs than the staminate. Each consists of a 3-locular pistil with a 3-lobed stigma. The ovulary has 6 ovules, but only one matures into a seed. A 6-lobed calyx is adherent to the ovulary and is in turn enclosed in a cup of overlapping involucral scales which by subsequent development form a cup in which the ripened ovulary (nut or acorn) is seated.

The oaks have an extremely variable foliage. Leaves of the same tree, on sucker shoots, or on lower or upper branches, may differ markedly. Moreover, leaves of young trees often differ notably from those of mature trees. On a given tree, the shade leaves of lower branches are commonly much larger and lobed to a lesser degree. If one particular kind of oak has lobed leaves, those of lower branches or of vigorous sucker shoots are frequently more shallowly or differently lobed than those of mature branches higher and nearer the periphery of the crown. The leaves of fertile branches are most nearly consistent in size and form for the species, but even in these, striking variation occurs from tree to tree. Allowing for variation of leaf forms, the student can still learn to seek prevailing characters which may be considered as distinguishing for each species. One should learn to restrict his observations to mature leaves of fertile branches high on the crown of the tree in order to come to know the various oaks. Later, then, after repeated observations, the necessary correlations of intergradations can be made which make possible identification of young trees, or of older ones by use of leaves from lower branches or sucker shoots. In the descriptions of the various species below, distinctive characteristics of the leaves are derived from those of mature branches in the crowns and the variation expected on most of the species is noted.

Identification of oaks is complicated somewhat because some of the species hybridize and the progeny of such hybrids exhibits characteristics of an intermediate nature. This hybridity is probably not so common as the frustrated student would like to believe, and once he is reasonably familiar with the various species and their characters it is often possible to "guess" the probable parentage of a supposed hybrid.

For purposes of identification of difficult or doubtful individuals, it is helpful to collect a range of leaves from different parts of the same individual and compare these with known material or with text descriptions. Acorns and/or the acorn cups may be distinctive enough to aid in identification. In some cases, the acorn and cup alone are so distinctive as to render determination possible.

With regard to persistence of live leaves into or over winter, the oaks of our region are of three general kinds: evergreen, partly evergreen, and deciduous. Some, as for example the laurel oak (*Q. hemisphaerica*) and myrtle-leaf oak (*Q. myrtifolia*), usually retain virtually all their leaves until new growth begins in spring. At this time, all or nearly all the old leaves fall, defoliation and appearance of new leaves occurring within a short time. For practical purposes, therefore, these oaks are evergreen even though few, if any, leaves of one season are borne through the next. The live oak (*Q. virginiana*), the sand-live oak (*Q. geminata*), and the dwarf-like oak (*Q. minima*) are in the same sense essentially evergreen but some individuals, or individuals growing under particular conditions, may become more or less defoliated in mid-winter.

The water oak (*Q. nigra*), diamond-leaf oak (*Q. laurifolia*), and the Chapman oak (*Q. chapmanii*) are partially evergreen. That is to say, they gradually lose their leaves during the winter. Even some trees of *Q. incana,* ordinarily considered deciduous, retain some live leaves into the winter if growing in protected sites.

The other oaks of our region are regularly deciduous, although many dead leaves may remain on the trees into the winter.

The leaves of the oaks are simple, entire, toothed, or lobed, and are borne alternately on more or less 5-angled twigs in 5 ranks. The winter buds are clothed with numerous overlapping scales and clusters of them characteristically occur near the tips of twigs. Seen in cross-section, the pith of the twigs is 5-angled or 5-pointed.

The fruits are nuts, known as acorns, and are seated in saucer-like or cuplike involucres composed of closely overlapping, dry, hardened scales. With respect to period of maturation of the acorns, the oaks comprise two groups: (1) the white oaks (section *Lepidobalanus*), in which the acorns are "annual," that is, they mature during one growing season; (2) the red oaks (section *Erythrobalanus*) in which the acorns are "biennial," that is, they mature over a period of two consecutive growing seasons. Thus, from autumn to spring, no acorns of any stage of development will be seen on white oak trees and during the growing season a set of developing acorns may be seen on the twigs. On the other hand, during the autumn to spring period, the red oaks bear partially developed acorns on the twigs, and during the growing season the twigs of the season have a set of developing acorns and the twigs of the previous season bear a more fully developed set of acorns. In addition, the inner surfaces of the nutshells of the white oaks' acorns are glabrous while in the red oaks they are tomentose.

In northern Florida, 25 kinds of oaks occur. Of these, 19 regularly attain tree stature, 4 small-tree or shrub stature, and 2 are low shrubs which form clones of shoots by underground runners. The dwarf oaks are included here as a matter of interest.

A. Fruit "annual"; inner surfaces of the nutshells glabrous; leaf apices, teeth, or
    lobes of the leaves, not usually bristle-tipped..........................................WHITE OAKS
    1. Leaves prominently lobed, or coarsely toothed.

2. Mature leaves mostly glabrous on their lower surfaces.
   3. Leaf blades whitish on their lower surfaces, those of fertile crown branches with 7 - 11 elongate, finger-like lobes............1. *Q. alba*
   3. Leaf blades green on their lower surfaces, those of fertile crown branches with 5 - 7 short-rounded lobes, or sinuate-toothed or lobed ................2. *Q. austrina*
2. Leaves uniformly pubescent on their lower surfaces, or pubescent at least on the veins or in the vein axils.
   4. Leaf blades having 3 upper lobes notably larger than the lobes lower on the blades.
      5. Involucre almost completely enclosing the acorns; some leaves with pointed lobes; trees of river bottomlands............12. *Q. lyrata*
      5. Involucre enclosing about ⅓ of the acorns; none of the leaves with pointed lobes; trees of uplands.
         6. Twigs densely short—pubescent............23. *Q. stellata*
         6. Twigs glabrous............13. *Q. margaretta*
   4. Leaf blades with numeorus subequal crenate lobes or teeth terminating each of the numerous straight lateral veins.
      7. Lobes or teeth of the leaf blades predominantly blunt or rounded; lower leaf surfaces with sparsely distributed short hairs; larger leaves exceeding 6 inches in length; acorns about 1½ inches long; involucral scales very large, thick, and predominantly large-keeled ............20. *Q. prinus*
      7. Lobes or teeth of the leaf blades predominantly sharp-pointed; lower leaf surfaces with a dense, closely appressed tomentum; larger leaves 5 inches long or less; acorns about ¾ inch in length; involucral scales small, thin, and flattish, scarcely, if at all, keeled ............16. *Q. muehlenbergii*
1. Leaves entire, sinuate, wavy, or slightly lobed near their apices.
   8. The leaves with a fascicled pubescence below, the hairs tightly appressed thus giving the surface a smooth effect as seen with the naked eye or long and feltlike.
      9. Leaf blades rolled downward on each side, conspicuously rugose-veiny............7. *Q. geminata*
      9. Leaf blades flat, their edges barely revolute, not conspicuously rugose-veiny.
         10. Plants becoming large trees............25. *Q. virginiana*
         10. Plants shrubby, mostly not exceeding 3 feet in height, spreading by underground runners and forming low thickets ............15. *Q. minima*
   8. Leaves glabrous or sparsely pubescent below, or pubescent only on the veins............4. *Q. chapmanii*

A. Fruit "biennial" (except in *Q. pumila*); inner surfaces of the nutshell pubescent; leaf apices, teeth, or lobes of the leaves, often bristle-tipped............ ............Red or Black Oaks

1. Leaves on fertile crown branches usually entire, or with only 3 - 5 shallow lobes or coarse teeth near their apices.
   2. Lower leaf surfaces glabrous, or pubescent only in the vein axils.
      3. Blades of the leaves linear-oblong to elliptic-lanceolate, predominantly broadest at their middles and tapering to both ends......19. *Q. phellos*

3. Blades of the leaves oblanceolate to obovate, elliptic, or lanceolate, predominantly broadest above or below their middles.

    4. Plants characteristically thicket-forming by underground runners, rarely a small, scrubby tree; inhabiting old dunes and white sand ridges and hills of evergreen oak scrub................17. *Q. myrtifolia*

    4. Plants characteristically erect scrubby trees or large trees; inhabiting woodlands of various sorts, not evergreen oak scrub.

        5. Leaf blades predominantly obovate or spatulate and commonly somewhat lobed.

            6. At their broadest places, the leaf blades are nearly or quite as broad as the entire leaves are long........3. *Q. caput-rivuli*

            6. At their broadest places, the leaf blades are about half or less than half as broad as the entire leaves are long...........................18. *Q. nigra*

        5. Leaf blades predominantly oblanceolate, spatulate, rarely obovate, rhombic, or lanceolate, very rarely lobed.

            7. The apices of the leaves bristle-tipped; to transmitted light the leaves are opaque, the reticulate venation inconspicuous................8. *Q. hemisphaerica*

            7. The apices of the leaves are predominantly rounded and not bristle-tipped; to transmitted light the reticulate venation of the leaves is readily apparent................11. *Q. laurifolia*

2. Lower leaf surfaces uniformly pubescent.

    8. Leaf blades broadly obovate in general outline; lower leaf surfaces scurfy-pubescent or the pubescence bright rusty-yellow........................14. *Q. marilandica*

    8. Leaf blades oblong, elliptic, lanceolate, oblanceolate, or narrowly obovate; lower leaf surfaces grayish-tomentose.

        9. Plants not commonly over 3 feet tall, the shoots from slender underground runners thus usually in low thickets; leaves green, not bluish or ashy-green, at least above................21. *Q. pumila*

        9. Plants small or scrubby trees, or medium-sized trees, or if occasionally forming thickets from underground runners, the shoots much more than 3 feet tall; leaves with a bluish or ashy-green color..........................9. *Q. incana*

1. Leaves on fertile crown branches with prominent lobes separated by deep sinuses.

    10. Leaf blades with a dense, dull gray or tan mat of tomentum below, not at all lustrous.

        11. The leaf blades of the crown branches predominantly with a long, strap-like terminal lobe below which are a pair of large ascending lateral lobes, and nearer the base a pair of short-triangular lobes, the base itself U-shaped................5. *Q. falcata* var. *falcata*

        11. The leaf blades of the crown branches with 5 - 11 more or less triangular and subequal lobes which spread nearly at right angles to the midrib, the leaf bases truncate-oblique to broadly cuneate, not U-shaped................6. *Q. falcata* var. *pagodaefolia*

    10. Leaf blades glabrous below, or pubescent only in the vein axils, or with a thin pubescence and the lustrous surface showing through.

        12. Upper scales of the involucre folding inward, there extending downward and appressed against the inner surface of the cup; petioles of the leaves twisted so that the broad blade surfaces are oriented

vertically to the ground..................................................10. *Q. laevis*

12.  Upper scales of the involucre not folding inward; leaf orientation not as above.

    13.  Leaf blades mostly with 7 - 9 primary lobes, each with 3 - 13 secondary bristle-tipped lobes and/or teeth; lower leaf surfaces lustrous, only the vein axils pubescent......22. *Q. shumardii*

    13.  Leaf blades mostly with 5 - 7 primary lobes, each with 2 - 7 bristle-tipped teeth; lower leaf surfaces sparsely tawny-pubescent, or tawny-pubescent in patches and in the vein axils, lustrous surfaces showing through............................24. *Q. velutina*

### 1. **Quercus alba** L. White oak

This is a large tree with light gray or whitish flaky and scaly bark which on the trunks of old trees is divided into broad flat ridges.

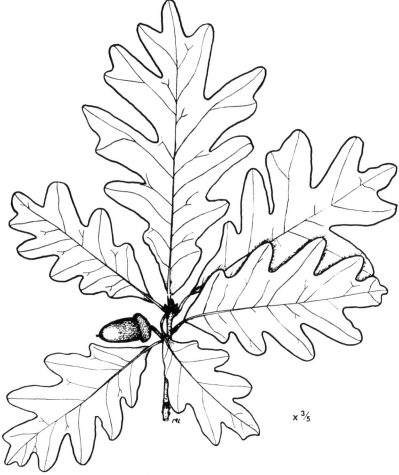

x ⅗

Fig. 38. *Quercus alba*

The leaves are deciduous, the blades 5 - 9 inches long and 2 - 4 inches broad. They are unevenly lobed, the lobes finger-like, narrow to broad, sometimes unevenly forked, forward-pointing and with rounded tips. The sinuses between the lobes are V- or U-shaped. The leaf bases are wedge- or U-shaped. The upper leaf surfaces are green, shiny and smooth, the lower whitish, not pubescent at maturity.

The cup of the fruit is sessile or short-stalked, shallowly bowl-shaped, its scales drab, warty, and puberulent. The annual acorn is ovoid or oblong, ½ - ¾ inch long, shiny tan to dark brown, and the inner surfaces of the nutshells are glabrous.

This oak occurs on well-drained, mixed hardwood sites, mostly in middle northern and western Florida.

The leaves of the white oak are distinguished by their whitish lower surfaces and finger-like, bristleless lobes. Those of the lower branches or of saplings may be broader and have shorter, less finger-like lobes. The leaves of the bluff oak (*Quercus austrina*) are similar but have broader lobes and are green underneath. Post oak leaves have more squarish lobes and they are more or less hairy below.

## 2.  **Quercus austrina** Small.  Bluff oak

*Q. durandii* Buckl., var. *austrina* (Small) Palmer

A medium-sized tree, this oak attains heights of 80 feet, and trunk diameters of 2 - 3 feet. The bark is light gray and scaly, similar to that of the white oak.

The leaves are deciduous, the blades 3 - 6½ inches long and 1 - 4 inches broad and have 3 - 9 (typically 5 - 7) rounded lobes, or occasionally they are unlobed or merely sinuate. The upper pair or two pairs of lobes point forward and are separated by narrow sinuses. The lower leaf surfaces are glabrous and green.

The involucres are sessile or short-stalked, shallowly bowl-shaped or cuplike and have small, thin, overlapping scales. The annual acorns are ovoid, ⅓ - ½ inch long, and the inner surfaces of the shells are glabrous.

The bluff oak inhabits rich wooded bluffs and limestone woodlands. We have records of its occurrence in the following north Florida counties: Marion, Alachua, Columbia, Liberty, Gadsden, and Jackson.

Of the oaks in our range, the bluff oak is most nearly like the white oak (*Quercus alba*). It is still more like *Q. durandii* Buckl., which occurs somewhat to the north and west of northern Florida and is considered by Palmer (1945) as a variety of that species.

The leaves of mature, crown branches of *Quercus alba* have longer, narrower lobes, and deeper, wider sinuses than do those of *Q. austrina;* the primary lobes of the former are themselves somewhat forked.    Moreover, the lower surfaces of the leaves of *Q. alba* are whitish, those of *Q. austrina* green.

x ⅔

Fig. 39.   *Quercus austrina*

3.  **Quercus caput-rivuli** Ashe.    Arkansas oak

*Q. arkansana* Sarg.

This is a small or medium-sized tree, commonly with a crooked trunk, and having thick, rough, blackish bark.

The leaves are deciduous, broadly obovate, broadly oval, or almost orbicular. The leaf blades are 3 - 5 inches long and 2 - 4 inches broad at their broadest parts. The summits of the leaves are broadly rounded and often wavy, or shallowly triangular-lobed, the lobes bristle-tipped, or if unlobed then with bristles scattered along the leaf margins. The obovate leaves are wedgelike, the sides straight-tapering to a rounded or acute base. The upper surfaces of the leaves are glabrous and green, the lower paler green and glabrous, or nearly so at maturity, or pubescent only in the vein angles.

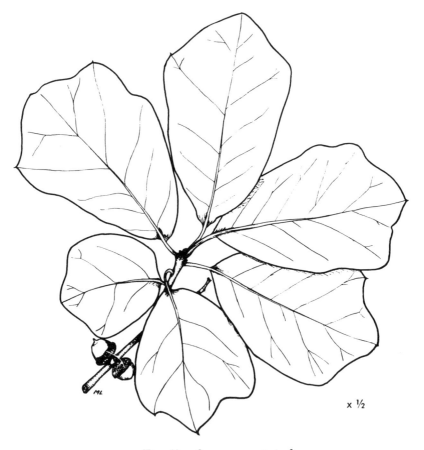

x ½

Fig. 40.  *Quercus caput-rivuli*

The involucres are saucer-like, enclosing only the base of the nut, the scales small, rounded or blunt, and tightly appressed.

The acorns are hemispheric or broadly ovoid, about ½ inch in diam-

eter, somewhat downy, the inner surface of the nutshells pubescent.
The fruits are borne singly or in pairs, sessile or short-stalked. They
are biennial.

In our area, the Arkansas oak appears to be restricted to sandy ravines
in the vicinity of Niceville, Okaloosa County.

The involucre and acorn of *Quercus caput-rivuli* are similar to those
of *Q. hemisphaerica*, although in leaf and bark characters these two
are quite unlike. In leaf form, *Q. caput-rivuli* resembles *Q. marilandica*.
Leaves of the former of these two tend to be round-obovate, tapering
wedgelike to an acute or rounded base, the lower surfaces essentially
glabrous at maturity, and its acorns enclosed only at their bases by
saucer-like involucres. Leaves of the latter of the two tend to be
blocky T-shaped, or broadly triangular-obovate, the sides abruptly narrowed and thus concave to a rounded to subcordate base, the lower
surfaces scurfy- or bright rusty-yellow-pubescent, and the involucres
turbinate-hemispheric enclosing ½ or slightly more of the acorns.

### 4. **Quercus chapmanii** Sarg.   Chapman oak

A small tree or shrub, this oak has light gray bark which exfoliates
in thin plates suggestive of that of the white oak.

The leaves are somewhat persistent, commonly turning yellow or
reddish and falling one by one during winter or early spring. The
blades are oblong, elliptic, obovate, or spatulate, 2 - 4 inches long and
¾ - 1¼ inches wide. They vary from unlobed, to irregularly wavy-
margined, to somewhat 3-lobed (or more rarely 5-lobed) at their apices.
In the lobed blades, the terminal lobe is rounded to triangular and
round-tipped, the lateral lobes shoulder-like. The leaf bases are cuneate
or U-shaped. The leaves are dark green and glabrous above, lighter
green, nonlustrous, and sparsely pubescent below, or pubescent only
on the veins below.

The involucres are hemispheric, enclosing ⅓ - ½ of the nut. The
annual acorns are ovoid, ½ - ¾ inch long, the inner surfaces of the shell
glabrous. The fruits are usually borne singly and are sessile or short-
stalked.

This oak occurs amongst the evergreen oak-sand pine scrub of coastal
dunes, or of hills or ridges of white sand near the east and Gulf coasts
of northern Florida, and locally in similar habitats elsewhere. Its associates are *Pinus clausa, Quercus myrtifolia,* and *Q. geminata,* but it
is usually less abundant in these communities than the latter two oaks.

Of the oaks occurring on hills and ridges of white sand in our area,
the Chapman oak is identifiable by its oblong, elliptic, obovate, or

spatulate leaves which are nonlustrous below, have cuneate to U-shaped leaf bases, and some of which are usually 3-lobed at their apices, the terminal lobe being rounded to broadly triangular and round-tipped, the laterals shoulder-like.

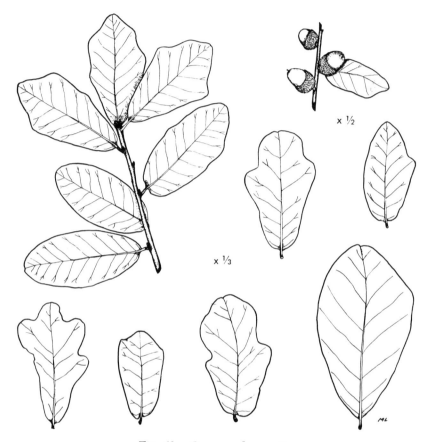

Fig. 41. *Quercus chapmanii*

5. **Quercus falcata** Michx., var. **falcata.**    Southern red oak; Spanish oak

The southern red oak is a large tree with nearly black, rough bark which is deeply fissured between flat ridges. The young branchlets are gray-pubescent, becoming glabrate and reddish the second year.

The leaves are deciduous, 4 - 9 inches long, prominently lobed, the number of lobes mostly 3 - 5, and the lobing pattern very variable. The lobes tend to be long and narrow, separated by wide sinuses, and the lobes or their subdivisions prominently bristle-tipped. Typically, the leaves have a terminal, straplike, elongated lobe with secondary lobes or teeth at its summit, a large pair of lateral lobes below the terminal one, the latter commonly pointed and curved upward, and a lowermost pair of small triangular lobes. The leaf base is conspicuously U-shaped. The upper surfaces of the blades are dark green and glabrous, the lower uniformly gray- or rusty-soft-pubescent. Leaves of saplings and vigorous shoots or sprouts are characteristically 3-lobed near their summits, the bulk of the blade appearing as a large U.

The involucres are saucer-like, enclosing about ⅓ of the nut, the scales densely gray-pubescent, closely appressed. The biennial acorns are ovoid to subglobose, about ½ inch long, the inner surfaces of the nutshells pubescent. The fruits are mostly borne singly on short stalks.

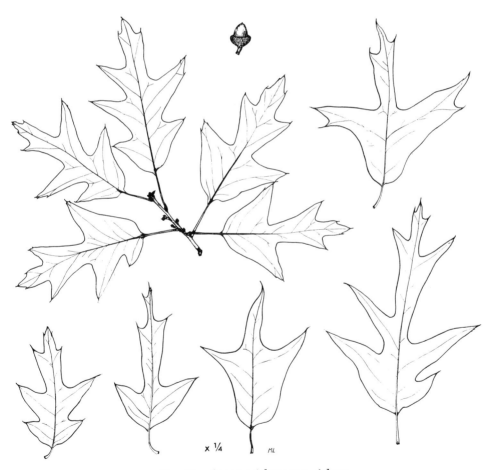

× ¼

Fig. 42. *Quercus falcata* var. *falcata*

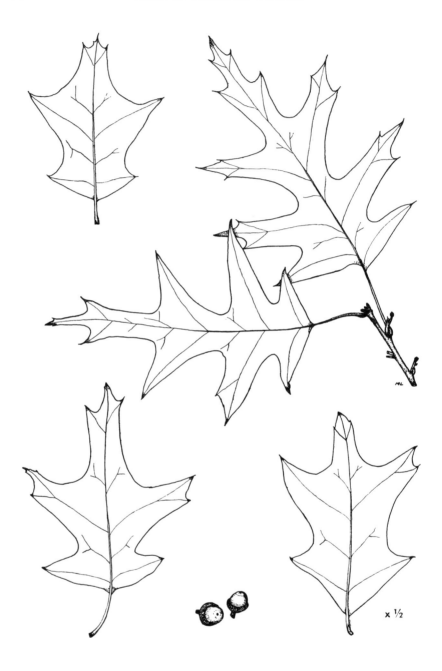

Fig. 43. *Quercus falcata* var. *pagodaefolia*

Throughout northern Florida, the southern red oak occurs in open upland woods on fertile soils. It is commonly associated with *Quercus stellata, Q. velutina, Carya tomentosa, Pinus echinata,* and/or *P. taeda.*

This is the only oak of our area with deeply lobed leaves, the lobes bristle-tipped, the undersurfaces of which are persistently and uniformly soft-pubescent and with conspicuously U-shaped leaf bases. (See also *Quercus falcata* var. *pagodaefolia.*)

6. **Quercus falcata** Michx., var. **pagodaefolia** Ell.   Cherrybark oak; swamp red oak

The cherrybark oak is very much like the southern red oak. Its bark is not as rough and forms narrow, flaky, or scaly ridges.

The leaves, in general, have more lobes and these form a different pattern. Those of the crown branchlets have 5 - 11 lobes which are more or less triangular, subequal and spread at nearly right angles to the midrib. The leaf bases are more or less truncate-oblique just below the lowermost lobes, not U-shaped. Leaves of lower branches are broader and 5 - 7-lobed, the lobes squarish or triangular and separated by more shallow sinuses. Their bases are short-cuneate, subtruncate, or rounded, but not conspicuously U-shaped. As in the southern red oak, the lower surfaces of the leaves are persistently and uniformly soft-pubescent, a characteristic which suffices to distinguish it from oaks of other species having leaves deeply lobed, the lobes bristle-tipped.

Our only record of the cherrybark oak in northern Florida is in floodplain woods along the Apalachicola River at Chattahoochee.

7. **Quercus geminata** Small.   Sand-live oak

*Q. virginiana* L., var. *maritima* (Michx.) Sarg.

This is a small to medium-sized tree. Where it occurs as component of evergreen oak scrub, it is commonly scrubby or thicket-forming. The bark is dark, thick, roughly ridged and furrowed, becoming blocky.

The leaves are oblong, oblong-elliptic, or lanceolate, 1 - 2½ inches long, the sides of the leaf tending to be rolled downward and the margins markedly revolute. This gives them an over-all appearance of an inverted shallow boat. They are thick and leathery, rugose-veiny, the veins being deeply impressed on the upper surfaces. The lower surfaces are densely and tightly tomentose.

The involucres and acorns are commonly borne in pairs on peduncles of varying lengths. The involucres are turbinate, enclosing about ⅓ of the nut. The scales are thinnish, acute, and closely appressed. The annual acorns are oblong-ellipsoid or ovoid, ½ - 1 inch long, tan-brown to nearly black, the inner surfaces of the nutshells glabrous.

x ⁴/₅

Fig. 44. *Quercus geminata*

The sand-live oak occurs on seacoast dunes, in the evergreen oak scrub on white sands, mostly near the Atlantic or Gulf coasts. The larger trees are usually on deep, more fertile sandy sites elsewhere throughout northern Florida. It is the most abundant and most consistently present component of the evergreen oak scrub. Many sites of intermediate nature as to soil texture, soil water, and soil fertility support live oaks which are intermediate in character between *Quercus virginiana* and *Q. geminata.* It is not unlikely that these are hybrids between them.

Many of the ornamental live oaks planted or otherwise used as shade trees are specimens of *Q. geminata* or possibly hybrids.

The sand-live oak is most likely to be mistaken for *Q. virginiana.* Its leaves are much more rugose-veiny, with the sides rolled downward, the edges markedly revolute, densely and loosely tomentose beneath. Those of the latter are not prominently rugose-veiny, the blades are relatively flat, the margins with a yellowish-opaque edge which is scarcely revolute, and they are tightly tomentose, the tomentum scarcely evident to the naked eye.

## 8. **Quercus hemisphaerica** Bartr.   Laurel oak

*Q. laurifolia* of authors, not Michx.

This is a handsome (although not a long-lived) evergreen oak which attains large size except for its apparent shrubbiness where small trees are in part buried in the sand of growing coastal dunes. The bark is dark gray, becoming blackish on older trunks. It is relatively smooth until the trunk reaches large size, when it is irregularly furrowed and ridged but not blocky.

The leaves are persistent until just before or during the time of resumed growth in early spring. The leaves of mature branches are 1 - 5 inches long, oblanceolate, elliptic, or lanceolate. The tips are bristle-tipped, the bases mostly cuneate or sometimes rounded. The margins are entire and have a yellow-opaque edge which is not revolute. Both surfaces are glabrous and lustrous. To transmitted light, the leaves are opaque and the reticulate venation is not at all conspicuous. The leaves of saplings, sprouts, or vigorous shoots commonly are bristle-toothed or have bristle-tipped lobes.

The involucres are shallowly saucer-like, with the scales very tightly appressed. The acorns are ovoid to hemispheric, ½ - ⅔ inch long, and are about ⅕ enclosed by the cups. The inner surfaces of the nutshells are pubescent. The biennial fruits are borne singly or in pairs and are sessile or short-stalked.

The laurel oak occurs in mixed open woods, hammocks, on sites back of old coastal dunes, along roadsides, and on city lots. It is common throughout northern Florida and is a popular shade tree.

Since this tree has come to be known popularly as laurel oak, it is unfortunate that the Latin name, *Quercus laurifolia,* by which it was long known, must be applied to the diamond-leaf oak. This is based

x ½

Fig. 45.  *Quercus hemisphaerica*

upon the International Rules of Botanical Nomenclature, however, and cannot be helped.

Leaves of *Q. hemisphaerica* are somewhat similar to those of *Q. phellos* and *Q. laurifolia*. Those of *Q. phellos* are generally broadest at their mid-points and taper toward both ends, while those of *Q. hemisphaerica* are mostly broadest above their mid-points. The leaves of *Q. laurifolia*, often blunt-tipped, have a reticulate venation which is easily apparent when viewed against the light. Those of *Q. hemisphaerica*, mostly pointed at the tip, are opaque and the reticulate venation is not easily apparent when so viewed. (See also *Q. virginiana*.)

x ¾

Fig. 46.  *Quercus incana*

## 9. Quercus incana Bartr.    Bluejack oak

*Q. cinerea* Michx.

A small tree, or shrublike, this oak commonly forms thickets from underground runners. The bark is thick, gray to blackish, becoming deeply corrugated and blocky. The young branchlets are heavily pubescent.

The leaves are ordinarily deciduous in autumn, tardily so only where protected or during very mild winters. The blades are oblong, elliptic, narrowly obovate, or lanceolate, 2½ - 5 inches long and up to about 2 inches wide. The leaf margins are entire, or occasionally irregularly dentate-toothed or lobed on sprouts. The leaf apices are blunt or rounded, tipped with a short bristle. The leaves are bluish- or ashy-green, both surfaces pubescent at first, the upper becoming glabrate, the lower remaining grayish- or silvery-tomentose.

The involucres are shallowly cuplike or bowl-like, enclosing about ¼ of the nut, the scales pale-pubescent and rounded or blunt. The acorns are subglabrous, about ½ inch long, bright brown, olive-brown, or blackish, sometimes neatly striped, the inner surfaces of the nutshells pubescent. The biennial fruits are clustered on short stalks or sessile.

The bluejack oak occurs throughout northern Florida on coarse, buff sandy ridges, or slightly elevated areas of flatwoods where drainage is good. It also often occurs with the turkey oak and sand post oak, but is usually on slightly more moist sites (see under *Quercus laevis*).

The bluish or ashy-green entire leaves with tomentose lower surfaces are distinctive for the bluejack oak. Restricted as it is to the deciduous oak scrub on buff sandy sites, it is not difficult to recognize.

## 10. Quercus laevis Walt.    Turkey oak

*Q. catesbaei* Michx.

The turkey oak is a common, small tree of the deciduous oak scrub. Not infrequently it forms clones by underground runners and this vegetative reproduction is stimulated by frequent burning. The bark is thick, blackish, deeply corrugated, and blocky.

The leaves are deciduous, 5 - 14 inches long, irregularly lobed and with the size and number of the lobes varying. Narrowly 3-lobed leaves suggest a turkey foot, hence the name turkey oak. The number of primary lobes is 3 - 7, and leaves with the several lobe numbers are common on single trees. The lobes are relatively long and are separated by broad, open sinuses. The lobes and their subdivisions are prominently bristle-tipped. A characteristic of the turkey oak, which is not

shared by other oaks having leaves with a similar lobe pattern, is that
the petioles are twisted so that the broad plain surfaces of the leaves
are virtually always oriented vertically to the ground.  The upper surfaces are glabrous, bright green, and lustrous.  The lower surfaces are
lighter green, lustrous, and pubescent only in the vein axils.  The leaf
bases are cuneate.

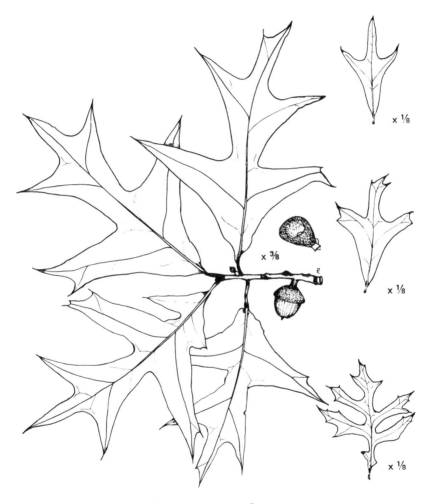

Fig. 47.  *Quercus laevis*

The involucres are turbinate, enclosing ⅓ - ½ of the nut, the scales
coarse, the tips of the uppermost scales rolled inward and downward
and appressed against the inner face of the cup, often giving the effect

of a terrace encircling the acorn. The acorns are ovoid, about 1 inch long, the inner surfaces of the nutshells pubescent. The biennial fruits are borne singly, in pairs, or clusters of 3, sessile or short-stalked.

Throughout our area, this oak is common on well-drained ridges and hills of coarse buff sand. Together with *Quercus margaretta* and *Q. incana*, it comprises the deciduous oak scrub, and where deforesting has not been too severe these are associated with the longleaf pine. On such sites, *Q. laevis* is much more abundant than its two oak associates. Although the three species occupy the same general habitat and may be intermixed, *Q. laevis* is most abundant in the drier places, *Q. margaretta* in the richer, and *Q. incana* in the more moist.

*Q. laevis* sometimes occurs intermixed with *Q. falcata* where mixed hardwood forests and deciduous oak scrub are adjacent. The leaves of these are somewhat similar in lobing pattern but those of the former are glabrous below, or pubescent only in the vein axils, and have a cuneate base, while those of the latter are uniformly gray- or rusty-soft-pubescent underneath and have a U-shaped base. The inwardly rolled upper scales of the cup are distinctive for *Q. laevis*.

### 11. **Quercus laurifolia** Michx. Diamond-leaf oak

*Q. obtusa* Willd.

This is a large tree with relatively smooth gray bark which on older trunks becomes scaly.

The leaves are tardily deciduous, falling gradually in late autumn and during the winter. Leaves of mature, fertile branches are prevailingly oblanceolate to narrowly obovate or oblong-obovate, or rhombic, or some of them elliptic or lanceolate, 2 - 5½ inches long and ½ - 2 inches wide. The leaves of some trees may be on the small side of that range, those of others on the large side. Occasional individuals have larger more distinctly obovate leaves. Occasional leaves on a tree may be somewhat 3-lobed at the apex. Normally, the apices of the leaves are blunt or rounded, occasional ones acute and bristle-tipped, the bases cuneate. The upper surfaces are smooth, the lower glabrous or pubescent in the vein axils. The reticulate venation of the leaf is readily apparent when viewed against the light. The margins are entire and have a yellow-opaque edge which is not revolute.

The leaves of small saplings, or sometimes of sucker shoots, are generally several-lobed and little resemble those characteristic of the mature branches of a well-developed tree.

The involucres are shallowly saucer-like, the scales tightly appressed. The acorns are ovoid to hemispheric, ½ - ⅔ inch long, and are about ⅕

enclosed in the cups.  The inner surfaces of the nutshells are pubescent.
The biennial fruits are borne singly or in pairs and are sessile or short-
stalked.

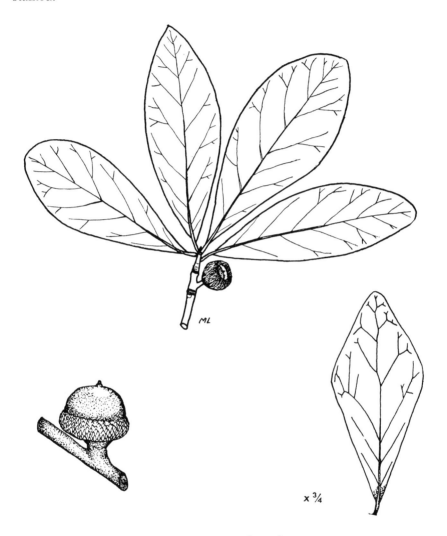

Fig. 48.  *Quercus laurifolia*

This oak occurs in lowland woods, or floodplain woods, from Clay
and Marion counties westward in northern Florida.

Trees of this species may sometimes have some leaves which are
obovate and 3-lobed, resembling those of *Quercus nigra*.  However,

the prevailing leaves are usually oblanceolate, only very narrowly obovate, or rhombic, and unlobed with rounded apices which are not
bristle-tipped. These are distinctive for the diamond-leaf oak. (See
also *Q. hemisphaerica.*)

### 12. **Quercus lyrata** Walt.   Over-cup oak

The over-cup oak is a medium to large tree, having light brownish-
gray bark which forms thick, irregular plates covered with thinner
scales.

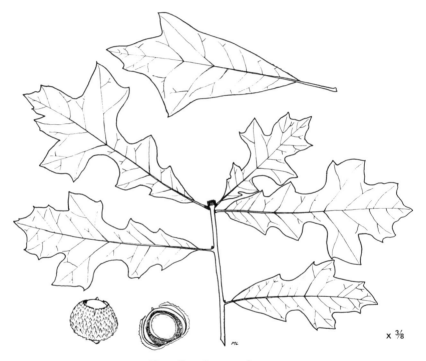

Fig. 49.   *Quercus lyrata*

The leaves are deciduous, 5 - 9 inches long and 1½ - 5 inches broad,
narrowly obovate in general outline.   They commonly have 7 lobes.
While the lobing pattern is variable, in many characteristic leaves there
are 3 relatively large, subequal, squarish terminal lobes.   Each of these
is commonly sublobed.   The 2 lateral lobes extend outward armlike
not necessarily opposite each other.   Two to 4 much smaller more or
less triangular lobes occur below.   The sinuses between the lobes are
broad and open.   Below the lowermost lobes the leaf tapers, forming

a long-acute-angled base.   In many other leaves the lobes are all more nearly short and broad-triangular, increasing somewhat in size upward, somewhat resembling stairsteps.   The young leaves are white-tomentose below, remaining whitish-downy in age or becoming nearly glabrous and green.   The branchlets are at first pubescent, then glabrate.

The involucres are subglobose, almost completely enclosing the nuts, the scales rough-tuberculate.   The annual acorns are subglobose or globose, about 1 inch in diameter, the inner faces of the nutshells glabrous.

This oak occurs in river-bottom woods or occasionally on slopes, westward from the Suwannee River in northern Florida.

Distinctive characteristics of the over-cup oak are the usually 7-lobed leaves which have broad, open sinuses between the lobes, the upper 3 lobes being relatively large and squarish, the lateral 2 extending outward armlike, the lower in general triangular, or triangular and stairstep-like.   Amongst our oaks, the nearly complete enclosure of the nuts by the involucral cup at maturity is unique to this species.

### 13.  Quercus margaretta Ashe.   Sand-post oak

The sand-post oak is generally a small, often a scrubby tree, which commonly forms small groves from underground runners.   The bark is rough and brown or reddish-brown.

The leaves are similar in form to those of the post oak, *Quercus stellata,* but are smaller, 2 - 3½ inches long and 1 - 2½ inches broad, and 3-lobed leaves or even unlobed ones are more frequent.   The squarish, "crosslike," 3-terminal lobes of the leaves are not so common on the sand-post oak but more often these lobes are shorter, less squarish, and more rounded.   The leaves are glabrate above, stellate-pubescent below, or the lower surfaces glabrate except on the veins.   The twigs are reddish-brown and usually glabrous.   The acorn cups and acorns are similar to those of the post oak.

The sand-post oak is an inhabitant of the deciduous scrub throughout northern Florida.   It is a frequent associate of *Quercus laevis, Q. incana,* and *Pinus palustris* on well-drained buff sandy soils; also, it occurs in open, dry woods of loamy soils.

In some cases, the sand-post oak and post oak are difficult to distinguish.   The former usually has glabrous reddish-brown twigs in contrast to the tomentose twigs of the latter.   The smaller, less commonly squarish-lobed and more commonly rounded-lobed leaves of the sand-post oak help to distinguish it.

Although not restricted to buff sandy sites, this oak is much more common on them than elsewhere and the post oak never occurs on such sites.

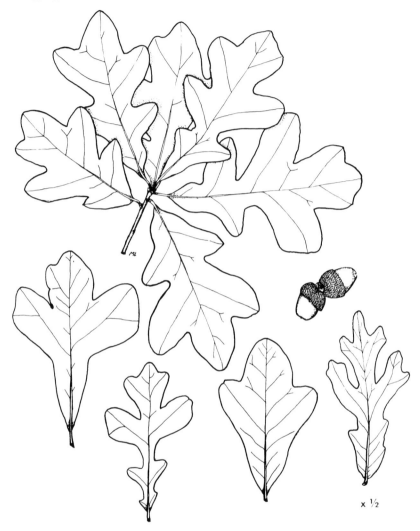

x ½

Fig. 50.  *Quercus margaretta*

## 14. **Quercus marilandica** Muench.  Blackjack oak

The blackjack oak is a small to medium-sized tree, not commonly over 50 feet tall, often scrubby and with drooping branches.  The bark is blackish and rough, being deeply fissured and broken into irregular blocks.

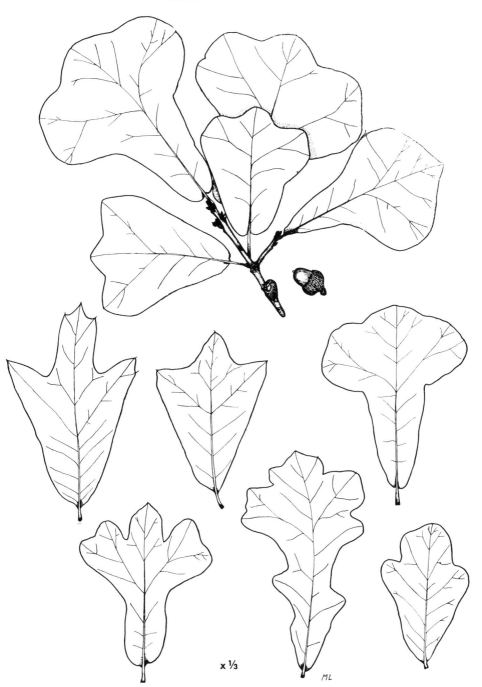

x ⅓

Fig. 51. *Quercus marilandica*

The leaves are deciduous, broadly obovate, or obovate-oblong, with 3 (or less frequently 5) bristle-tipped lobes at the broad end. The sides of the blades from the broadened or lobed summit abruptly narrow to a rounded or subcordate base, the sides thus concave. The over-all shape approximates a block T. Sometimes the summit of the blades is unlobed, the sides straight-tapering, and the over-all shape corresponds to a broad triangle. The upper surfaces are dark green and glabrous, the lower surfaces scurfy-pubescent, or bright, rusty-yellow-pubescent.

The involucres are turbinate-hemispheric, enclosing ½ or slightly more of the nuts, the scales relatively large and loosely imbricated, the rim of the cup thickened by the tips of several series of scales reaching it, the scale tips sometimes curled inward. The acorns are globose or ovoid, about ¾ inch long, light brown and downy, the inner surfaces of the nutshells pubescent. The biennial fruits are borne singly or in pairs and are usually stalked.

This oak occurs locally in our area in dry, sandy, open woodlands where the sand is underlain by clay or limestone. Its frequent associates are *Carya tomentosa, Quercus falcata, Q. stellata, Pinus echinata,* and/or *P. taeda.*

The broadly obovate, blocky T, or broadly triangular leaf shape, and scurfy- or rusty-yellow-pubescent lower surfaces of the leaves characterize the blackjack oak. (See also *Quercus caput-rivuli.*)

### 15. *Quercus minima* (Sarg.) Small.  Dwarf-live oak

This is an evergreen shrub which has underground runners and forms thickets. The erect branches are 3 feet tall, frequently less. Rarely they reach 6 - 8 feet tall.

The leaves are persistent, thick leathery, and very stiff, 1½ - 5 inches long, narrowly oblong, lanceolate, or oblanceolate, their tips rounded to acute, sometimes with a short narrow abrupt tip. Those of mature branchlets are entire and revolute. Those of sprouts arising after fire injury often produce spiny-toothed, or lobed, holly-like leaves. The leaf blades are smooth above and usually dark green, the lower surfaces tightly tomentose, rarely becoming glabrate.

The involucres are cuplike or turbinate, enclosing about ⅓ of the nut, the scales ridged or slightly humped at base, densely pubescent except at the tips, which are blackish-brown, and they are closely appressed. The acorns are ovoid to narrowly ellipsoid, shiny brown or blackish, the inner surfaces of the nutshells glabrous. The annual fruits are borne singly or in pairs on stalks up to 1½ inches long.

The dwarf-live oak occurs throughout our area in pine flatwoods, or in seepage areas of sandy-clay upland; it is restricted to sites subject to burning.

Quercus minima often occurs in the same general habitat as Q. pumila, another dwarf oak which spreads by underground runners. In habit,

Fig. 52.   Quercus minima

it may resemble Q. geminata, but the latter occurs on deep, well-drained sands, for the most part. The leaves of Q. minima are flat and smooth above in contrast to those of Q. geminata, in which the sides of the leaves roll downward and the surfaces are notably rugose-veiny. Q. minima can best be distinguished from Q. pumila, with which it is more

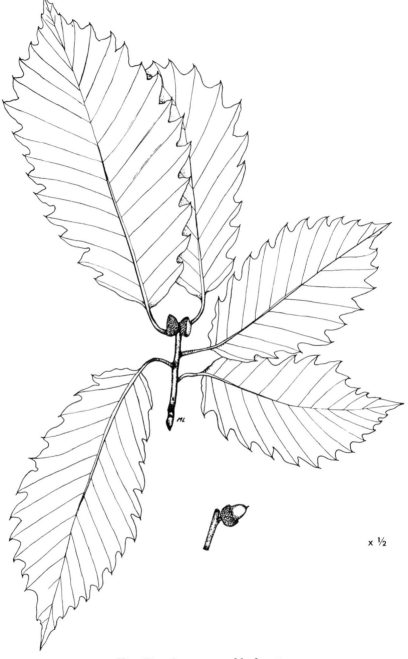

Fig. 53. *Quercus muehlenbergii*

x ½

often associated, by characters of their fruits. Those of the former are long-stalked, and the inner faces of the nutshells are glabrous, while those of the latter are sessile or essentially so and the inner faces of the nutshells are pubescent. Ordinarily, fruits can be found on or under at least some shoots of a clone, making this comparison a possible and useful one.

### 16. Quercus muehlenbergii Engelm.   Chinquapin oak; yellow oak

This is a small or medium-sized tree which resembles the swamp-chestnut oak in bark and leaf characters.

The leaves are deciduous, broadly lanceolate, oblanceolate, elliptic-lanceolate, or obovate, 4 - 7 (rarely exceeding 5) inches long and 1 - 4 inches broad. The blades are coarsely serrate, or dentate-serrate, the teeth upwardly curved, each terminated by a colorless glandular mucro. Their upper surfaces are dark green and glabrous, lustrous, the lower whitish or tan with a closely appressed tomentum.

The involucres are cuplike, enclosing about ½ of the nut, the scales thin and closely appressed. The annual acorns are ovoid, ⅓ - ¾ inch long, the inner surfaces glabrous. They occur singly or in pairs and are sessile or nearly so.

The chinquapin oak is of much more restricted occurrence than the swamp-chestnut oak. It occurs on clay or limestone soils on the Apalachicola River bluffs in Gadsden and Liberty counties, and in Jackson County.

This oak will be mistaken for no other except *Quercus prinus*. (See the latter for a comparison.)

### 17. Quercus myrtifolia Willd.   Myrtle oak

Usually a thicket-forming shrub, the myrtle oak occasionally forms a small scrubby tree. Its bark is light gray, smoothish, becoming shallowly furrowed and ridged, or transversely wrinkled at the joints or where the trunks bend.

The leaves are leathery, evergreen, ¾ - 2 inches long and ½ - 1 inch wide. The blades are oval, obovate, elliptic, or narrowly oblong, the apices rounded (sometimes bristle-tipped), the bases broadly cuneate to rounded. The leaf margins are mostly entire and revolute, both surfaces smooth dark green and shiny. The sides of the leaf blades are commonly rolled downward.

The involucres are shallowly saucer-like, enclosing about ¼ of the nuts, the scales small and closely appressed. The acorns are ovoid to subglobose, the inner surfaces of the nutshells pubescent. The biennial fruits are borne singly, in pairs, or in clusters, and are sessile or on short stalks.

This oak is a characteristic component of the evergreen oak-sand pine scrub, both of coastal dunes along the Atlantic and Gulf coasts of northern Florida, and locally on ridges and hills of white sand elsewhere in the area.

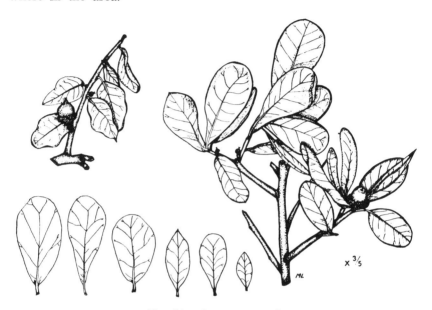

Fig. 54.   *Quercus myrtifolia*

The oak associates of the myrtle oak in the evergreen scrub are *Quercus geminata* and *Q. chapmanii*.   Its glabrous, shiny leaves distinguish it from both of the latter.   The lower surfaces of the leaves of *Q. geminata* are clothed with a dense, closely appressed tomentum. The lower surfaces of the leaves of *Q. chapmanii* are dull, light green, and sparsely pubescent or pubescent on the veins.

## 18.  **Quercus nigra** L.   Water oak

The water oak is a large tree having smoothish gray-brown bark which on older trunks is only shallowly and irregularly furrowed and ridged.

The leaves are semipersistent, falling gradually throughout the winter.   They are very variable in size and form on saplings, sprouts, and vigorous shoots, even on fertile branches from tree to tree.   Basically, in outline, they are broadest toward their tips, spatulate to obovate, with 3 terminal rounded lobes, the lobes bristle-tipped, or the apical lobe notched. Both leaf surfaces are glabrous and green.

The involucres are shallowly saucer-like, enclosing only the base of the nut, the scales acute, closely appressed. The acorns are ovoid to hemispheric, ½ - ⅓ inch long, the inner surfaces of the nutshells pubescent. The biennial fruits are borne singly or in pairs, and are sessile or on short stalks.

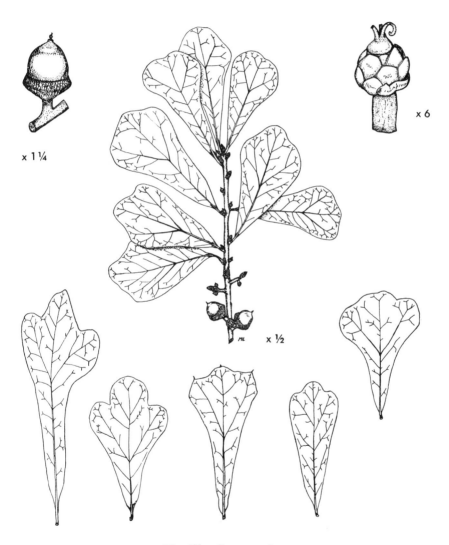

x 1¼

x 6

x ½

Fig. 55.  *Quercus nigra*

The water oak occurs in a wide variety of places, open woods, mixed forests, fence rows, roadsides, locally in flatwoods, bottomlands, and on city lots.  It is common throughout northern Florida.

Fig. 55a.  *Quercus nigra.*  Leaves of saplings or sprouts

In general, the leaves of the water oak tend to be broadest toward their apices, spatulate to obovate in outline, and are commonly shallowly 3-lobed, tapering wedgelike to their bases, and glabrous on both surfaces.

### 19. **Quercus phellos** L.  Willow oak

The willow oak, a large tree having dark gray bark which is smoothish on smaller trunks, shallowly fissured and split irregularly into plates on older trunks, is not at all common in our area.

The leaves are deciduous in autumn, 1½ - 5½ inches long and ⅓ - 1 inch broad, linear-oblong to elliptic-lanceolate, sometimes falcate, mostly broadest near their middles and tapering to both ends, the apices often bristle-tipped.  The margins are entire, the upper surfaces glabrous and with finely reticulate, elevated veinlets, the lower surfaces glabrous, or hairy in the vein angles or along the midrib.

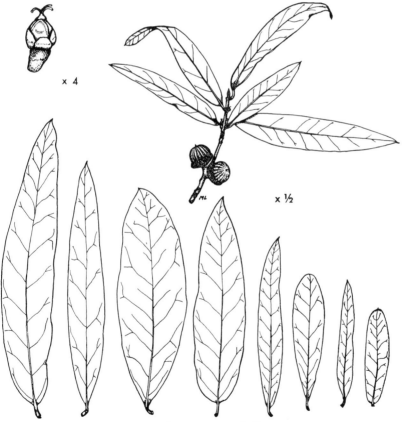

Fig. 56.  *Quercus phellos*

The involucres are shallowly saucer-like, enclosing just the base of the nut, the scales gray-pubescent, round-tipped, and closely appressed. The acorns are subglobose, about ⅓ inch high, the inner surfaces of the nutshells pubescent. The biennial fruits are borne singly or in pairs, and are sessile or on short stalks.

The willow oak inhabits lowland or floodplain woods. We have records of its occurrence in several north Florida counties from Duval westward to Escambia.

*Quercus phellos* is most easily confused with *Q. hemisphaerica.* The former is deciduous in autumn, while the leaves of the latter are persistent virtually through the winter. The leaves of the former are on the average narrower, usually widest at their middles and tapering to both ends, usually pubescent at least along the midvein below. Those of the latter tend to be wider and more of them oblanceolate, the lower surfaces glabrous and lustrous.

### 20. **Quercus prinus** L.  Swamp-chestnut oak; cow oak; basket oak

*Q. michauxii* Nutt.

A large tree, this oak has light gray or whitish scaly bark resembling that of the white oak.

The leaves are deciduous, obovate or oval, 4½ - 11 inches long and 2 - 6½ inches broad. The blades are regularly crenate-lobed, crenate, or crenate-dentate, the teeth or lobes mostly ascending, blunt or rounded at their tips, more rarely pointed, the tips of the lobes or teeth sometimes with a glandular mucro. The teeth may be so shallow as to render the margins wavy, or may be deep enough to be considered lobed. The upper leaf surfaces are green and glabrate, not lustrous, the lower whitish or rusty with persistent sparsely distributed short hairs.

The involucres are cuplike or bowl-shaped, have coarse, thickened, tuberculate, loosely imbricated scales and enclose about ½ the nut. The acorns are ovoid to subcylindric, large, up to 1⅔ inches long and 1¼ inches broad. Their outer surfaces are somewhat pubescent, slightly lustrous, the inner surfaces glabrous. They are annual and are borne singly or in pairs, sessile or short-stalked.

This oak is of wide occurrence in northern Florida in mixed hardwoods of low grounds, river bottoms, and ravines.

*Quercus prinus* is more closely similar to *Q. muehlenbergii* than to any other of our oaks, their leaves being much alike in shape and lobing or toothing. Typically, the leaves of the former are crenate-lobed or crenate, the teeth or lobes blunt and with stubby tips while those of the latter are usually sharp pointed. The lower leaf surfaces

of *Q. prinus* are beset with sparsely distributed short hairs, those of
*Q. muehlenbergii* with a dense, closely appressed tomentum. The larger
leaf blades of *Q. prinus* commonly exceed 6 inches in length, whereas
the larger ones of *Q. muehlenbergii* are commonly 5 inches long or
less. The acorns offer the best means of distinguishing these oaks.

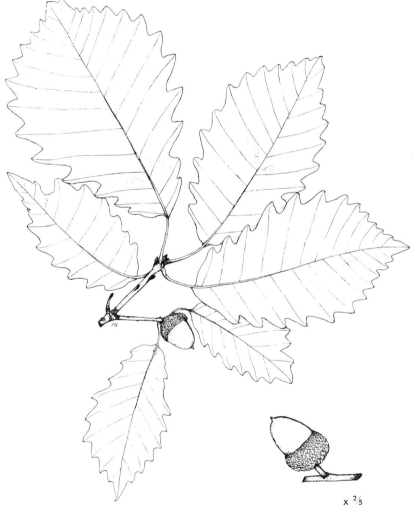

Fig. 57. *Quercus prinus*

Those of *Q. prinus* are large, averaging about 1½ inches long, the scales
of the cup very large, thick, and very prominently large-keeled. The

acorns of *Q. muehlenbergii* do not exceed ¾ inch in length, and the scales of the cup are thin, small, and flattish, only slightly, if at all, keeled.

### 21. **Quercus pumila** Walt.   Running oak

This is a shrub which forms low thickets from underground runners, the erect shoots generally being about 3 feet tall, more rarely 6 - 8 feet tall.

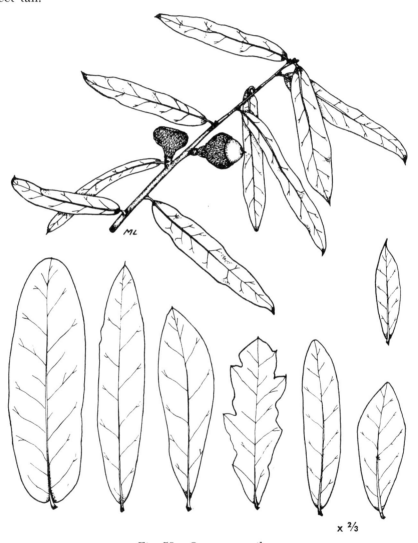

x ⅔

Fig. 58.   *Quercus pumila*

The leaves are deciduous, thin-leathery, commonly 1½ - 3 inches long, narrowly lanceolate, elliptic, or oblanceolate, acute to rounded and with a prominent mucro at their apices. The margins are entire and revolute, sometimes somewhat crisped, occasionally irregularly toothed. The lower leaf faces are usually grayish and soft-tomentose (rarely glabrate).

The involucres are bowl-shaped, turbinate at their bases, the scales strongly humped at the base, long-acuminate and pubescent. The annual acorns are ovoid, about ½ inch long, the inner surfaces of the nutshells pubescent. They are sessile or essentially so.

The running oak occurs throughout northern Florida in pine flatwoods and open sandy pine-oak scrub. (See *Quercus minima* for comparative features.)

### 22. **Quercus shumardii** Buckl.   Shumard oak

A large tree with handsome, lustrous foliage, the Shumard oak has thick bark with deep dark fissures and grayish scaly ridges.

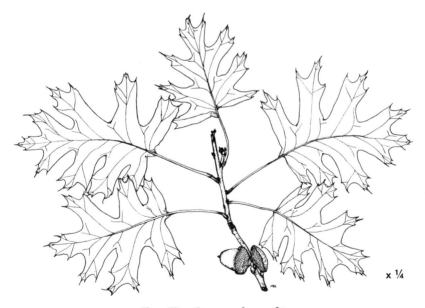

x ¼

Fig. 59.   *Quercus shumardii*

The leaves are deciduous, 4 - 7 inches long and 2 - 4 inches wide, and have 7 - 9 (rarely 5) primary lobes. The lobes are usually squarish, with approximately truncate bases, and have 3 - 13 secondary bristle-tipped lobes or teeth at or near their summits. The primary lobes spread nearly at right angles or are slightly ascending. The base of the leaf blade is truncate or oblique-truncate on crown branchlets, or broadly cuneate on leaves of lower limbs. The upper leaf surfaces are glabrous and glistening deep green, the lower scarcely paler green, lustrous, glabrous except in the vein axils.

The involucres are saucer-like or sometimes shallowly cup-shaped, enclosing about ⅓ of the nut, the scales small, somewhat tuberculate, and closely appressed. The acorns are ovoid to oblong, ¾ - 1 inch long, the inner surfaces of the nutshells pubescent. The biennial fruits are borne singly or in pairs, and are sessile or short-stalked.

In northern Florida, the Shumard oak occurs locally in mixed hardwood forests of hammocks or on rich wooded slopes, often where the soil is underlain by limestone. We have records of its occurrence in Marion, Levy, Columbia, Jefferson, Leon, Wakulla, Gadsden and Jackson counties.

Although intermixed with a variety of other hardwoods, this is a tree of surpassing beauty. Its glistening, glabrous (except in the vein axils below), multi-bristled, deeply lobed leaves are distinctive. (See also *Quercus velutina*.)

### 23. **Quercus stellata** Wang.   Post oak

Under favorable conditions the post oak becomes a large tree. The bark is dark gray, rather finely checked on smaller trunks and becoming divided by fissures into broad flat ridges on older trunks.

The leaves are deciduous, firm and stiffish, the blades of the mature, fertile branches 4 - 5 inches long and 3 - 4 inches broad, generally 5-lobed. The upper pair of lobes and the terminal one are much the larger; the terminal one and/or the lateral pair below often have subordinate lobes. The lobes are all broad at base; the upper 3 tend to be squarish, the lower pair triangular or thumblike. The lower surfaces of the leaf blades are grayish or brownish with stellate hairs, the upper sparsely hairy or roughish with the persistent bases of the hairs. The petioles and twigs are tomentose.

The involucres are cup-shaped, enclosing about ⅓ - ½ of the acorn, the scales small, closely appressed, and finely pubescent. The acorns are ovoid or oblong-ovoid, ½ - ¾ inch long, the inner surfaces of the shells glabrous. They are borne singly or several-clustered, are sessile or short-stalked, and are annual.

This oak inhabits open, upland woods the soils of which are frequently underlaid by clay or marl, from the Santa Fe River westward in northern Florida. Its characteristic associates are *Carya tomentosa*,

*Quercus falcata, Pinus echinata, P. taeda,* and sometimes *Q. velutina.*

Distinctive features are the broad, 5-lobed leaf whose upper 3 lobes are much the larger and squarish, resembling a cross, and the stellate-pubescent lower leaf surfaces. It is most nearly like the sand-post oak (*Quercus margaretta*).

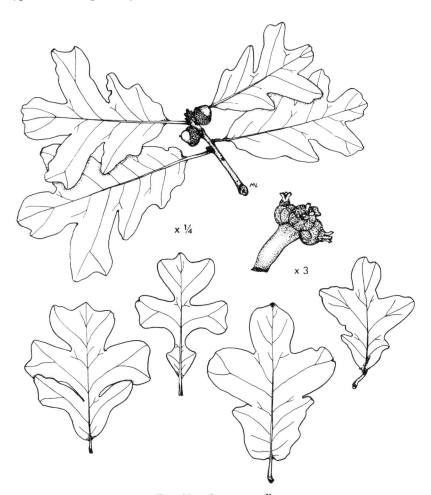

Fig. 60.  *Quercus stellata*

## 24. **Quercus velutina** Lam.  Black oak; yellow-barked oak

The black oak is a large tree with dark, rough, blocky bark. The bark is thick and the inner bark is conspicuously yellow-orange in color. The leaves are deciduous, 5 - 9 inches long and 3 - 6 inches broad.

The blades are 5 - 7-lobed, the lobes squarish, slightly widened at their bases, usually somewhat ascending, the primary lobes with 2 - several bristle-tipped teeth.  The bases of the blades are broadly cuneate to subtruncate, often somewhat oblique.  The upper leaf surfaces are deep green and glabrous; at maturity the lower are pubescent in the vein axils, the surfaces otherwise sparsely tawny-pubescent, or tawny-pubescent in patches, or glabrate.

The involucres are bowl-like or hemispheric, enclosing ¼ - ⅓ of the nuts; the scales reddish-tan, pubescent, coarse, loosely overlapping, or on the upper part of the cup spreading.  The acorns are ovoid, broad at their bases, ⅔ - ¾ inch in diameter, the inner surfaces of the nutshells pubescent.  The biennial fruits are borne singly or in pairs, sessile or nearly so.

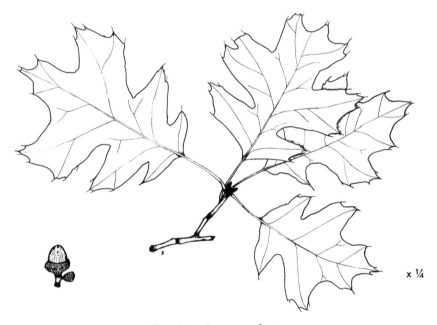

x ¼

Fig. 61.  *Quercus velutina*

The black oak is not common in northern Florida.  It occurs in open woods with a clay subsoil in the Tallahassee Red Hills, and upland woods along the Apalachicola River in Liberty and Gadsden counties. Its frequent associates are *Quercus falcata, Q. stellata, Carya tomentosa, Pinus echinata,* and/or *P. taeda.*

In leaf characters, the black oak most closely resembles the Shumard oak.  The inner bark of the black oak is notably yellow-orange in color;

that of Shumard oak is tan or buff, often pinkish. The involucres of the black oak are bowl-like with coarse, loosely imbricated scales, those of Shumard oak are saucer-like and have small, closely appressed scales. The leaves of the black oak have 5 - 7 (usually 5) primary lobes with 2 - several bristly teeth, the leaf bases mostly broadly cuneate; those of the Shumard oak have 7 - 9 primary lobes which have 2 - several secondary lobes and/or up to 13 bristly teeth, the leaf bases being mostly oblique-truncate, only those of the lower branches broadly cuneate.

## 25. Quercus virginiana Mill. Live oak

The live oak does not commonly attain great heights, but is nonetheless of great stature and magnificent proportions. It is certainly one of the most picturesque trees of our area. Older specimens exhibit short, bulky trunks 3 - 4 feet or more in diameter. From these several large, horizontally spreading, often descending limbs arise. The crown is broad and rounded, attaining a spread of 100 feet or much more, the tips of the lower limbs often touching the ground. In relatively dense forests, the trunks may be tall, the crown high and irregular.

The rugged proportions and hard, tough wood of the live oak have led to the popular fancy that the trees are slow-growing and that large specimens are of ancient age. Special studies have revealed, however, that they grow relatively rapidly.

The bark is dark, thick, roughly ridged and furrowed, commonly becoming blocky.

The leaves are normally persistent until just before growth is resumed in spring, although in cold or dry winters defoliation may occur earlier. The leaf blades are leathery, oblong, elliptic, or narrowly obovate, 1½ - 4 (sometimes to 5½) inches long and ⅓ - 2½ inches broad. The leaf margins are commonly entire and unlobed on the mature twigs. Occasionally on summer shoots the leaves may have 3 small rounded terminal lobes, or vigorous shoots or sprouts may have sharply toothed or lobed blades in form resembling those of American holly.

The leaf blades tend to be flat or flattish, the margin bony-opaque, scarcely revolute. The lower surfaces are tightly tomentose, the tomentum scarcely evident to the naked eye.

The involucres are turbinate, enclose about ⅓ of the nut, the scales thinnish, acute, and closely appressed. The annual acorns are oblong-ellipsoid or ovoid, ½ - 1 inch long, tan-brown to nearly black, the inner faces of the nutshells glabrous. They are borne singly or in clusters, on stalks of varying lengths.

In northern Florida, the live oak is common on a wide variety of sites. It occurs in hammocks, flatwoods, borders of salt marsh, along the margins of depressions, on open roadsides, in city lots, and in open upland woods. It is not fire-tolerant and occurs in almost any place free from fire where not too wet or where the soil is moderately fertile.

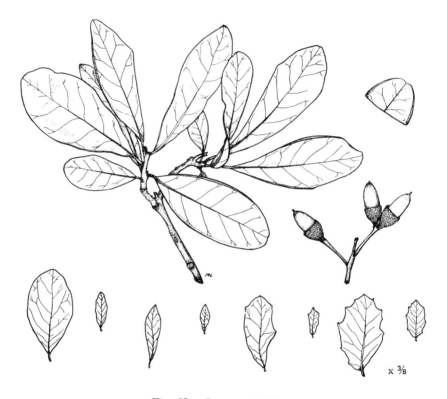

Fig. 62.  *Quercus virginiana*

*Quercus virginiana, Q. hemisphaerica,* and *Q. nigra* occur together in this region and all are common shade trees in towns and cities. The leaves of *Q. virginiana* are conspicuously leathery, their lower surfaces tightly tomentose, the apices rounded or blunt and not bristle-tipped. Those of *Q. hemisphaerica* are at most thin-leathery, their lower surfaces glabrous and lustrous, the apices bristle-tipped. Those of *Q. nigra* are prevailing obovate, commonly 3-lobed, and taper wedgelike to an acute base. Both surfaces are glabrous. (See also *Q. geminata.*)

# ULMACEAE.  ELM FAMILY

1. Lateral veins of the leaves unequal, the lower much exceeding the others; pith at the nodes chambered; bark smoothish, but commonly becoming warty or short-corky-ridged; fruit a fleshy drupe................................................................CELTIS

1. Lateral veins of the leaves essentially equal; pith at the nodes solid; bark rough-ridged and furrowed or with large, loose, scaly plates; fruit a samara or dry bur-like drupe.

    2. Leaf blades symmetrical, rhombic-ovate to deltoid-ovate; fruit a dry burlike drupe................................................................................................PLANERA

    2. Leaf blades mostly asymmetrical, lanceolate to oblong, or if ovate neither rhombic nor deltoid; fruit a samara................................................ULMUS

## CELTIS

### 1. **Celtis laevigata** Willd.  Sugarberry; hackberry

This is a medium-sized tree having variable leaves and characteristic bark.  The bark is gray-smooth, or bearing corky outgrowths in the form of warty bumps, beehive-like masses, or irregular ridged masses.  When smooth, it is not unlike the bark of beech, and like the latter, it offers a temptation to sentimental bark carvers.  Carving apparently stimulates the development of the corky outgrowths.  In 1923, the senior author saw a tree on the trunk of which was a prominently raised, neat corky development in the form of 1898.  The pith of the twigs is chambered in the nodal areas.

The leaves are simple, alternate, and 2-ranked, the blades very variable.  In shape, the leaf blades are ovate to ovate-lanceolate, often somewhat falcate, generally up to 3 inches long (longer occasionally) and up to 2 inches broad.  Their bases vary from abruptly short-tapering to truncate or subcordate, commonly asymmetrical, and the apices from long-tapering acute or acuminate to abruptly short-acuminate.  The margins may be entire, wavy, irregularly-closely or remotely serrate, to regularly and saliently serrate.  The longer, narrower entire leaves tend to be characteristic of mature, older trees, or their older branches; the shorter, wider, more serrated ones are characteristic of saplings, sprouts, or younger branchlets.  Diverse kinds may be found on individual trees.  The lower lateral veins of the leaves tend to be much more prominent than the upper laterals.  When observed with a lens against strong light, the network of veinlets is prominent and translucent and in the islets between the veinlets are numerous tiny translucent dots.

The flowers are unisexual (the plants monoecious) and are small and greenish.  The pistillate flowers are borne solitary or in pairs mostly in the axils of the emerging leaves toward the branchlet tips; the staminate flowers are borne in small fascicles mostly lower on the branchlets, many of them at leafless nodes of older branchlets. The calyx is 5 - 6-parted, not persistent, the corolla lacking, stamens 5 - 6, the pistil 1-locular and 1-seeded, and with recurved stigmas.

The fruits are thin-fleshed, globose drupes, ¼ - ⅓ inch in diameter. At maturity, they are orange or brownish-red.

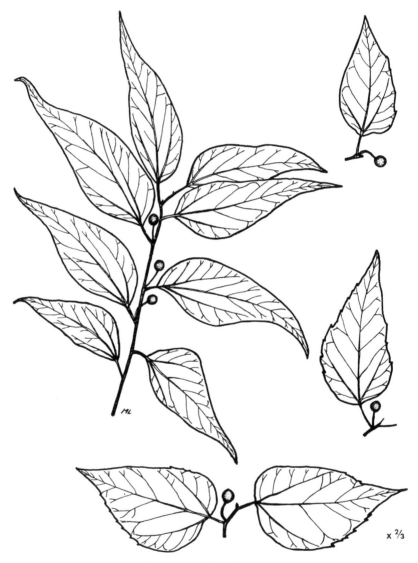

Fig. 63.  *Celtis laevigata*

This tree occurs throughout northern Florida in a wide variety of habitats, river-bottom woods, hammocks, low limestone woods, upland woods, roadsides, and fencerows.

The sugarberry may be recognized by its smooth, gray, warty or corky-ridged bark, chambered pith in the nodes, and variable ovate to ovate-lanceolate, asymmetrical leaves whose margins vary from entire to irregularly or regularly serrate. Its leaves somewhat resemble those of the planer-tree. Those of the latter, however, are always serrate, tending to doubly-serrate; the veinlets of the leaves are not translucent as seen with a lens against bright light; neither do they have translucent dots in the vein islets. The bark of the planer-tree is reddish-brown and conspicuously flaking and shredding in contrast to that of the sugarberry, which is gray and smooth or warty or irregularly corky-ridged.

## PLANERA

### 1. **Planera aquatica** Gmel. Planer-tree

This is a small-to-large tree usually having a short trunk and a low, spreading crown. Not uncommonly, clusters of scraggly sprouts grow from the trunk at or near its base. Most authors do not credit this tree with attaining any appreciable size. Along Lloyd Creek in Jefferson County, Florida, there are a number of large trees, one of which is about 60 feet high, with a trunk diameter of 4 feet at breast height, and a spread of about 90 feet. The principal trunk is about 12 feet high and supports 12 limbs ranging from 6 - 15 inches in diameter.

The leaves are simple, alternate, 2-ranked, and deciduous. Their blades are rhombic-ovate, or deltoid-ovate, 1 - 3½ inches long, the bases broadly wedge-shaped to rounded, slightly if at all asymmetrical, the apices acute to acuminate. The leaf margins are irregularly serrate to somewhat doubly-serrate. The upper leaf surfaces are glabrous and dark green, the lower glabrous or sparsely very short-pubescent, the veins below becoming brownish.

The bark is conspicuously scaly and flaky, is sloughed in long grayish-brown plates and exposing reddish-brown inner bark.

The flowers are small, lacking petals and with a 4 - 5-cleft calyx. They may be bisexual or unisexual; plants may have only bisexual flowers or staminate, pistillate, and bisexual on the same plant.

The fruits are dry nutlike drupes which are clothed with crooked, blunt, simple, or slightly lobed, soft projections which give them a burlike appearance. They are ⅓ - ½ inch long.

The planer-tree occurs on alluvial floodplains subject to temporary, periodic flooding in Alachua County (West and Arnold, 1946), and

locally westward in northern Florida.  Although not common, it sometimes occurs in pure stands.

Distinguishing characteristics are the scaly, flaky bark which sloughs
in strips exposing reddish-brown inner bark, the rhombic-ovate to del-

x ¼

x ⅔

Fig. 64.  *Planera aquatica*

toid-ovate, serrate leaves which are slightly, if at all, oblique at their
bases, and the small, soft, burlike fruits.  Leaves of the elms are uniformly doubly-serrate; those of the sugarberry have the lower lateral
veins co-equal with the midrib, which is not true of those of *Planera*.

## ULMUS. ELMS

The elms have ridged and furrowed or scaly bark. The leaves are simple, alternate, and deciduous, short-petioled, the blades tending to be asymmetrical, and have small, quickly deciduous stipules. The leaf margins are doubly-serrate. The principal lateral veins of the leaves are essentially equal, straight, and parallel.

The flowers are small, greenish, borne in short racemes or fascicles in winter much before the leaves unfold, the fruits developing to maturity and usually shedding prior to leaf development. The flowers are bisexual, apetalous, the calyx 3 - 9-lobed, the stamens of the same number as the calyx lobes and opposite them. The ovularies are bicarpellate, with 2 styles, but producing a 1-seeded, flat, membranous samara which is usually surmounted by the 2 persistent styles.

1. Leaves lanceolate to narrowly elliptic; twigs often corky-winged.............1. *U. alata*
1. Leaves broadly elliptic, oblong, oval, ovate, or obovate; twigs never corky-winged.
    2. The leaves very harsh-scabrous on their surfaces; bud scales, especially the inner, having long brown pubescence; samaras about 1 inch long, essentially glabrous..................................................................................................4. *U. rubra*
    2. The leaves smooth, or only slightly scabrous on the upper surfaces; bud scales glabrous or with short grayish to brown pubescence; samaras ⅓ - ½ inch long, glabrous on the faces, the margins ciliate.
        3. Leaves all very inequilateral; larger leaves on any given tree up to 6 inches long by 2½ inches broad, the primary marginal teeth long-acuminate, curved upward and inward and hooked......2. *U. americana* var. *americana*
        3. Leaves varying from equilateral to slightly inequilateral, or distinctly inequilateral; larger leaves on any given tree not usually exceeding 4 inches long by 2 inches broad, the primary marginal teeth short acuminate, not curved upward and inward or hooklike........3. *U. americana* var. *floridana*

### 1. **Ulmus alata** Michx. Winged elm; cork elm

This medium-sized tree's common names are attributable to corky wings which are usually present on the twigs. Wings form on either side of the twigs during the second year and on older but still small twigs attain a breadth of ½ inch on each side. On twigs of about ¼ inch in diameter or a little more, the corkiness is more irregular, having been broken up and partially sloughed. Although this winged feature is in general characteristic of the species, not all twigs on a given tree exhibit them; moreover, some trees have no twigs which are winged. Ordinarily, however, in a given restricted locality where the tree occurs, there will be some individuals having winged twigs.

The leaf blades are lanceolate to narrowly elliptic, mostly 1 - 2½ inches long by ½ - 1 inch broad, narrowly rounded and often somewhat oblique-cordate at their bases, the apices acute to acuminate. The leaf

margins are doubly and regularly to irregularly and saliently serrate.
The upper surfaces appear smooth but are sparsely pubescent with
inconspicuous very short, stiff, forward-pointing hairs, the lower surfaces
are mostly sparsely pubescent with short hairs on the principal veins.

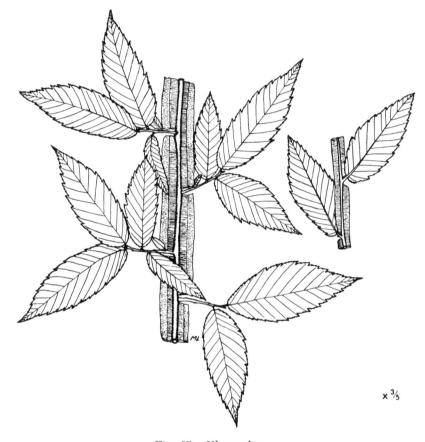

x ⅗

Fig. 65.   *Ulmus alata*

The fruits are oblong, about ⅓ inch long, 2-pronged at the tips, both
the fruit bodies and the wings downy-pubescent on their surfaces and
margins.

This tree occurs in upland woodlands, on wooded slopes, and in well-
drained hammocks and floodplains, throughout northern Florida.

Characteristic features of the winged or cork elm are the doubly-
serrate, lanceolate or elliptical leaves and 2-winged younger twigs.   If
a given individual tree has no winged twigs, one can usually locate
others in the vicinity which have them.   Our only other tree with corky-

winged twigs and branches is the sweetgum. Its twigs are seldom winged in but one plane. Moreover, its corky outgrowths are in various patterns—warts, ridges, knobs, regular and irregular wings.

### 2. **Ulmus americana** L., var. **americana.** American elm

A large, handsome tree whose branch system widens upward like a vase with concave sides, the crown consisting of dense, delicate sprays of branchlets and twigs. The bark is grayish-brown, fissured and ridged, or with flaky plates.

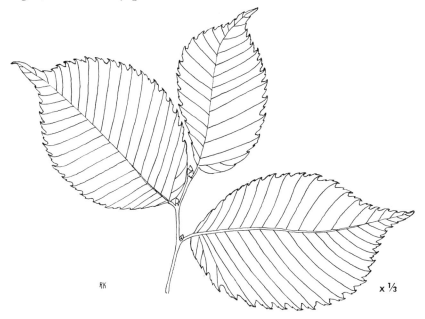

Fig. 66. *Ulmus americana* var. *americana*

The leaf blades are more or less oblong or broadly oval but very inequilateral, one side convex and with a broadly rounded half-cordate base, the other oblique or oblique-concave and much shorter. In size the leaves vary greatly on the same tree and the toothing of their margins appears to vary with the size. Mostly they are from 2 to 4 inches long (some as long as 6 inches) and from about 1 to 2 inches broad (the broadest 2½ inches). The leaves are all doubly-serrate. The smaller ones tend to have smaller primary teeth which are very abruptly short-pointed and have 1 - 2 secondary teeth. The larger ones tend to have much larger, more deeply cut primary teeth whose tips are longer acuminate, often curved upward and inward and hooklike, and have

2 - 4 secondary teeth. One extreme grades into the other. The upper leaf surfaces are smooth, rarely scabrous, the lower glabrous to sparsely soft-pubescent.

The samaras are oval to oblong, ⅓ - ½ inch long, notched at their apices and having two straight or often clawlike beaks. Their faces are glabrous, the margins long-ciliate.

In northern Florida, the American elm occurs in bottomland woods along the Apalachicola River in Liberty and Gadsden counties, along Little River in Gadsden County, and in Jackson County along the Chipola River and in limestone woods in the vicinity of Marianna.

In leaf, this tree can be distinguished from the slippery elm very readily in that its leaves are essentially smooth above, whereas those of the latter are very harsh-scabrous. In fruit, the samaras of this one are long-ciliate, those of the slippery elm glabrous throughout.

For a comparison to the Florida elm, see under *Ulmus americana* var. *floridana*.

x ½

Fig. 67.  *Ulmus americana* var. *floridana*

3. **Ulmus americana** L., var. **floridana** (Chapm.) Little.  Florida elm

*Ulmus floridana* Chapm.

The Florida elm is very much like the wider-ranging American elm. It differs in a number of characteristics only in degree and is, therefore, regarded by us as a variety.

The trees do not attain so great a stature as do those of the American elm, the larger individuals being medium-sized. The branches and branchlets are more stiff, the ultimate branchlets much less dense, the crown thus more open and not so vaselike. The leaves have about the same over-all outline shape. None of them, however, on any given tree, have as great a range in size or as great a range in marginal tooth characters. Moreover, they are in general much less asymmetrical. The leaf blades are mostly up to 3 inches long and 2 inches broad, the largest rarely exceeding 4 inches by 2 inches. They vary from equilateral to slightly inequilateral (or more rarely markedly inequilateral). The leaf margins are mostly doubly-serrate, occasional teeth having no secondary teeth; usually there are 1 - 2 secondary teeth. The primary teeth are abruptly acuminate, not long acuminate or curved upward, inward, and hooklike as is characteristic of the larger leaves on any American elm.

We have been unable to discern any consistent differences in the fruits of these two elms.

The Florida elm inhabits moist to wet hammocks and river bottoms throughout northern Florida.

## 4. **Ulmus rubra** Muhl.  Slippery elm

*U. fulva* Michx.

A medium-sized tree, the common name derives from a distinctive quality of its inner bark. This is mucilaginous, a feature which can be demonstrated easily by peeling the bark from vigorous sprouts. In earlier times, the slippery inner bark of this elm was used a great deal medicinally. The crown is open, the branches and twigs stiffish and relatively few and far apart.

The leaf blades are variable in shape, oblong, oval, obovate, broadly elliptic, or ovate, up to 7 inches long and 2 - 2½ inches broad. Their bases are rounded to broadly cuneate, often asymmetrical, the apices abruptly acuminate. The margins are doubly, saliently serrate. Both surfaces are pubescent, the upper uniformly so, harsh and very scabrous, the lower soft, tawny-pubescent, particularly along the veins, and with conspicuous tufts of whitish hairs in the principal vein axils.

The fruits are suborbicular, ½ - ¾ inch in diameter, the wings broad, wavy-margined but not notched at the apex, essentially glabrous throughout.

The slippery elm is of sporadic occurrence in northern Florida. It is known to us from Jefferson to Jackson counties: on rich wooded slopes at Lake Miccosukee, rich woodlands of the Tallahassee Red Hills, flood-plain woodlands and bluffs along the Apalachicola River, and in rich clay and limestone woodlands in the vicinity of Marianna.

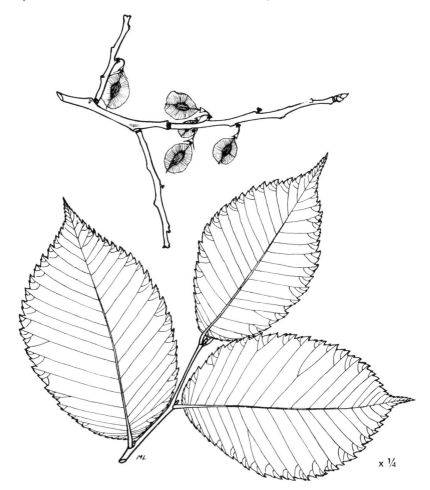

Fig. 68.  *Ulmus rubra*

Diagnostic features of this elm are the mucilaginous inner bark, the doubly-serrate, strongly but abruptly acuminate, oblong-obovate, oblong, or oblong-ovate leaves which are very scabrous above and soft-pubescent below. The leaf bases are in general not nearly so asymmetrical as those of *Ulmus americana,* which it most nearly resembles. Moreover, the upper leaf surfaces of the latter are relatively smooth. The American elm's twigs and branchlets are numerous, curved, and graceful while those of the slippery elm are more scanty and stiffish, making its crown open.

## MORACEAE.  MULBERRY  FAMILY

1. Leaves entire; some branches with stout axillary thorns; fruit orange-like..............
   ..............................................................................................................2. MACLURA
1. Leaves variously toothed and/or lobed, stems thornless; fruit a syncarp (superficially blackberry-like).
   2. Leaves all alternate, glabrous or pubescent but neither markedly rough-scabrous above nor velvety below; buds with 3 - 6 scales; female flowers compacted into an oblong-cylindric catkin....................................................3. MORUS
   2. Leaves alternate, opposite, or in whorls of 3, markedly rough-scabrous above, velvety below; buds with 2 - 3 scales; female flowers compacted into globular catkins...................................................................................1. BROUSSONETIA

### BROUSSONETIA

### 1. **Broussonetia papyrifera** (L.) Vent.   Paper mulberry

Originally introduced from Asia, now widely naturalized in the vicinity of human habitations, the paper mulberry is a small tree. It usually has a short trunk and a beautifully spreading crown, grows rapidly, and is commonly used as a shade tree. It produces root suckers prolifically and thus forms thickets. The sap is milky. The bark is tan and smooth or only slightly furrowed.

The leaves are deciduous, chiefly alternate, sometimes opposite or in whorls of 3. The leaf blade is serrate or crenate, its form variable, even on a single specimen. Some leaves are broadly ovate-cordate and unlobed, others are 2-lobed and mitten-like, or 3 - 5-lobed, the apices or lobe apices acuminate. The leaves of sprouts and seedlings tend to be more variously lobed, those of mature trees more often unlobed. They may be palmately or pinnately veined. The upper surfaces are harsh-scabrous, the lower velvety-pubescent. Yellowish-green stipules are present as the leaves unfurl but these are soon shed. First- and second-year twigs are conspicuously pubescent.

The flowers are unisexual, the plants dioecious. Staminate flowers are borne in pendant, cylindrical, axillary catkins, the pistillate in globular, axillary catkins which become globose multiple fruits at maturity. From these multiple fruits the individual red or orange fruits protrude.

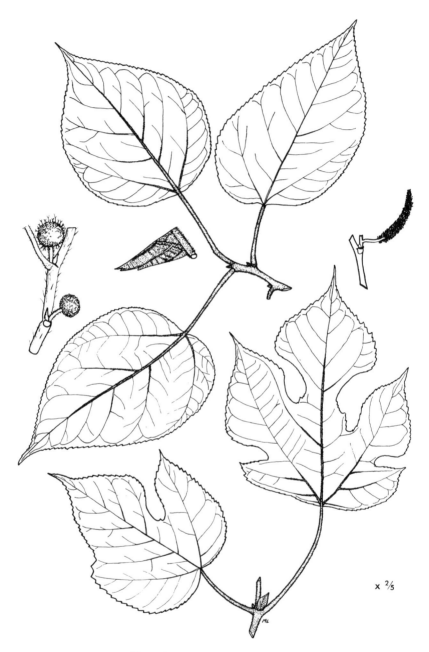

x ²/₅

Fig. 69. *Broussonetia papyrifera*

The paper mulberry is in cultivation and becomes naturalized in waste places and along fences and roadsides.

Distinctive features of the paper mulberry are the smoothish tan bark, a mixture of unlobed and lobed ovate, serrate leaves, the upper surfaces of which are harsh-scabrous and the lower velvety-pubescent.

## Maclura

### 1. **Maclura pomifera** (Raf.) Schneid.   Osage-orange

A small tree or shrub, rare and probably introduced in our area, the osage-orange is much more abundant northward.   Sucker growth is a notable characteristic and leads to thicket forming.   The bark is yellowish-brown, irregularly fissured, and the stems bear stout, simple, axillary thorns.   The sap is milky.

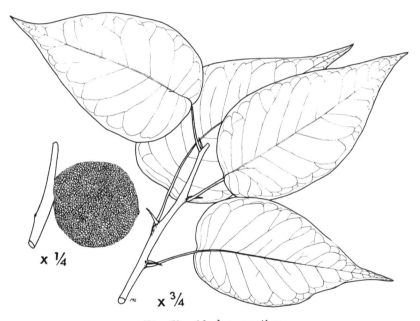

x ¼

x ¾

Fig. 70. *Maclura pomifera*

The leaves are simple, alternate, deciduous, their blades lustrous, ovate to oblong-lanceolate, pinnately veined, and entire.   Their bases are cuneate, rounded, or subcordate, the apices blunt to acuminate.

The flowers are unisexual, the plants dioecious.   Staminate and pistillate flowers are greenish-yellow, borne in globular to short-oblong, axillary catkins.   The pistillate flowers, numerous and closely approximate, produce a large, globular, wrinkled syncarp (each flower produces a fruit and these collectively are massed into an orange-like ball).

This tree is known to us in northern Florida in waste places or fence rows only in the vicinity of Tallahassee and Marianna.

Simple, entire, ovate or oblong-lanceolate leaves, simple stout axillary thorns, a milky sap, and orange-like fruits, are distinctive characteristics of the osage-orange.

## MORUS.  MULBERRIES

The mulberries have simple, alternate, serrate, deciduous leaves. The leaf blades are variable in form, unlobed, mitten-like, palmately 3 - several-lobed, or pinnately several-lobed. The sap is milky. The flowers are unisexual, the plants mostly dioecious. The staminate flowers are borne in elongate-cylindrical catkins, the pistillate in short-oblong catkins. Each flower has a 4-lobed calyx and is apetalous. Staminate flowers bear 4 stamens, pistillate flowers a pistil with a 2-locular ovulary and 2 styles. A pistillate catkin produces a fleshy syncarp resembling a blackberry, the numerous, closely approximate flowers each producing a juicy drupelet, and these collectively form the syncarp or mulberry.

1. Twigs glabrous; leaves glabrous and lustrous on both surfaces, or pubescent only in the principal vein axils below................................................................1. *M. alba*
1. Twigs pubescent; leaves glabrous to slightly short-scabrous and dull-green above, pubescent below................................................................2. *M. rubra*

### 1. **Morus alba** L.  White mulberry

The white mulberry is a small spreading tree, introduced from Asia, and is now widely naturalized.

The leaves are ovate and unlobed varying to ovate-oblong and pinnately 3 - 9-lobed. The upper surfaces are glabrous and lustrous, the lower glabrous, or pubescent only in the vein axils. The twigs are glabrous.

The syncarpic fruits are cylindric-oblong, ½ - ¾ inch long. At maturity, they are white or pink; occasional trees have black fruit [var. *tartarica* (L.) Ser.].

Throughout northern Florida, this tree occurs in vacant lots, waste grounds and moist second-growth woods, mostly near human habitation.

Distinguishing features of the white mulberry are its glabrous, shiny, ovate, unlobed to ovate-oblong, 7 - 9 pinnately lobed leaves.

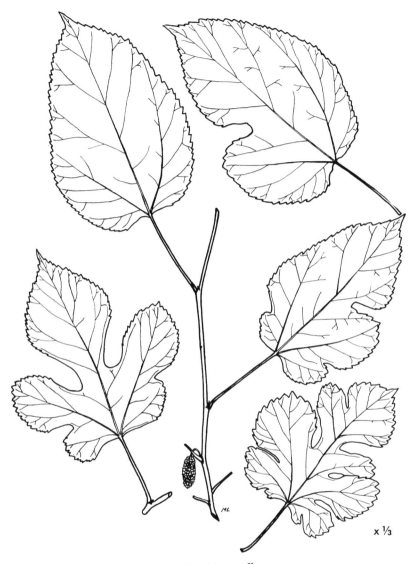

Fig. 71. *Morus alba*

## 2. **Morus rubra** L.   Red mulberry

This is a small tree whose bark is smooth or thin-scaly.

The leaves are variable in shape from broadly ovate and unlobed to mitten-like, or 3 - several-lobed.   The lobed leaves are more character-istic of sprouts and saplings than of the normal branches of mature

trees.  Leaf venation is palmate or pinnate.  The apices of the leaves
(or of the lobes) are acuminate, the leaf bases cordate to truncate.  The
upper surfaces are dull-green, glabrous to slightly short-scabrous, the
lower pubescent with short appressed hairs.  The twigs are pubescent.

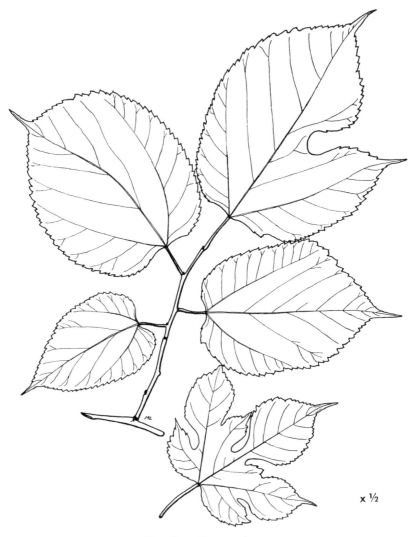

x ½

Fig. 72.  *Morus rubra*

The syncarpic fruits are juicy, cylindric-oblong, 1 - 2 inches long,
dark red to black.

The red mulberry is a native forest tree which inhabits hammocks, rich wooded slopes, and floodplain woodlands. It is not anywhere abundant, but occurs throughout northern Florida.

This tree, if its ovate, variously lobed leaves are present, is unlikely to be mistaken for any other of our forest trees. Its unlobed leaves are similar to those of basswood, but the leaves of the latter are mostly asymmetric and oblique at base and do not have a milky sap.

## MAGNOLIACEAE. MAGNOLIA FAMILY

1. Leaves 4 - 6 lobed, truncate or broadly V-notched at their apices; pistils on the cone ripen into dry, terminally-winged, indehiscent samaras...........LIRIODENDRON
1. Leaves not lobed (except for basal auricles in some); pistils ripening into woody dehiscent follicles, the seeds remaining attached and hanging by slender threads for some time after dehiscence .......................................................MAGNOLIA

### LIRIODENDRON

#### 1. Liriodendron tulipifera L.   Yellow-poplar; tulip-tree

The yellow-poplar is a tall tree with a pyramidal or ovate crown. The limbs are ascending, long and straight when young, becoming spreading in age. Large, old trees are rarely seen in our range any longer. Farther north, in the Appalachians, where it is still a commercially valuable species, specimens of superb dimensions may still be seen. The only large trees of which we know in our area are near Tallahassee. A specimen 7 feet in diameter grows near the Wacissa River in Jefferson County. Several large specimens may be seen in a particularly fine hardwood stand on Governor Millard F. Caldwell's plantation just north of Tallahassee.

The leaves are alternate, simple, long-petioled, glabrous, and deciduous. Their blades are 4 - 6-lobed, the lobes in 2 - 3 pairs. One pair is on either side of a widely truncate or widely V-notched apex, and another pair on either side of the blade, the latter often with secondary lobes. The leaf bases are truncate, widely notched, or rounded. Other than the lobing, the margins are entire. The leaf buds are covered by membranous stipules, which, when they are shed, leave ring-scars around the twigs. The twigs are glabrous, somewhat glaucous, and are brown or gray.

The flowers are large, 2½ - 3 inches broad, 1 - 1½ inches deep, shaped like a broad inverted bell (or tulip-shaped). There are 3 reflexed, freely deciduous sepals, 6 petals whose tips are reflexed, their color greenish-yellow and each with a blotch of orange, and many stamens and pistils spirally arranged on a long-conical axis.

The fruiting cone consists of numerous dry terminally-winged, boat-shaped, cohering, indehiscent fruits, the cone partially persisting into the winter. The lowermost scales, together with the central axis, form characteristic dry cups, some of which remain on the tree into the next blooming period.

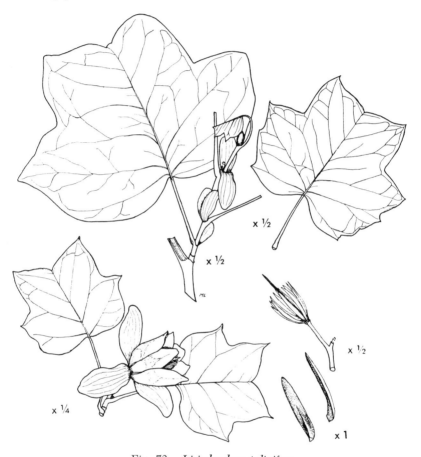

Fig. 73.   *Liriodendron tulipifera*

The yellow-poplar occurs in low woodlands, swamps, bays, along small streams, or on stream slopes. It is sporadic in eastern north Florida, more common in west Florida.

Three distinctive characters mark the yellow-poplar; the apically truncate or broadly notched, 4 - 6-lobed leaves; the tulip-shaped greenish-yellow corolla with orange blotches on the petals; and the scaly cones or cups on the leafless tree in winter.

## MAGNOLIA. MAGNOLIAS

The magnolias are trees or shrubs, some evergreen, some deciduous. The buds are covered by spathelike structures, each consisting of 2 united stipules. The twigs are marked by ring-scars made when the bud spathes are shed, or by similar paired stipules shed by each embryonic leaf of the developing shoot. The leaves are simple, alternate, petioled, and entire (except for basal lobes in some). Flowers are large and showy. Each has 3 sepals and 6 - 12 petals, the sepals and petals often much alike. Stamens and pistils both are numerous and are spirally arranged on a long, conical axis. The anthers open along the side toward the axis. The pistils mature into follicles which open on the side away from the axis, the follicles becoming hard, woody, and coalesced into a fruiting cone. At the base of these cones, the sepal and petal scars are prominent. When the follicles open the seeds are shed but remain hanging for some time on slender threads.

1. Leaves evergreen.
  2. The leaves with rusty-brown pubescence below, or less frequently green below, dark bright green and very lustrous above; follicles densely velvety-pubescent.............................................................................3. *M. grandiflora*
  2. The leaves silvery or sooty-gray below, lustrous above but not dark bright green; follicles glabrous or glabrate.................................5. *M. virginiana*
1. Leaves deciduous.
  3. The leaves cordate or auricled at base.
    4. Twigs and petioles pubescent; leaves chalky-white below........1. *M. ashei*
    4. Twigs and petioles glabrous; leaves green below.............4. *M. pyramidata*
  3. The leaves cuneate, or rounded at base...................................2. *M. cordata*

### 1. Magnolia ashei Weatherby. Ashe magnolia

The Ashe magnolia is a small tree, usually less than 30 feet tall, and not over 4 inches in diameter (or a shrub), with spectacularly large deciduous leaves.

The leaves are broadly obovate or spatulate, more or less constricted from about their middles toward the bases, 8 - 24 inches long by 4 - 11 inches broad. The bases are auricled or cordate, the apices broadly obtuse-angled to acute. They are light green and smooth above, the lower surfaces chalky-white-glaucous, pubescent or glabrous. The pubescent petioles are 2 - 4 inches long, the twigs very hairy to almost glabrous, and the bud-spathes densely pubescent.

The fragrant flowers are creamy-white, large, about 12 inches in diameter at full anthesis. In early anthesis, the corollas form a beautiful urn or inverted bell, the petals recurved at their tips. The petals are

6 in number, the inner 3 sometimes purple-blotched (the outer may be purple-blotched, too, but this is less pronounced).

The fruiting cones are subcylindric to ovoid, 1¾ inches long by 1¼ - 2¼ inches in diameter. They are rose-red during maturation, dark brownish at maturity. The seeds are reddish or dark brown.

Fig. 74. *Magnolia ashei* (except lower left which is a cone of *M. macrophylla*)

This tree or shrub inhabits open, or dense, upland deciduous woods, steepheads and bluffs. Formerly, it was known in Florida from Walton, Okaloosa, and Santa Rosa counties (and in Liberty County as *M. macro-*

*phylla*). To these we add recent discoveries at Wausau in Washington County, and upland woodlands along the Ochlockonee River in Wakulla and Leon counties. Vines (1960) records it for eastern Texas.

The huge, broadly obovate, or spatulate leaves with auricled or cordate bases, chalky-white lower surfaces, and large, creamy-white flowers make this magnolia strikingly distinctive.

*Magnolia macrophylla* Michx., a closely related tree, is reported for Florida by a number of authors, including Chapman. (It should be noted that in Chapman's day *M. ashei* had not been described.) Such reports are probably either a result of misidentification of *M. ashei* or are based on the opinion that *M. ashei* is identifiable with *M. macrophylla*. The authors find that there are characteristics by which the two may be distinguished. Whether the rank of distinction should be specific or varietal is beyond the objectives of this book.

The maximum size of specimens, flower size, fruit size and shape, are measurable characters by which *M. macrophylla* and *M. ashei* differ. Weatherby (1926), who described *M. ashei*, states: "It will be noted that the differential characters of *M. ashei* are for the most part of a rather comparative nature, and with the exception of the shape of the fruit and structure of the follicle not wholly constant, in Mr. Ashe's fine series of specimens." With his statements we are in agreement. The fruiting cones of *M. macrophylla* are globular or subglobular, averaging about 3¼ by 3 inches. Those of *M. ashei* are subcylindric to ovoid, averaging about 3 by 1¾ inches. The mere figures do not sufficiently suggest the contrast, particularly the striking narrowness of the *M. ashei* cone.

We are of the opinion that *M. macrophylla* does not occur in Florida.

### 2. **Magnolia cordata** Michx. Cucumber-tree

This is a medium-sized tree, which in our range attains a height of 75 feet and a diameter of 3 feet.

The leaves are oval, elliptic-ovate, or obovate, 4 - 8 inches long, their bases broadly cuneate, rounded, or rarely slightly subcordate, the apices abruptly short-acuminate. Their margins are entire, but sometimes slightly wavy-curled. The upper leaf surfaces are pubescent when young, glabrate with age, the lower whitish-pubescent when young, glabrate and darker with age. The petioles, young twigs, and bud-spathes are pubescent.

The flowers are lemon-yellow, brownish-yellow to orange-yellow. There are 6 petals, up to 2 inches long, and these are narrowly obovate. The flowering period is mid-March in our area.

The fruiting cone is usually knotty, oblong-cylindrical, about 1½ inches long.

This cucumber-tree is known in our range only in deciduous woods of the rolling hill country south of Ponce de Leon, Holmes County, and near Knox Hill in Walton County. These stations were discovered by Kurz in 1948. Only 6 trees were found, one of which was 75 feet high and 3 feet in diameter. This last has since succumbed to a bulldozer.

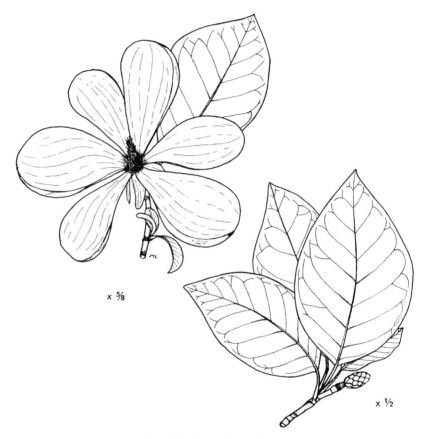

Fig. 75.  *Magnolia cordata*

Of the three deciduous magnolias occurring in Florida the cucumber-tree may be distinguished by its cuneate or rounded (non-ear-lobed) leaf bases, and by its relatively small, brownish-yellow flowers.

### 3. **Magnolia grandiflora** L.  Southern magnolia; bullbay

This is a large and handsome evergreen tree whenever it grows under optimal, mesic conditions. In the southern, coastal part of its range, where it occurs as a dune plant, it may appear as a sprawling shrub because of burial of its lower parts by shifting sands.

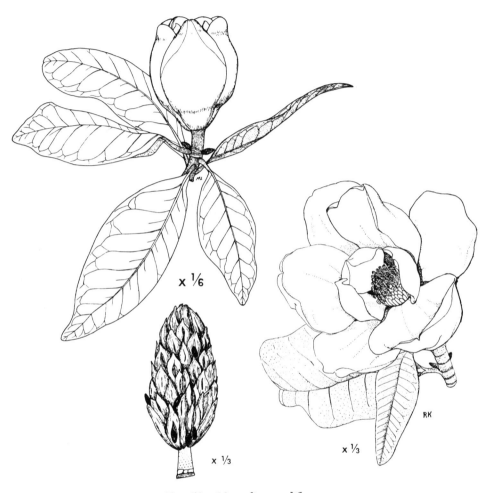

Fig. 76. *Magnolia grandiflora*

The leaves are oblong or broadly elliptic, sometimes slightly broader above or below their middles. They are relatively large, 4 - 8 ( - 13) inches long, and although the margins are entire they may appear wavy because of curling of the blades. They are thick and leathery, dark, lustrous-green above, and rusty-tomentose (rarely green) below. When bruised, they have a peppery aromatic odor.

The young twigs are clothed with a brown, feltlike pubescence.

The flowers are creamy-white, very fragrant, and large (6 - 8 inches across). When in process of opening, they are beautifully urnlike in form. Fully opened flowers, also handsome, exhibit irregularly spreading petals. The petals number 6 to 12, and are variable in size and shape. The perianth parts and stamens are soon deciduous, leaving their scars on the cone axis below the fruits. The spathes covering both flower and leaf buds are velvety.

The fruiting cones, 3 - 4 inches long, are tawny-felty-pubescent, turning buff-pink or rose-red during maturation and becoming brown with age. The seeds are bright lustrous-red.

The southern magnolia occurs in high or low hammocks, on bluffs and ravine slopes, in river bottoms, even on coastal dunes, throughout northern Florida. Optimal sites for its establishment are shady, well-drained situations with abundant leaf mulch and freedom from fire.

This tree is easily distinguished from the sweetbay, its only evergreen relative. Its leaves are much larger, lustrous dark green above, mostly rusty-brown below, compared to those of the sweetbay which are dull, light green above, and silvery below.

4. **Magnolia pyramidata** Bartr. ex Pursh. Pyramid magnolia

The pyramid magnolia is a small, sparsely-branched, deciduous tree whose leaves tend to be clustered at the ends of the branches in umbrella-like rosettes.

The leaves are rhombic-obovate or broadly rhombic-spatulate (kite-shaped), up to 9 inches long by 5 inches broad. Their bases are auricled, the auricles extended outward, the apices rounded, or wide-angled. Their surfaces are green and glabrous. The twigs and petioles are glabrous, as are the spathes covering the buds.

The flowers are white, 6 - 7 inches across, urn-shaped during anthesis and spreading irregularly at full anthesis.

Fruiting cones are glabrous, oblong, 1¼ - 3½ inches long, bright-rose-colored during maturation and turning tawny or purple.

This tree occurs in deciduous forests of slopes, bluffs, and uplands along the Ochlockonee, Apalachicola, and Escambia rivers in western Florida. It is not common.

Although the larger leaves of *Magnolia pyramidata* do not reach nearly the proportions of those of *M. ashei*, the larger of the former and the smaller of the latter may be similar in size and shape. However, *M. pyramidata* leaves are glabrous, not chalky-white below, and its twigs and buds are glabrous. The leaves, twigs, and buds of *M. ashei* are pubescent, and its leaves are strikingly chalky-white below. In

*M. pyramidata,* the terminal leaves, radiating symmetrically in one plane like the petals of an immense green flower, are beautiful to behold. As many as 7 crowded leaves may encircle a stem segment no more than ¼ - ½ inch long.

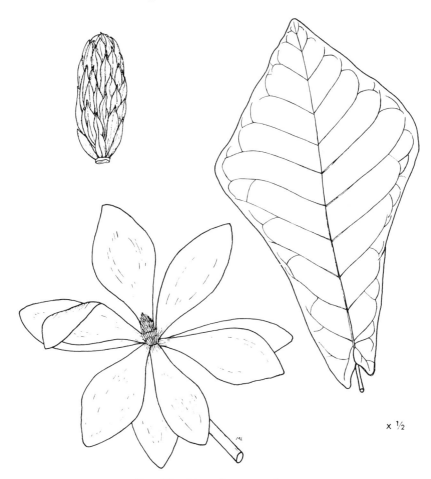

x ½

Fig. 77.   *Magnolia pyramidata*

5. **Magnolia virginiana** L.   Sweetbay

In our area the sweetbay normally forms a fairly large, evergreen tree (up to 90 feet high and 30 inches or more in diameter). It is scrubby or shrubby on certain sites, but, by and large, develops a tree form in contrast to its predominantly shrubby form northward of our range.

The leaf blades are oval to broadly elliptic, 4 - 6½ inches long, narrowing toward both ends which are mostly acute. They are thin-leathery, dull-green above and silvery-pubescent beneath, the hairs appressed, appearing "brush-swept" in one direction. The foliage is pleasantly aromatic. The young twigs are silvery-pubescent becoming ashy and dark.

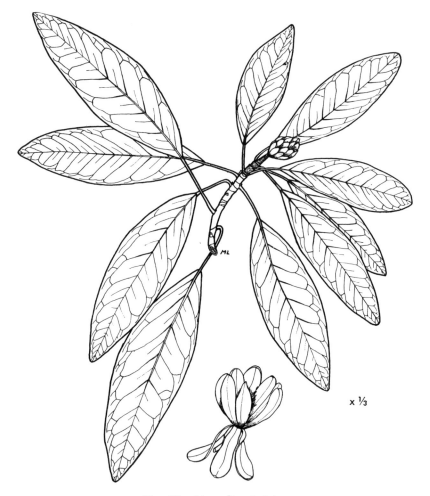

x ⅓

Fig. 78. *Magnolia virginiana*

The flowers are fragrant, creamy-white, 2 - 3 inches across, symmetrically urn-shaped at first, spreading later, the many stamens giving it a disheveled appearance. The petal number is 8 - 12, usually 8.

The fruiting cones are glabrous, ellipsoid or ovoid, about 2 inches long, sometimes appearing knobby. The seeds are dark red or brown.

The tree inhabits flatwoods, depressions, branches, sandy bottom-lands, bays, and swamps, throughout northern Florida. It is particularly conspicuous along streams and in bays in the western part of the state.

The silvery lower surfaces of the leaves of the sweetbay make it discernible from a distance, especially if any breezes are blowing. In sites infrequently and not severely burned, the trees are large and conspicuous. Shrubby forms are commonly seen in shallow depressions, flatwoods, or on low, gentle slopes where periodic fires are severe. These shrubby forms bear flowers and fruit and are not to be mistaken for young trees for they have large, old, underground parts. (See also *Nyssa biflora*.)

## ILLICIACEAE. ANISE-TREE FAMILY

### ILLICIUM

1. **Illicium floridanum** Ellis. Florida anise-tree; stinkbush

This is a shrub or small tree whose flowers or crushed foliage emit a strange, rather overwhelming odor, obnoxious to some persons, doubtfully pleasant to others.

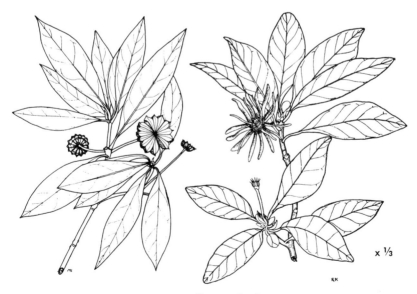

Fig. 79. *Illicium floridanum*

The leaves are alternate, simple, and evergreen. Their blades are long-elliptic to elliptic-lanceolate, 3 - 6 inches long, entire, glabrous and green on both surfaces, but copiously glandular-dotted beneath. When bruised they have a curious odor rather on the order of a concoction of turpentine, spice, and fresh fish! This odor is at first pleasant, then tolerable, finally obnoxious after prolonged exposure to it. The leaves tend to be crowded at the ends of the twigs.

The flowers are showy and attractive but are often more or less hidden in the foliage. They emit much the same odor as the foliage though more nearly clamlike or fishlike.

The flowers have 3 - 6 sepals, numerous, straplike, maroon-red petals, numerous stamens, and numerous pistils arranged in a single whorl. The flowering period extends over several weeks in spring.

The Florida anise-tree inhabits moist, wooded ravines, bayheads, and swamps, from Gadsden and Liberty counties westward in Florida.

Of our native woody plants, this one is unique in having flowers with numerous, dark red petals, fruits arranged in a whorl like a cut cake, and all parts with an offensively odd odor.


# ANNONACEAE.   CUSTARD-APPLE FAMILY

## ASIMINA

### 1. **Asimina triloba** (L.) Dunal.   Pawpaw

*Asimina triloba,* which to the north of our range reaches tree stature, apparently occurs in northern Florida only in the vicinity of Marianna, Jackson County, and along the Apalachicola River. There the plants do not exceed shrub form.

The leaves are membranous, oblong-obovate, 6 - 12 inches long. The tips are short-acuminate to acute, the bases gradually tapering to the short petiole. The upper surfaces are sparsely appressed-pubescent, the lower densely reddish-hairy when young, becoming glabrous above and sparsely hairy on the veins below in age.

The flowers are borne on short, nodding pedicels from the axils of leaf scars before or during the time of leaf emergence. They are maroon in color, have a calyx of 3 subequal triangular-deltoid sepals which are brownish-pubescent on their outer surfaces. There are two series of 3 petals each, the outer oblong-elliptic and 1¼ - 1 inch long, their tips recurved, the inner elliptic, saclike at the base, ½ - ⅓ as long as the outer, and their tips recurved. There are numerous stamens arranged into a compact ball and mostly 3 - 7 pistils. The crushed foliage and the flowers are fetid-aromatic.

The fruit is an oblong-cylindric, pulpy, edible berry 2 - 6 inches long.

*Asimina parviflora* (Michx.) Dunal, a shrub, is very similar except that its flowers and leaves are smaller. The flowers do not exceed ½ - ⅔ the size of those of *A. triloba*.

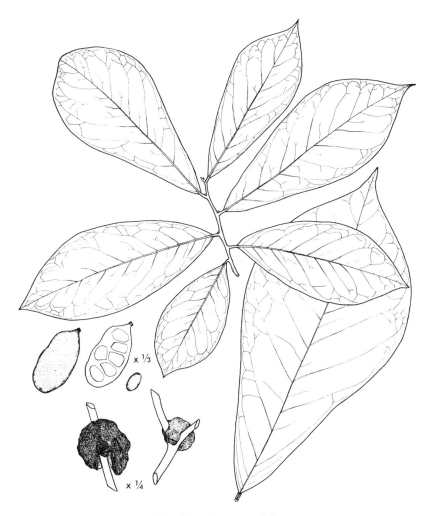

Fig. 80. *Asimina triloba*

An interesting fungal parasite, *Inonotus amplectens* Murrill, commonly occurs on both *Asimina triloba* and *A. parviflora*. The brown-fleshy mass of the fungus (Fig. 80, lower left) occurs in the forks of branches or between a petiole and a branch.

# LAURACEAE. LAUREL FAMILY

1. Leaves evergreen, not lobed; flowers bisexual.
   2. The leaf blades curled in such a way that the edges appear wavy; prominent callosities in the principal vein angles on upper leaf surfaces....CINNAMOMUM
   2. The leaf blades flat, but mature leaves normally have irregular or kidney-shaped, wax-coated galls near their margins; no callosities in the vein angles ........................................................................................................PERSEA
1. Leaves deciduous, most trees having some leaves 2-lobed and mitten-like, or 3-lobed; flowers functionally unisexual, the staminate each with 9 stamens and a rudimentary pistil, the pistillate with 6 staminodia, the plants thus functionally dioecious................................................................................................SASSAFRAS

## CINNAMOMUM

1. **Cinnamomum camphora** (L.) Nees & Eberm.   Camphor-tree

The camphor-tree is an eastern Asiatic evergreen tree which is widely planted for ornament and which is to some extent naturalized throughout our range.   It normally has a short main trunk with numerous ascending secondary trunks.   Its crown supports a dense, handsome foliage.   Cut stems and bruised leaves both are highly aromatic with the odor of camphor.

The leaves are simple, alternate, petioled, persistent, elliptic to ovate, and 2 - 4 inches long.   Their bases are broadly cuneate to rounded, the apices acuminate.   Although the leaf margins are distinctly hyaline and entire, the blades are somewhat curled so that the edges appear wavy. The upper surfaces are bright green and glabrous, the lower pale green and with a thin waxy bloom.   The venation of the blades merits special description.   The midrib is markedly wide from the base to the point of departure of the two principal lateral veins where it abruptly narrows and tapers to the tip.   In the bases of the angles formed at the points of departure of the two main lateral veins from the midrib (on the upper surface) are distinct yellowish callosities.   Similar callosities are in other larger vein angles.

The twigs are glabrous, green or reddish.   The young foliage of developing shoots is often somewhat reddish.

The flowers are greenish-white, small, and are borne abundantly in small axillary panicles.   They are bisexual.

The fruits are globose black drupes, about ⅜ inch in diameter.   They are normally abundant on mature trees and during a certain short period in late winter birds frolic and feast in and around the camphor-trees.

This is a popular shade tree and is frequently encountered as an escape from cultivation in woods, thickets, and along fence rows in the vicinity of human habitation.

Fig. 81. *Cinnamomum camphora*

The prominent odor of camphor, and glossy, wavy leaves with hyaline margins and distinctive callosities in the main vein angles are features which mark the camphor-tree.

## Persea.  Redbays

The redbays are small to medium-sized trees or shrubs having aromatic herbage and simple, alternate, leathery, and persistent leaves. A singular characteristic of the leaves of all species is the occurrence of irregular or kidney-shaped, wax-coated growths (insect galls) along the edges of the leaves. The leaves are commonly "eaten into" at the sites of the galls. The flowers are bisexual. They have 3 greenish outer perianth parts, and 3 larger, greenish-creamy inner ones. There are 9 fertile stamens in whorls of 3 each, and an inner whorl of 3 staminodes. The pistil has a long style with a capitate stigma. The fruits are dark blue or blackish single-seeded drupes.

1. Twigs thinly and minutely pubescent to glabrous; leaves glabrous, glaucous below; peduncles about 1 inch long; inhabiting drained hammocks, mesic woods, or dunes.................................................................................1. *P. borbonia*
1. Twigs densely pubescent; leaves heavily pubescent below; peduncles from nearly an inch to 2 or more inches long; inhabiting sand pine-evergreen oak scrub or swamps.
    2. Pubescence of twigs and leaves short, silky-lustrous; leaves averaging 1½ - 4 inches long; inhabiting evergreen-oak-sand pine scrub.................2. *P. humilis*
    2. Pubescence of twigs and leaves long, dull; leaves averaging 2 - 8 inches long; inhabiting swamps.................................................................3. *P. palustris*

### 1.  **Persea borbonia** (L.) Spreng.   Redbay

Including *P. littoralis* Small

The redbay is a small to medium-sized tree or a shrub. The bark of larger specimens is brownish-gray, roughened with more or less vertical, interlacing fissures between the ridges.

The leaves are broadly lanceolate, elliptic, or oblong, their bases cuneate to rounded, the apices obtuse to acute; often they taper from about their middles to both ends. They average 2 - 8 inches long by 1 - 1½ inches wide. They are dark green and glabrous above, lighter green, smooth and glaucous below, or with short sparse pubescence below. The bloom may be tinged with orange or brown, especially along the veins. The leaf margins are entire or slightly wavy. The twigs are mostly sparsely pubescent with short hairs, and they are variously tinged from green to reddish.

The drupes are subglobose, lustrous, blue or black, and are borne on orange peduncles about ½ - 1 inch long. They are subtended by enlarged, persistent, orange perianth parts in 2 whorls of 3 each.

This plant occurs on coastal dunes, or more generally in drained hammocks or mesic woods, from central and east Florida westward to the vicinity of Marianna in Jackson County.

The redbay has glabrous leaves, fruits on peduncles about ½ - 1 inch long, and grows in drained, mesic sites. The swamp bay, superficially similar, has leaves which are pubescent below, fruiting peduncles 1 - 2 inches long, and grows in poorly drained or wet sites.

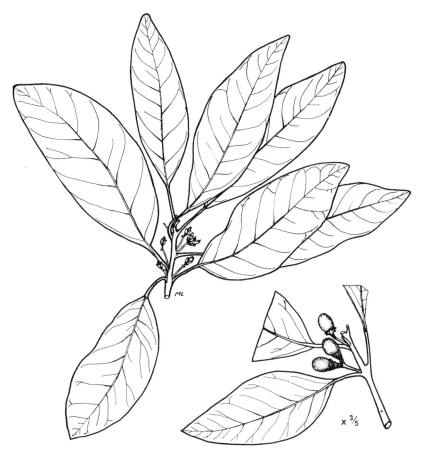

Fig. 82. *Persea borbonia*

We consider *Persea littoralis* Small as a scrubby, dune-inhabiting variant of *P. borbonia*. Its smaller stature and smaller leaves are not unlike similar environmental forms of *Carya glabra*, *Prunus caroliniana*, *Osmanthus americana*, and *Quercus hemisphaerica*.

## 2. **Persea humilis** Nash. Silkbay

This is a small tree or a shrub, of very limited distribution in our range.

RK                                    x 1

Fig. 83.  *Persea humilis*

The leaves are narrowly elliptical, 2 - 3 inches long by ¾ - 1½ inches wide, the margins entire but revolute. The twigs, peduncles, and lower surfaces of the leaves are heavily clothed with a lustrous-silky, appressed, tan or brown pubescence, becoming sooty in age.

The drupes are globose, ⅜ - ⅝ inch long, purplish-black and with a waxy bloom. The peduncles are about 1 inch long.

The silkbay is common in our range only east of Ocala in the ever-green oak-sand pine scrub having white sandy topsoil.

This *Persea* is easily distinguished from the other species by the silky sheen of its twigs and leaves and by its distinctive scrub habitat.

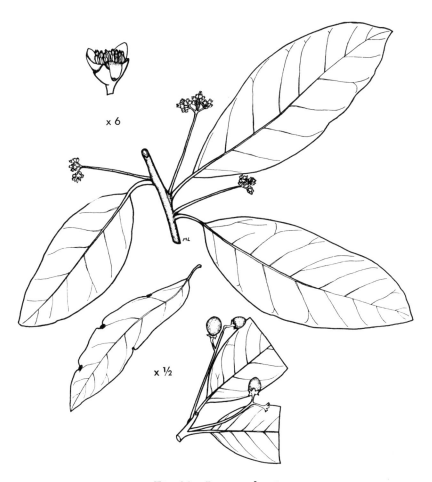

Fig. 84. *Persea palustris*

### 3. **Persea palustris** (Raf.) Sarg. Swampbay

*P. pubescens* (Pursh) Sarg.

The swampbay is similar to the redbay in general habit, and with respect to size and shape of its leaves.

The twigs and lower surfaces of the leaves are coated with a down of long, dull, tan or brown hairs. The lower leaf surfaces, besides being hairy, have a bluish-white bloom accentuated by a buff or orange bloom on the veins.

The drupes are dark blue or black and have a thin whitish bloom somewhat obscuring the color. They are ⅓ - ½ inch long, and are borne on peduncles 2 or more inches long.

The swampbay inhabits poorly drained, nonalluvial swamps and wet grounds from northeastern to western Florida.

There is much disagreement as to whether or not the redbay and swampbay constitute separate species. In our area, at least, we find each, as described, restricted to a very distinct type of habitat. It seems practical, therefore, to distinguish them. (See *Persea borbonia* for comparative notes.)

### SASSAFRAS

### 1. **Sassafras albidum** (Nutt.) Nees. Sassafras

*S. sassafras* (L.) Karst.

Ordinarily this is a small tree but it is commonly found forming shrub or small-tree thickets. The bark of small trees is reddish-brown and shallowly fissured. In older, larger trees it is rough with thick, scaly, broad ridges separated by shallow furrows.

The leaves are simple, alternate, and deciduous. They are variable in size and shape, unlobed, 2-lobed and mitten-like, or 3-lobed and resembling a 3-fingered glove (rarely 5-lobed). Trees with all unlobed leaves are infrequently encountered. Leaf lengths are from 3 - 5 inches, or up to 8 inches in shade. Their margins are entire except for the lobing. The undersurfaces are pubescent, conspicuously so when young.

Parts of the entire plant, roots, stems, and leaves are spicy-aromatic.

The flowers are unisexual, the plants dioecious. Flowers are borne in clusters at the summits of twigs of the previous year and prior to the appearance of the leaves. The perianth consists of 6 greenish-yellow parts, all alike, in 2 whorls. Staminate flowers have 9 stamens, 3 each in three whorls, the inner 3 each with a pair of stalked glands at its base. The pistillate flowers have 6 short staminodia.

The fruits are ellipsoidal, blue drupes.

Distinguishing characters of the sassafras are the variable, entire, unlobed, mitten-like or glovelike leaf forms, together with the spicy-aromatic qualities of the vegetative parts.

This tree is common throughout northern Florida.  It occurs in well-drained woodlands, old fields, and along roadsides.

x ½

Fig. 85.  *Sassafras albidum*

## HAMAMELIDACEAE.  WITCH-HAZEL FAMILY

1.  Leaves pinnately-veined, their margins wavy, coarsely crenate to crenate-dentate; flowering in late autumn, the flowers borne in short axillary clusters............
........................................................................................................HAMAMELIS

1.  Leaves palmately-veined and lobed, the 5 acute lobes giving much the effect of a star; flowering in spring, monoecious, the staminate flowers borne in tight-

rounded clusters on stiff spikes, the pistillate borne in tight spherical heads on dangling stalks............................................................................................................LIQUIDAMBAR

## HAMAMELIS

### 1. **Hamamelis virginiana** L.   Witch-hazel

The witch-hazel, usually a shrub, occasionally attains the stature of a small tree.   The bark is grayish-brown and shallowly furrowed and ridged.   The twigs tend to zigzag in one plane in relation to a 2-ranked, alternate leaf arrangement.   The terminal winter buds are asymmetrically curved, stalked, and with a dense covering of tawny hairs.

Fig. 86.  *Hamamelis virginiana*

The leaves are simple, alternate, deciduous, and 2-ranked.   The leaf blades are oval, ovate, obovate, or suborbicular, asymmetrical, mostly 3 - 5 inches long and 2 - 3 inches broad, those of sprouts and suckers generally larger.   The base of the blade of the larger half of the leaf extends farther down the side of the petiole and is usually rounded, that of the shorter side tapering.   The leaf apices are rounded to short-acuminate, the latter being especially characteristic of the larger leaves of suckers or sprouts. The leaf margins are wavy, or coarsely crenate to crenate-dentate. The upper leaf surfaces are sparsely stellate-pubescent or glabrate, the lower sparsely stellate-pubescent.

The flowers are borne in short axillary clusters. The flowers buds appear several months before they open, the clusters appearing in the leaf axils or in the axils of leaf scars. Actual flowering occurs in late autumn, beginning about the time the leaves begin to fall, and reaches its height after or when nearly all the leaves have been shed. The flowers have a cuplike calyx with 4 densely hairy, dirty-brown lobes, 4 elongate-linear, bright yellow petals, 4 short stamens and 4 scalelike staminodia, a pistil with 2 styles.

The fruit is an ovoid, hard-bony, 2-beaked capsule, the base of which is invested by the cuplike calyx. The capsule is 2-loculed, each locule bearing a single shiny black seed, and it dehisces along 2 sutures. In splitting, each of the beaks is dissected, making the opened capsule appear 4-beaked. The fruit is densely granular and stellate-hairy.

The witch-hazels inhabit rich woodlands more or less throughout our range. Commonly a shrub, it attains tree stature in calcareous, mesic, mixed flatwoods hammocks.

Distinctive features of *Hamamelis virginiana* are the wavy or coarsely crenate-dentate leaves, the asymmetrically curved, stalked, tawny-hairy terminal buds, and the axillary clusters of densely hairy flower buds. At time of flowering in late autumn, the clusters of flowers with elongate-linear yellow petals make it unmistakable.

## LIQUIDAMBAR

### 1. Liquidambar styraciflua L.   Sweetgum

This is a large and beautiful tree having aromatic foliage, balsamic juices, and (frequently) corky-winged twigs.

The leaves are simple, alternate, palmately-veined, palmately 5-lobed, the 5 acute lobes giving much the effect of a star. They are 5 - 7 inches long by 4 - 5 inches broad. Their lobed margins are sharply and evenly serrate, the blades glabrous on both surfaces. They turn deep winy-crimson in autumn.

The twigs are often (not always) beset with corky outgrowths which take the form of wings, ridges, or warts. The buds are ovoid, pointed, and are covered by conspicuously glossy-brown overlapping scales. The bark of the trunks is dark gray, with many vertical interlacing ridges and furrows.

The flowers are unisexual, the plants monoecious. The staminate are greenish-yellow, borne in tight-rounded clusters on a stiff spike; the pistillate are pale green, consisting of 2-beaked pistils subtended by small scales, borne in large numbers which cohere in tight, spherical heads at the ends of long drooping or dangling stalks.

Fruiting clusters mature into semiwoody, pendant balls.

Fig. 87.   *Liquidambar styraciflua*

The sweetgum inhabits a variety of wooded, mesic sites nearly throughout our range.

The sharply serrated, regularly 5-lobed, semistarlike leaves which have an aromatic odor suffice to identify this tree.   Should there be any tendency to mistake it for a maple, the oppositely arranged, nonaromatic leaves of the latter are in contrast.

## PLATANACEAE.  SYCAMORE  FAMILY

### Platanus

#### 1.  Platanus occidentalis L.   American sycamore

This is a large tree, picturesque because of its bright varicolored bark and large, yellow-green leaves.   The bark sloughs off in thin, irregular plates and appears exquisitely mottled or dappled in several colors.   The outer is light gray, the inner blends of tan, green, or chalky-white, the pattern depending upon the degree of flaking off of the older bark.

The leaves are simple, alternate, and deciduous. The large blades are mostly wider than long, usually 3 - 6 inches broad and slightly less in length (up to 10 by 10 inches on vigorous sprouts). They are palmately-veined, their margins with large, irregular teeth or lobes. They are thick-downy when young, becoming glabrous except along the veins at maturity. The bases of the blades are truncate, or commonly they are decurrent-winged along the summits of the petioles. The petioles are long and enlarged at their bases, these enlarged bases enveloping the axillary buds. Large, leaflike stipules at the petiole-bases are completely united around the twigs forming a sheathing crown the edges of which spread horizontally and are toothed or lobed. Frequently the remains of these crownlike stipules persist after leaf-fall, lending the otherwise naked twigs an odd and distinctive appearance.

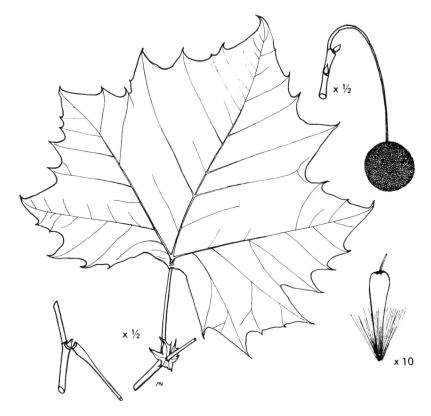

Fig. 88. *Platanus occidentalis*

The flowers are unisexual, the plants monoecious. All the flowers are individually very small, those of each sex borne in separate, globular heads on the same shoots, the male reddish, on short, stiffish peduncles, the female much larger, greenish, and dangling on long peduncles.

The fruiting head ("button balls") are about 1 inch in diameter and they dangle on stalks 3 - 6 inches long. They consist of many nutlets, each nutlet subtended by numerous long hairs.

In Florida the American sycamore is apparently restricted to floodplain woodlands along the Apalachicola, Choctawhatchee, and Escambia rivers.

This tree is readily identified. It is our only large tree with simple leaves in which the petiole-bases enclose the axillary buds. This character is common to the box-elder and the smooth sumac, but both of them are shrubs or small trees with pinnately compound leaves. Other distinctive features of the American sycamore are the crownlike sheathing stipules and the conspicuously mottled bark. Sometimes, especially in winter, the outer bark is all sloughed off, making the trunks spectacularly white.

## ROSACEAE. ROSE FAMILY

1. Principal lateral veins of the leaves appressed to the midribs for a short distance (visible with a 10x lens); petals elongate, linear or oblong............AMELANCHIER
1. Principal lateral veins of the leaves departing abruptly from the midribs (as seen with a 10x lens); petals nearly as broad as long.
   2. Flowers having a floral cup fused to the ovulary, the sepals, petals, and stamens borne apparently on the summit of the ovulary; fruit a pome or pomelike, remnants of the sepals and stamens persisting at its summit, several-seeded.
      3. Thorns not leafy, nor bearing leaf scars; flowers and fruits borne terminally on leafy branchlets of the season; seeds enclosed in hard-bony nutlets
          ....................................................................................................CRATAEGUS
      3. Thorns leafy or bearing leaf scars; flowers and fruits borne terminally on spur-shoots; seeds enclosed in cavities with stiff-papery walls.........MALUS
   2. Flowers having a floral cup free from the ovulary; on the upper margin of the floral cup are borne the sepals, petals, and stamens; fruit a 1-seeded drupe with no remnants of calyx or stamens persisting.....................................PRUNUS

### AMELANCHIER

1. **Amelanchier arborea** (Michx. f.) Fern. Downy serviceberry

A small, slender tree or shrub with a narrow crown and ascending branches. The bark is ashy-gray, smooth on younger trunks or branches and becoming shallowly furrowed in age. The twigs and branches are not thorny.

The leaves are simple, alternate, deciduous, their blades oblong-oval, slightly ovate or obovate, 1 - 2½ inches long and ¾ - 1½ inches broad. The bases are rounded to subcordate, the apices acute to short-acuminate. The principal lateral veins are appressed to the midribs for a very short distance, then abruptly extend outward to the leaf margin. The leaf margins are serrulate or doubly serrulate, the teeth abruptly contracted to incurving tips. As the leaves expand they are pilose above, tomentose below, the petioles and young twigs tomentose. Grad-

Fig. 89.   *Amelanchier arborea*

ually, the pubescence is mainly lost on the upper leaf surfaces, somewhat more of it retained on the lower leaf surfaces and on the petioles.
The winter buds are mostly linear-elliptic, ½ - ¾ inch long.

The flowers are white, about an inch across, borne in erect or drooping, showy racemes. The petals are linear or linear-oblong, ¾ - ½
inch long, much longer than broad. The ovulary is inferior and remains of the calyx persist at the summits of the fruits. Flowering occurs as the leaves unfurl in early spring.

The fruit is a reddish-purple, berry-like pome, 10-seeded, sub-globose,
becoming about ⅓ inch in diameter.

The downy serviceberry is rare and local in western Florida: in rich
woodlands of Leon County and from Washington to Escambia counties.

During the flowering period, the showy racemes of white flowers,
which have elongate petals, make this small, slender, rich woodland
tree distinctive. Subsequent to flowering, and until about midsummer,
the racemes of subglobose reddish-purple, 10-seeded pomes distinguish
it. A characteristic of the leaf venation which is peculiar to this tree
in contrast to the other genera in the family is that the principal lateral
veins are appressed to the midribs for a short distance, then abruptly
extend outward to the leaf margin. This character is not very evident
to the naked eye.

## CRATAEGUS* HAWTHORN; THORN; RED HAW

This is a large genus of small trees or shrubs, usually armed with
simple or compound naked thorns. The leaves are deciduous, alternate,
simple, usually serrate or dentate and often more or less lobed, those
at the ends of sterile shoots differently shaped, larger, and usually more
deeply cut than on the flowering branchlets. Flowers are borne in simple or compound corymbs or cymes (rarely singly or two or three together); hypanthium cup-shaped or campanulate; ovary inferior, of 1 - 5
carpels; petals normally 5; stamens 5 - 25; styles 1 - 5, distinct. The
fruit is a haw or pome, subglobose, ovoid, or pyriform, with 1 - 5 bony
nutlets embedded in the firm or succulent flesh. The pomes are red,
yellow, or orange in our species, or sometimes remaining green or
mottled.

For convenience of treatment the genus has been divided into a number of groups or series, seven of which are represented in this treatment.

---

* This treatment of *Crataegus* was prepared and contributed, with minor modifica-
tion, by Mr. Ernest J. Palmer, Arnold Arboretum, retired. It will be noted that
measurements used by Mr. Palmer are metric, unlike others in the book.

*Crataegus* is the largest genus of woody plants in North America; it is also one of the most difficult for taxonomic treatment. Many species that have been named and described differ from others only in slight and inconstant characters, and there are a number of hybrids.

Besides the species described here, several others have been reported from northern Florida. Among them may be mentioned *Crataegus youngii* Sarg., *C. flava* Ait., *C. sororia* Beadle, *C. michauxii* Pers. and *C. grosseserrata* Ashe. Other species described by Beadle, Ashe, and Murrill are regarded as of doubtful validity; some have been omitted because they are not known to attain the form and size of trees. Many species are on the border line between shrubs and trees, usually flowering and fruiting as shrubs, but rarely becoming small trees under favorable circumstances. One striking example is *C. uniflora* Muenchh. It is usually a slender shrub throughout its wide range, but there is a form or closely related species (*C. grosseserrata*) that becomes a small tree in Florida.

In the distribution of each species we have listed the counties in which we have collected specimens of the species. These records are not meant to indicate that a given species is restricted to those counties for we have made no special effort to gather distributional data for the hawthorns.

### KEY TO THE SERIES

1. Veins of the leaves running both to the sinuses and to the points of the lobes; fruit small, usually under 5 mm. thick................................................1. Microcarpae
1. Veins of the leaves running only to the points of the lobes; fruit larger, usually 5 - 12 mm. thick.
    2. Flowers single or few in simple clusters; plants usually shrubby but rarely becoming small trees.
        3. Leaves obovate, oblong-obovate or elliptic, mostly 3 - 5 cm. long on flowering branchlets or twice as long at the ends of shoots; flowers usually 3 - 4; fruit becoming soft and edible....................................2. Aestivales
        3. Leaves mostly obovate, 1.2 - 3.2 cm. long; flowers usually single or rarely 2 - 3 in a cluster; fruit remaining hard and inedible............3. Parvifoliae
    2. Flowers more numerous (3 - 20) in simple or compound cymes or corymbs; plants becoming trees but sometimes fruiting as arborescent shrubs.
        4. Leaves mostly obovate or spatulate, rather uniform in type but larger and relatively broader at the ends of the shoots; nutlets usually 1 - 2............
................................................................................4. Crus-galli
        4. Leaves variable, mostly obovate, elliptic or ovate in outline, or sometimes broadly ovate at the ends of shoots, usually lobed.
            5. The leaves not conspicuously glandular.
                6. Flowering branchlets having leaves sharply lobed or sometimes nearly unlobed, but more deeply lobed at the ends of the shoots; flowers mostly 8 - 20 in compound corymbs; fruit 5 - 8 mm. thick; nutlets 3 - 5, usually 5....................................5. Virides
                6. Flowering branchlets having leaves sharply and uniformly lobed

or often deeply incised at the ends of shoots; flowers mostly 3 - 10 in simple corymbs; fruit usually 0.6 - 1 cm. thick; nutlets 2 - 5, usually less than 5..................................................................6. PULCHERRIMAE

5. The leaves conspicuously glandular, those of the flowering branchlets mostly obovate or oblong-obovate, narrowed or cuneate at the base; entire or serrate near the apex or sometimes coarsely dentate and with small toothlike lobes, or at the ends of shoots often broadly obovate to orbicular, more deeply lobed or incised; flowers mostly 3 - 7 in simple corymbs.........................................................................7. FLAVAE

## SERIES 1: *Microcarpae*

1. Leaves obovate or spatulate, distinctly longer than broad except sometimes at the ends of shoots; foliage and inflorescence glabrous; fruit subglobose................
..................................................................................................1. *C. spathulata*

1. Leaves ovate or deltoid, often as wide as long or wider than long; foliage and inflorescence pubescent at least when young; fruit obovoid.........2. *C. marshallii*

### 1. Crataegus spathulata Michx.    Small-fruited thorn;  red haw

A small tree up to 5 - 7 m. high with spreading branches, stoutish, usually thorny branchlets, and thin, scaly bark; sometimes fruiting as an arborescent shrub.  Leaves cuneate at the base, with strongly ascending or nearly parallel primary veins.  Flowers 6 - 8 mm. wide in many-flowered corymbs; stamens about 20; anthers pale yellow; fruit 4 - 7 mm. thick, with thin, mellow flesh and 3 - 5 nutlets.

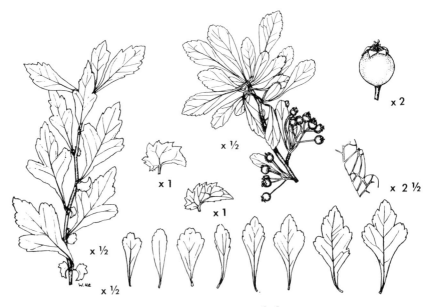

Fig. 90.  *Crataegus spathulata*

Moist to wet depressions and stream banks from Marion County westward.

## 2. Crataegus marshallii Egglest.   Parsley haw

*C. apiifolia* Michx. not Medic.

A small tree up to 6 - 8 m. high, or sometimes a stout shrub, with slender thorny or nearly thornless branchlets, pubescent while young, and with thin, scaly bark.   Leaves at the ends of the shoots often truncate or subcordate at the base.   Flowers 1 - 1.5 cm. wide, in many-flowered corymbs; stamens about 10; anthers red; fruit bright red, succulent at maturity.   Nutlets 1 - 5, usually 2.

Bottomland or floodplain woodlands throughout the area.

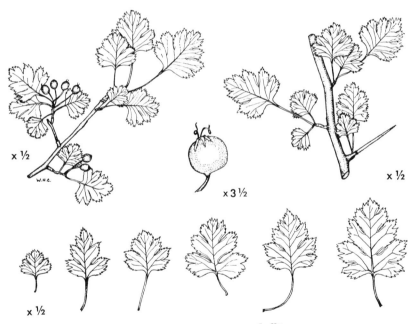

Fig. 91.   *Crataegus marshallii*

## Series 2.   *Aestivales*

### 3. Crataegus aestivalis (Walt.) T. & G.   May haw; apple haw; shining haw

Usually a large arborescent shrub or rarely becoming a tree up to 6 - 8 m. high, with erect or spreading branches; slender, usually thorny branchlets, and pale gray, scaly bark over reddish inner bark. Flowers about 2 cm. wide; stamens 15 - 20 or sometimes 25; anthers pink or purplish; fruit short-oblong or depressed globose, about 1 cm. thick, scarlet, with yellow, juicy flesh. The fruit is slightly acid and highly flavored and is eaten and sold on the market.

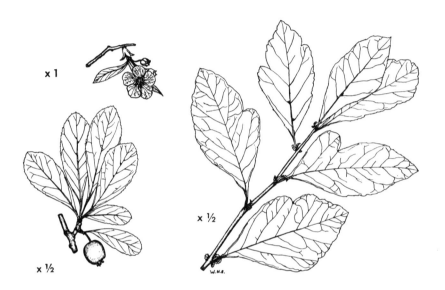

Fig. 92.  *Crataegus aestivalis*

Shallow ponds, wet woodlands, and along streams throughout the area.

## Series 3: *Parvifoliae*

### 4. **Crataegus uniflora** Muenchh.   One-flowered haw; dwarf haw

*C. grosseserrata* Ashe ?

Usually a slender shrub but sometimes becoming a small tree 4 - 5 m. high, with stout, flexuous, thorny branchlets. Flowers 1 - 1.5 cm. wide; stamens about 20 or rarely 25; anthers white or pale yellow; sepals usually deeply glandular-serrate, somewhat foliaceous and persistent on the fruit. *Crataegus grosseserrata*, which was described as a small tree, may be distinct but the complex needs further study.

Dry open woods, deciduous woodlands, and borders of woods from about Alachua County westward.

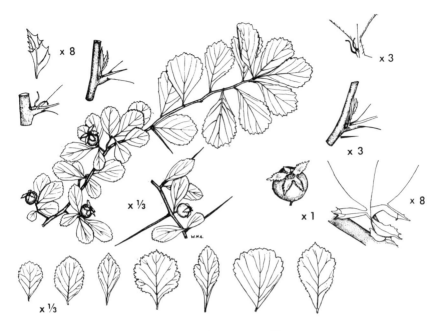

Fig. 93.    *Crataegus uniflora*

## Series 4:  *Crus-galli*

1. Leaves thick at maturity, finely and sharply serrate above the middle; stamens 10 or less; branchlets usually very thorny.............................................5. *C. crus-galli*
1. Leaves comparatively thin at maturity, serrate with shallow or crenate teeth; branchlets thornless or sparingly thorny..................................6. *C. pyracanthoides*

### 5.  **Crataegus crus-galli** L.   Hog-apple; cockspur haw

*C. algens* Beadle; *C. armata* Beadle

A tree up to 10 m. high, typically with a broad crown of wide spreading intricate branches, thorny flexuous branchlets, and dark, slightly scaly bark.   Leaves glossy above or sometimes dull and thinner in shade.   Flowers 1 - 1.5 cm. wide; stamens about 10; anthers pink or rarely yellowish.   Fruit subglobose or obovoid, sometimes slightly 5-angled, dull red or remaining green and dark mottled at maturity, with thin, dry, inedible flesh.   *C. crus-galli* var. *pyracanthoides* Ait. has smaller, relatively narrower leaves and smaller fruit.

Upland open woodlands, pastures, abandoned fields, from about Taylor County westward.

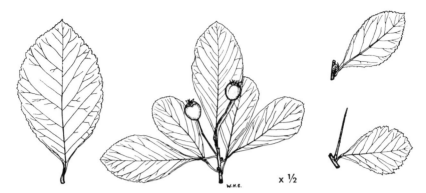

Fig. 94.   *Crataegus crus-galli*

6. **Crataegus pyracanthoides** Beadle.    Wakulla  haw

An arborescent shrub or a small tree up to 5 - 6 m. high with open ascending or spreading branches and slender unarmed or slightly thorny branchlets.    Flowers 1 - 1.5 cm. wide; stamens 10 - 20; anthers pink; fruit subglobose, 5 - 8 mm. thick, bright red.    In *C. pyracanthoides* var. *arborea* (Beadle) Palmer, the leaves are slightly larger and relatively broader, and the flowers slightly larger with 20 stamens and light yellow anthers.    In *C. pyracanthoides* var. *limnophila* (Sarg.) Palmer, the foliage and inflorescence is more or less villous, the stamens number 10 or 20 with pink anthers.

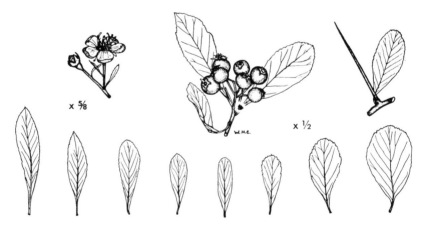

Fig. 95.   *Crataegus pyracanthoides*

Mixed  pine-deciduous  flatwoods  and  occasionally  floodplain  woodlands, locally  from Lafayette to Jackson counties.

## Series 5: *Virides*

1. Leaves of the flowering branchlets mostly 2 - 4 cm. wide; anthers pale yellow or rarely pink; nutlets usually 5.............................................................7. *C. viridis*
1. Leaves of the flowering branchlets mostly 1 - 2 cm. wide; anthers pink or purple; nutlets 3 - 5.............................................................8. *C. paludosa*

### 7. **Crataegus viridis** L.    Green haw

*C. arborescens* Ell.

A tree up to 8 - 10 m. high with wide spreading or ascending branches, slender unarmed or sometimes sparingly thorny branchlets, and thin, scaly, brownish-gray bark over cinnamon-colored inner bark.    Leaves

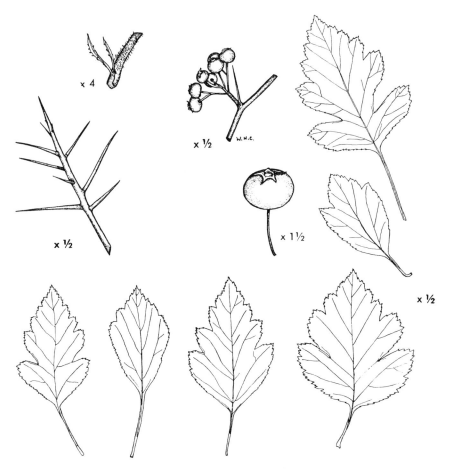

Fig. 96.    *Crataegus viridis*

mostly ovate, oblong-ovate or elliptic, usually more or less lobed or some-times unlobed except at the ends of the shoots, thin, glabrous except for small tufts of tomentum in the axils of the veins at maturity. Flowers 1.2 - 1.5 cm. wide, mostly 8 - 20 in compound corymbs; stamens about 20; fruit subglobose, 5 - 8 mm. thick, red at maturity.

Lowland woodlands and pond margins from Taylor County west-ward.

### 8. **Crataegus paludosa** Sarg.   Pond haw; swamp haw

An arborescent shrub or a small tree up to 4 - 5 m. high with open spreading or depressed branches and slender flexuous thorny branch-lets, slightly villous when they first appear. Flowers 1.3 - 1.8 cm. wide, mostly 5 - 10 in slightly villous corymbs; stamens 20 - 25. Fruit oblong or subglobose, red or orange-red at maturity.

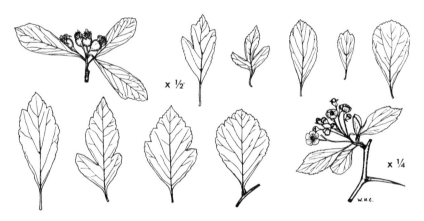

Fig. 97.   *Crataegus paludosa*

Lowland woodlands and pond margins from Lafayette County west-ward.

## SERIES 6: *Pulcherrimae*

1.  Leaves of terminal shoots seldom over 4 - 5 cm. long; flowers mostly 5 - 7, 1.4 - 2 cm. wide; fruit 5 - 7 mm. thick.
    2.  Terminal shoot leaves broadly ovate; flowers 1.6 - 2 cm. wide; fruit subglo-bose or oval, yellowish-green at maturity; nutlets 2 - 3.........9. *C. pulcherrima*
    2.  Terminal shoot leaves sometimes suborbicular; flowers 1.5 - 1.8 cm. wide; fruit subglobose, bright red at maturity; nutlets 3 - 5...............10. *C. opima*
1.  Leaves of terminal shoots 5 - 6 cm. long; flowers mostly 5 - 10, 1.5 - 1.8 cm. wide; fruit 0.7 - 1 cm. thick; nutlets 3 - 5....................................11. *C. robur*

### 9. **Crataegus pulcherrima** Ashe

*C. abstrusa* Beadle

A small tree up to 4 - 6 m. high, or oftener an arborescent shrub with crooked ascending branches and slender sparsely thorny branchlets. Leaves elliptic or oblong-ovate or broadly ovate at the ends of shoots, with 2 - 3 pairs of sharp lateral lobes, thin but firm, glabrous at maturity. Flowers few in compact glabrous corymbs with about 20 stamens and purplish-red anthers. Fruit with thin flesh, remaining hard and dry at maturity.

Wet hammocks, Wakulla County.

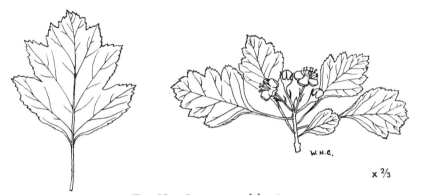

x ⅔

Fig. 98.   *Crataegus pulcherrima*

### 10. **Crataegus opima** Beadle

*C. assimilis* Beadle; *C. illustris* Beadle

A tree up to 6 - 7 m. high or often a large shrub with slender, thorny branchlets and dark gray, slightly scaly bark. Leaves oval or ovate or

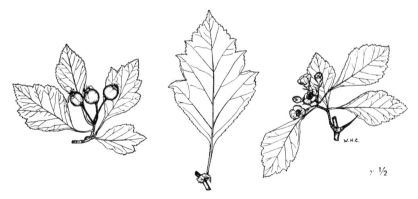

× ½

Fig. 99.   *Crataegus opima*

sometimes nearly orbicular at the ends of shoots, indented with 2 - 3 pairs of shallow but acute lateral lobes, firm, glabrous at maturity. Flowers few in glabrous corymbs; stamens about 20; anthers dark rose-colored.  Fruit with thin, dry flesh and 3 - 5 nutlets.

Deciduous woodlands, Leon and Wakulla counties.

### 11.  Crataegus robur Beadle

A tree up to 7 - 8 m. high or sometimes a stout shrub with slender, sparingly thorny branchlets and brownish-gray, slightly scaly bark. Leaves mostly oval or ovate, rather deeply indented with 2 - 3 pairs of acute or rounded spreading lobes.  Flowers in mostly 5 - 10-flowered slightly compound glabrous corymbs.  Fruit with thin, firm flesh, becoming orange-red at maturity.

Upland woodlands and abandoned fields, Leon and Wakulla to Jackson counties.

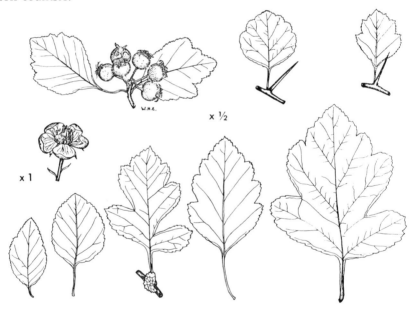

Fig. 100.  *Crataegus robur*

## Series 7: *Flavae*

1. Terminal leaves of sterile shoots up to 5 - ? cm. wide, broadly ovate to suborbicular or sometimes wider than long.
    2. Leaves of terminal shoots often wider than long with small acute lobes above the middle; stamens about 20; anthers pale yellow; fruit 1 - 1.8 cm. thick, becoming succulent........................................................12. *C. ravenelii*

2. Leaves of terminal shoots seldom wider than long, stamens about 20; anthers pink; fruit 0.9 - 1.2 cm. thick, with firm flesh becoming mellow..................
..............................................................................................................................13. *C. leonensis*

1. Terminal leaves of sterile shoots seldom over 3 - 4 cm. wide, usually longer than wide.

   3. Lower branches and branchlets depressed; leaves of the flowering branchlets cuneate or narrowly obovate, entire or finely serrate or sometimes with a few toothlike lobes at the rounded or nearly truncate apex, or at the ends of shoots broadly obovate, elliptic or ovate, more or less lobed and sometimes deeply laciniate.

      4. Branchlets very slender and repent; foliage and inflorescence glabrous or nearly so; flowers mostly 3 - 5 in simple corymbs or rarely single; nutlets usually 3................................................................................14. *C. lacrimata*

      4. Branchlets slender and slightly drooping but not distinctly repent; foliage and inflorescence pubescent at least while young; nutlets 3 - 5.................
..............................................................................................................................15. *C. floridana*

   3. Lower branches spreading or ascending; branchlets often flexuous; leaves of the flowering branchlets mostly obovate or oval, or at the ends of the shoots ovate to suborbicular.

      5. Leaves mostly spatulate-obovate, rounded or nearly truncate at the apex, or at the ends of shoots broadly obovate to suborbicular and more or less irregularly lobed; flowers 1.6 - 2 cm. wide; anthers pink or purplish
..............................................................................................................................16. *C. visenda*

      5. Leaves mostly oblong-obovate, oval or ovate, pointed or rarely rounded at the apex; flowers 1.5 - 1.7 cm. wide; anthers white, pale yellow or pale pink.

         6. The leaves glabrous and lustrous above at maturity; stamens about 20; anthers light yellow; fruit pyriform or oblong; nutlets usually 3
..............................................................................................................................17. *C. audens*

         6. The leaves glabrous but dull above at maturity; stamens 15 - 20; anthers white or pale pink, fruit subglobose; nutlets 3 - 5..................
..............................................................................................................................18. *C. egregia*

## 12. Crataegus ravenelii Sarg.   Ravenel haw

A tree up to 10 - 20 m. high with a trunk 4 dm. in diameter, stout wide-spreading branches, stoutish, flexuous thorny branchlets and dark brown, thick and deeply ridged bark, or sometimes fruiting as an arborescent shrub. Leaves of the flowering branchlets mostly obovate, 3 - 4 cm. long, 2 - 2.5 cm. wide, attenuate at the base into slender petioles ½ to ⅔ as long as the blades, or on sterile shoots often broadly obovate to suborbicular or broader than long and often 3-lobed, or with 2 - 3 pairs of small shallow lobes and up to 5 cm. long and wide, pubescent at least while young. Flowers 1.6 - 2 cm. wide, mostly 3 - 5 in slightly villous corymbs; stamens about 20; anthers pale yellow. Fruit subglobose or short-oblong, 1.5 - 1.8 cm. thick, orange-red or yellow with red cheek at maturity; nutlets usually 5.

Sandy upland, open woodlands, Hamilton to Holmes counties.

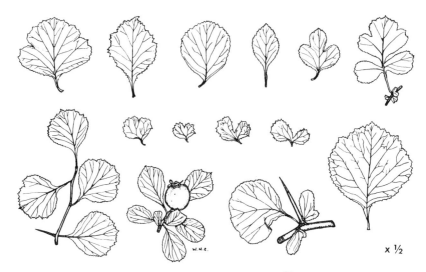

Fig. 101.  *Crataegus ravenelii*

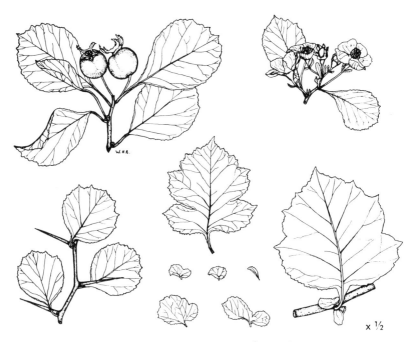

Fig. 102.  *Crataegus leonensis*

### 13. **Crataegus leonensis** Palmer.   Leon haw

A tree up to 10 - 12 m. high with a round or depressed top of wide-spreading intricate branches and slender, flexuous, sparingly thorny branchlets.   Leaves of the flowering branchlets mostly ovate or rhombic, coarsely dentate and obscurely lobed above the middle, or at the ends of shoots broadly ovate to suborbicular and up to 5 - 6 cm. long and wide, glabrous or nearly so from the first.   Flowers 1.6 - 2 cm. wide, in simple, mostly 5 - 7-flowered, slightly villous corymbs.   Fruit orange-red or russet when ripe or sometimes remaining green; nutlets 3 - 4 or rarely 5.

Upland woodlands, Leon County.

### 14. **Crataegus lacrimata** Small.   Weeping haw; sandhill haw; yellow haw; Pensacola haw

A tree up to 5 - 6 m. high, or sometimes a stout shrub, with depressed branches and slender, drooping branchlets armed with short stout thorns; bark dark gray, slightly scaly or deeply furrowed on old trunks.   Leaves subcoriaceous, glabrous and lustrous above at maturity.   Flowers 1.6 - 1.8 cm. wide; anthers pale yellow.   Fruit subglobose, dull orange or russet at maturity; nutlets usually 3.

Deciduous oak scrub, Walton to Escambia counties.

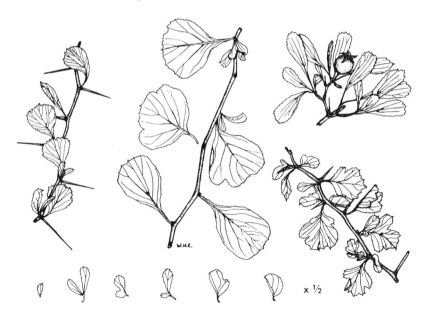

Fig. 103.   *Crataegus lacrimata*

### 15. **Crataegus floridana** Sarg.   Jacksonville haw; Florida haw

*C. adjusta* Beadle; *C. egens* Beadle; *C. inopina* Beadle; *C. recurva* Beadle; *C. rimosa* Beadle

A tree up to 5 - 6 m. high with spreading or depressed branches, slightly pendulous, flexuous, thorny branchlets, villous while young, and thick, nearly black, deeply fissured and ridged bark on old trunks. Leaves mostly obovate, rounded or abruptly pointed at the apex, pubescent while young and somewhat pubescent beneath throughout the season.   Flowers 1.6 - 1.8 cm. wide in few-flowered, simple villous corymbs.   Fruit subglobose with thin, dry, mealy flesh.

Deciduous woodlands and pine flatwoods, from the Atlantic Coast westward to Liberty County.

Several closely related species have been described; the following should perhaps be considered as varieties of *Crataegus floridana*: *C. anisophylla* Beadle, *C. clara* Beadle, *C. integra* (Nash) Beadle, and *C. lanata* Beadle.   The names of these have not been published with varietal status.

x ½

Fig. 104.   *Crataegus floridana*

### 16. **Crataegus visenda** Beadle

A tree up to 8 - 10 m. high with crooked spreading or ascending branches, stout, flexuous, thorny branchlets, villous when they first appear, and dark brownish-gray, deeply ridged bark. Leaves glabrous or nearly so, thin but firm and lustrous above at maturity. Flowers mostly 3 - 6 in simple, slightly villous corymbs. Fruit obovoid or pyriform, orange or orange-red at maturity; nutlets 3 - 5.

Upland woodlands, Liberty County.

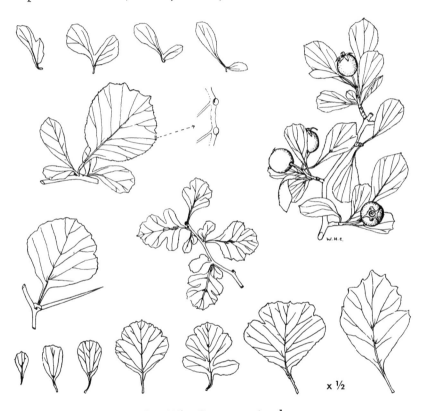

Fig. 105. *Crataegus visenda*

### 17. **Crataegus audens** Beadle

An arborescent shrub or a small tree up to 5 - 6 m. high with crooked ascending branches, stout, thorny or nearly thornless branchlets and dark brown, rough or slightly scaly bark. Flowers 1.5 - 1.6 cm. wide, mostly 2 - 5 in simple, slightly pubescent corymbs, or sometimes single.

Dry open uplands, Jackson County.

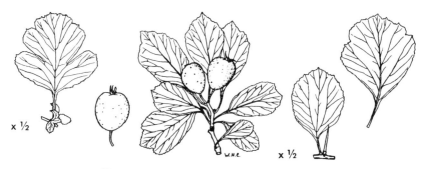

x ½

x ¾        Fig. 106. *Crataegus audens*

## 18. **Crataegus egregia** Beadle

An arborescent shrub or a small tree up to 5 - 6 m. high with erect or spreading branches, slender, flexuous, thorny or nearly thornless branchlets, and dark brownish gray, deeply furrowed bark. Flowers mostly 3 - 5 in simple, villous corymbs. Fruit yellow or orange; flesh yellow, becoming soft and mellow.

Longleaf pine, scrub oak ridges, Liberty County.

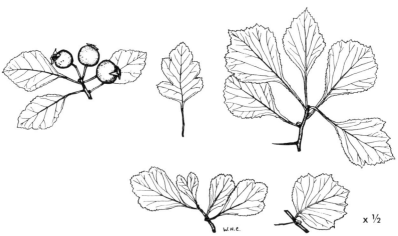

x ½

Fig. 107. *Crataegus egregia*

## MALUS. APPLE

### 1. **Malus angustifolia** (Ait.) Michx.  Southern crab apple

*Pyrus angustifolia* Ait.

The southern crab apple is a small tree with a rounded crown, spreading limbs, stiff twigs, and commonly bearing leafy thorns. During early spring, in flower, it makes a beautiful show.  The bark breaks up into irregular grayish plates, exposing reddish-brown inner bark.

The branches bear long, straight, vegetative shoots.  From these eventually are produced short, slow-growing spur shoots which bear leaves and flowers.  In addition, the branches may bear leafy thorns which, of course, remain as naked thorns after the leaves are shed.

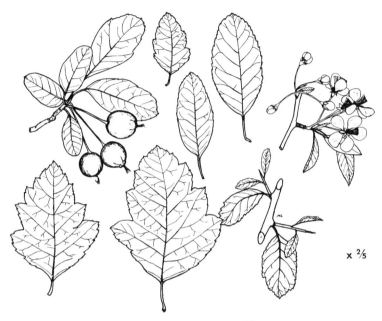

x ⅖

Fig. 108.  *Malus angustifolia*

The leaves are simple, alternate, and deciduous.  Those of the vigorous shoots are generally larger than those of the spur shoots and are not uncommonly incised-lobed.  The spur-shoot leaves are 1 - 2 (sometimes 3) inches long and up to about 1 inch broad, oblong, elliptic, or ovate-oblong, their bases broadly cuneate, the apices rounded or rounded-cuspidate, sometimes emarginate.  Their margins are crenate-serrate, serrate, or almost entire.  The upper surfaces are dark green, the lower pale green, both surfaces glabrous or nearly so.  Leaves of the vigorous shoots are somewhat larger, their margins commonly incised-lobed.

The flowers are borne as the leaves are emerging, in umbels of 3 - 5 terminating growth from the spur-shoots.  They are about 1 inch broad, having 5 clawed, spreading, deep pink to white petals, and are pleasantly fragrant.

The fruits are yellow-green pomes, about 1 inch in diameter, with the shrunken remains of sepals and stamens persisting at their summits. Within the fruit are 5 tough-papery-walled cavities, each containing 1 - 2 loose black seeds. The pomes ripen and drop in autumn; shrunken ones commonly can be found beneath the tree during winter.

This tree occurs in open woods of a variety of sites (sandy, clayey, or calcareous), often along fence rows, from about the Suwannee River westward in northern Florida.

To distinguish the southern crab apple from the hawthorns (*Crataegus*), the type of thorns is helpful. Those of the former are leafy thorns, or bear leaf scars, whereas those of the hawthorns are naked. With reference to the fruits, those of the crab apple have 5 tough-papery cavities, each containing 1 - 2 loose seeds; those of the hawthorns have 1 - 5 seeds each enclosed in a hard, stony covering.

## PRUNUS. CHERRIES AND PLUMS

Our species of *Prunus* are small to medium-sized trees with simple, alternate leaves which are deciduous except in one species, *P. caroliniana*. The bark is astringent, exudes a gummy substance, is at first smooth and somewhat shiny, has conspicuous transverse lenticels, and at length peels away in papery horizontal plates. The flowers are borne in racemes, in umbels, or singly. Each has a cuplike floral tube which bears at its upper margin 5 petals and numerous stamens, and seated within which is a solitary pistil. The petals are soon shed, the floral cup shrinks or falls, and the ovulary ripens into a drupe.

1. Flowers and fruits borne in racemes.
   2. Leaves membranous, deciduous, evenly serrate, the tips of the teeth appressed-incurved..............................................................................................4. *P. serotina*
   2. Leaves stiff-leathery, evergreen, entire or with a few remote, straight, sometimes bristle-tipped teeth.................................................................3. *P. caroliniana*
1. Flowers and fruits borne singly or in umbels of 2 - 5.
   3. Bark shaggy, the plates tan or buff; flowers about 1 inch across; mature leaves acuminate at their tips.................................................................1. *P. americana*
   3. Bark not shaggy, dark; flowers not exceeding ½ inch across; mature leaves acute at their tips.
      4. Flowers fragrant; at time of flowering, the developing leaves of non-flowering branches having marginal teeth with red-glandular tips; mature leaves folded upwards from the midribs and troughlike, the marginal teeth red-glandular-tipped................................................2. *P. angustifolia*
      4. Flowers not fragrant; at time of flowering, the developing leaves have nonglandular marginal teeth; mature leaves flat and their teeth nonglandular................................................................................5. *P. umbellata*

### 1. **Prunus americana** Marsh. American plum

This is a small tree which usually has a single trunk and spreading branches, with tan or buff bark which becomes shaggy, and with somewhat thorny stems or branches.

The leaves are deciduous, the blades oblong-oval, elliptic, or slightly obovate, 3 - 5 inches long and 1 - 2 inches broad. Their bases are broadly cuneate to rounded, the apices abruptly contracted and short-acuminate. They are finely sharp-serrate, often double-serrate. The upper surfaces are glabrous, the lower sparsely pubescent. The petioles commonly have 1 or 2 glands about ⅛ inch from their summits, or the glands may be at the very base of the leaf blade.

The flowers are about an inch across, have white petals, and are borne in umbels of 2 (more rarely up to 5) their peduncles ½ - ¾ inch in length. The flowers are pleasantly fragrant. Flowering occurs before the leaves emerge or as they emerge.

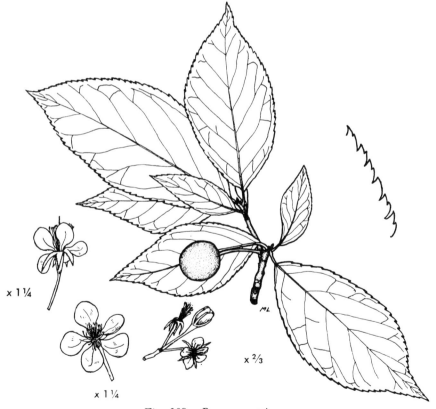

x 1¼

x ⅔

x 1¼

Fig. 109. *Prunus americana*

The drupes are globose or subglobose, about 1 inch long, bluish or purplish, and without a waxy bloom. They ripen in midsummer. *Prunus americana,* throughout most of its range to the north of our area, has red or yellow fruits. The north Florida population, having bluish fruits, has been called *P. americana* var. *floridana* Sarg.

The American plum inhabits rich loamy and calcareous woodlands of Leon, Wakulla, and Jackson counties, and floodplain woods along the Apalachicola River.

This plum may be distinguished from the others of our range by its large flowers which are about 1 inch across (in contrast to those of *P. angustifolia* and *P. umbellata* which do not exceed ½ inch across). Moreover, its branches usually bear developing leaves together with the flowers whereas the flowering branches of the other two are essentially leafless until the blooming period is over. Its leaves are acuminate at their apices while those of the other species are acute.

## 2. **Prunus angustifolia** Marsh.   Chickasaw plum

The chickasaw plum is a small tree or shrub with spreading branches. Characteristically, the plants are extended by underground runners and form thickets. The bark of the twigs and branchlets is reddish-brown to blackish, that of the older trunks scaly but not particularly shaggy. The stems are commonly thorny.

The leaves are deciduous, the blades lanceolate to lanceolate-oblong or oval, 1½ - 3 inches long and ¼ - 1 inch broad. They tend to be somewhat upwardly folded and troughlike. The leaf bases are cuneate, the apices acute, the margins finely toothed, the teeth tipped with tiny red glands. The upper leaf surfaces are glabrous, rather glossy, the lower sparsely pubescent, pubescent along the veins, or essentially glabrous. At the summit of the petiole, about ⅛ inch below the base of the blade, 1 or 2 glands are present, or the gland may be very near or on the base of the leaf blade.

The flowers are ⅓ - ½ inch across, have white petals, and are borne in umbels of 2 - 4, their peduncles mostly about ¼ inch long. The flowers have a strong but insipid odor. Flowering occurs mostly before the leaves emerge.

The drupes are globose or subglobose, ½ - ¾ inch long, have a waxy bloom, and at maturity are reddish or yellowish. They ripen in early summer.

The chickasaw plum is common throughout our range, mostly forming thickets in open sunny situations, edges of woods, along roadsides and fence rows.

*Prunus angustifolia* characteristically is a thicket-former as a consequence of its production of shoots from underground runners. The other two plums of our range, *P. americana* and *P. umbellata,* are single-trunked unless injured by cutting or burning.

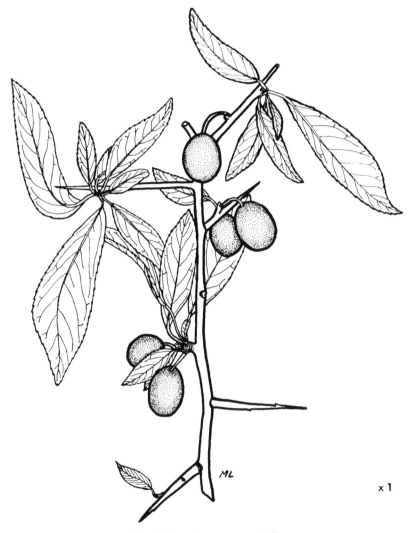

Fig. 110. *Prunus angustifolia*

The mature leaves of *P. angustifolia* are distinctive in that their marginal teeth are tipped by red glands and the blades tend to fold upwards, making them troughlike. The leaves of the other two plums lack the glandular tips on the marginal teeth and the blades are flat. At the time of flowering, *P. angustifolia* and *P. umbellata* are extremely difficult to distinguish. Usually, however, a given plant will have at time of flowering a few lower branches which lack flowers or have few flowers and which bear developing leaves. If these leaves bear the red-glandular-tipped teeth, the specimen is *P. angustifolia;* if not, it is *P. umbellata.*

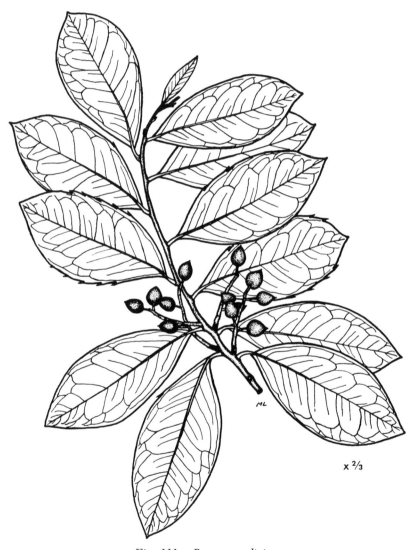

x ⅔

Fig. 111.   *Prunus caroliniana*

3. **Prunus caroliniana** (Mill.) Ait.   Carolina laurelcherry

This is a small, handsome evergreen tree which is widely used as an ornamental.   The bark is dark gray, tight and smooth, with prominent transverse lenticels on younger trunks, the older ones roughened by shallow vertical and horizontal fissures between which are squarish thin plates.

The leaves are persistent, leathery, dark glossy-green above and light green below, both surfaces glabrous.   The blades are oval, elliptic, or lanceolate, 2 - 4 inches long and mostly 1 - 1¼ inches broad.   Their bases are mostly cuneate, the apices acute or short-acuminate, the tips sharp.   The margins may be entire or have widely spaced, short, sharp, bristle-like dentations.   The short petioles are not glandular.

The flowers are small, white, in short compact racemes which are borne in the axils of the leaves or leaf scars in early spring before new growth begins.

The drupes are oval or oblong, about ½ inch long, short-pointed, black at maturity and with a dry flesh.   Usually but a few fruits develop on each raceme and they may persist on the trees until the next flowering period.

The Carolina laurelcherry is so widely used as an ornamental and it so readily becomes naturalized in woodlands that its natural range is difficult to establish.   It occurs in coastal dune hammocks, locally in rich woodlands or on shady slopes and bluffs of the Tallahassee Red Hills and Appalachicola River, and commonly in vacant lots and the like in towns and cities.

The distinctive combination of features of *Prunus caroliniana* are the dark gray bark marked by prominent transverse lenticels, leathery, evergreen, entire, or bristly-dentate leaves, and flowers or dry-black drupes borne in short racemes from axils of old leaves or leaf scars. Especially notable is the fact that the drupes tend to persist long after maturation in the autumn, even into the next flowering period.

4. **Prunus serotina** Ehrh.   Black cherry

The black cherry is a large tree with ascending branches.   The bark is grayish-black, or light gray on trees growing near the Gulf Coast. On young branches it is reddish-brown and marked with prominent transverse lenticels.   The sap is bitter and has an almond-like odor. Bark on older trunks forms an irregular patchwork of thin, grayish plates separated by a network of shallow fissures.   On very large trunks, the plates are smaller, thicker, and darker.

The leaves are deciduous, the blades oval-oblong, elliptical, or more rarely lanceolate or ovate, of varying size up to 5 inches long and 2 inches broad.  Their bases are rounded to cuneate, the apices abruptly short-acuminate and the margins finely appressed-serrate, the tips of the teeth purplish-red.  The upper surfaces of the leaves are dark shiny green, the lower dull whitish-green, both glabrous.  There are 1 - several reddish glands on the upper parts of the petioles and/or on either side of the bases of the blades.

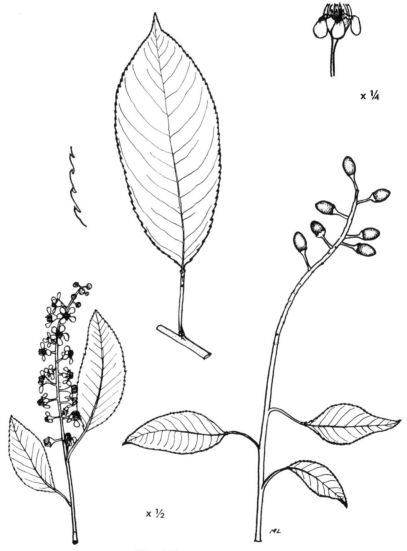

x ¼

x ½

Fig. 112.  *Prunus serotina*

The flowers are small, white, and numerous, in ascending or drooping racemes 3 - 6 inches long. The racemes are borne at the tips of the new leafy shoots of the season or in the axils of the leaf scars.

The drupes are globose to oval, mostly about ⅓ inch in diameter. At maturity they are dark purple to black, the flesh bittersweet to taste.

The black cherry occurs locally throughout our range in woodlands, along roadsides and fence rows, and in cut-over or disturbed areas.

Distinguishing characteristics by which *Prunus serotina* may be recognized are the bark of younger stems which is reddish-brown and marked by conspicuous transverse lenticels, the deciduous, oval-oblong leaves which are finely and evenly appressed-serrate, and racemes of flowers or drupes.

### 5. **Prunus umbellata** Ell.    Flatwoods plum

A small tree with a short, crooked trunk and spreading branches, it occasionally forms thickets. Bark is much as in *P. angustifolia,* but

x 1

Fig. 113. *Prunus umbellata*

rather more shiny on the branchlets. The stems and branchlets are only occasionally thorny.

The leaves are deciduous, the blades elliptic, oval, or oblong, mostly 1 - 2 inches long and ½ - ¾ inch broad. They are broadly cuneate to round at base, acute at their apices. The margins are finely toothed, the teeth not gland-tipped. The upper leaf surfaces are sparsely short-pubescent to glabrous, the lower hairy along the veins. A gland is usually present on one or both sides of the very base of the leaf blade and/or at the very summit of the petiole.

The flowers are ⅓ - ½ inch across, the petals white, and they are borne in umbels of 2 - 5, the peduncles mostly ¼ inch long. The flowers are not fragrant. Flowering occurs mostly before the leaves emerge.

The drupes are globose, ½ - ⅔ inch in diameter, dark purple at maturity (or red in the population on the Florida east coast dunes), and with a pronounced waxy bloom. They are bitter-sour and astringent to taste and mature in late summer.

This plum occurs widely in northern Florida in open pine or hardwood forests, calcareous flatwoods, and on the dunes along the Atlantic Coast.

For features by which *Prunus umbellata* may be distinguished from our other two plum species, see *P. americana* and *P. angustifolia*.

## LEGUMINOSAE.  LEGUME  FAMILY

1. Leaves simple................................................................................................................2. CERCIS
1. Leaves compound.
   2. Stems without thorns or spines; leaves evenly bipinnate, the ultimate leaflets ⅜ - ½ inch long, the blades developed only on one side of the midribs; flowers in tassel-like clusters.............................................................................1. ALBIZZIA
   2. Stems with thorns or spines; leaves once-odd-pinnate, or evenly pinnate or bipinnate, the leaflets much larger than above; flowers in dangling racemes or in spikes.
      3. Leaves once-odd-pinnate; stems bearing paired stipular spines at the nodes; flowers borne in dangling racemes.............................................4. ROBINIA
      3. Leaves evenly pinnate or bipinnate; stems bearing long, simple or branched thorns; flowers borne in spikes..................................................3. GLEDITSIA

### ALBIZZIA

#### 1. **Albizzia julibrissin** Durazz.   Silk-tree

A widely used, introduced ornamental, to some extent naturalized, the silk-tree is a small tree with handsome feathery or lacy foliage and beautiful flower clusters. The trunks are generally short, the crown somewhat umbrella-like with spreading-arching branches.

The leaves are deciduous, alternate, evenly twice-pinnately compound, the over-all length of the blades up to 16 inches. A leaf may have 10 - 25 primary leaf divisions which bear, in all, 500 - 1200 small leaflets. The blades of the latter are ⅜ - ½ inch long, oblong, asymmetrical, the midrib very near one margin of the leaflet, each thus appearing like a falcate half leaflet. They are glabrous and have entire margins. A saucer-shaped gland is present near the base of the petiole, and often one on the base of the stalk of each of the two lowermost primary leaf divisions. A pulvinus is present at the base of the petiole, and at the base of each succeeding leaf segment. These are sensitive to changes in light and/or temperature and moisture so that at night and during cloudy or rainy weather, the primary leaflets droop, the ultimate leaflets fold against each other. The leafs are then said to be "closed" or "asleep."

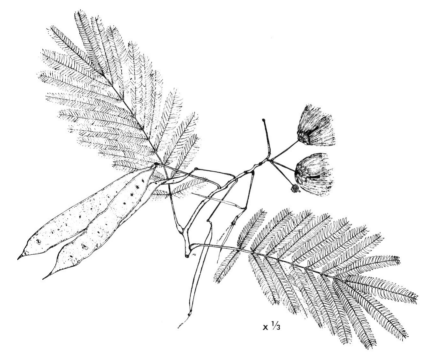

x ⅓

Fig. 114.  *Albizzia julibrissin*

The flowers are pink or pinkish and are borne at branch tips in stalked, fluffy, tassle-like clusters. The numerous, clustered flowers each have long, exserted stamens and styles giving a silky appearance. The central flower or one other of each cluster is larger and more conspicuous than the others.

The fruit is a yellowish, thin, flat legume, up to 6 inches long and about ¾ - 1 inch broad. The seeds are thin and wafer-like.

An ornamental introduction from Asia, this tree is naturalized throughout our range, occurring along roadsides, in waste places, borders of woodlands, and in clearings.

Distinctive characteristics which make the silk-tree easily identifiable are the evenly twice-pinnately compound leaves, the ultimate leaflets of which have the blades developed only on one side of the midrib.

Unfortunately, a parasitic fungus, *Fusarium perniciosum* Heptung, which enters the roots and destroys the sapwood, threatens to exterminate this valuable ornamental tree in our area.

### CERCIS

#### 1. Cercis canadensis L. Redbud

A small tree, the redbud is well known as a harbinger of spring; its early, abundant clusters of showy pink to magenta flowers borne all over its leafless stems make it a favorite in woodland or garden.

The leaves are deciduous, alternate, simple, long-petioled, and 2-ranked, the 2 ranks mostly oriented in 1 plane, the twigs zigzagged. The leaf blades are ovate or ovate-reniform, palmately-veined, cordate to truncate at their bases, the apices mostly short-acuminate. The margins are entire or irregularly wavy. The leaf surfaces are glabrous above, pubescent below. The summits of the petioles are conspicuously swollen, the bases somewhat swollen.

The flowers appear before the leaves in early spring and are borne in clusters almost anywhere on the stems. The flowers are pedunculate, the peduncles mostly slightly longer than the flowers, the corollas bilaterally symmetrical (imperfectly papilionaceous) and pink to magenta in color.

The fruits are flat, oblong legumes, 3 - 4 inches long, reddish-purple at maturity. The ripened legumes usually persist on the trees through most of the summer, frequently into the winter.

The redbud occurs in rich woodlands throughout northern Florida. It is commonly used as a garden ornamental and in street and roadside plantings.

Distinguishing features of the redbud are the palmately-veined, ovate to reniform, 2-ranked leaves with conspicuous pulvini at the summits of the petioles, and zigzagging twigs. In flower, it is unlike any other of our trees in having conspicuous clusters of pink to magenta flowers borne all over the leafless twigs.

Fig. 115. *Cercis canadensis*

## GLEDITSIA. HONEY-LOCUSTS

The honey-locusts are trees having large, simple or branched, reddish-brown thorns on the branches and trunks, those on older stems often much branched and clustered. The leaves are alternate, evenly 1 - 2-pinnately compound, a single leaf sometimes unequally divided, partly 1-pinnate, partly 2-pinnate. The flowers are greenish, small and inconspicuous, borne in spikes. The fruits are broad, reddish-brown legumes which are abruptly narrowed into a stalklike structure at base.

1. Legume short, elliptic, ovate, or suborbicular, usually asymmetric, 1 - 2 inches long, 1 - 3 seeded.............................................................................................1 *G. aquatica*

1. Legume elongate, linear-oblong, 8 - 24 inches long, heavy, and with many seeds ...........................................................................................................2. *G. triacanthos*

### 1. **Gleditsia aquatica** Marsh.   Water-locust

Ordinarily the water-locust is a small tree but occasional specimens reach sizable proportions.   The largest of which we know is about 80 feet high and 36 inches in diameter.   The bark is smoothish to warty.

The leaflets number 14 - 20 on once-pinnate leaves and up to 200 on twice-pinnate leaves.   In general, the leaflet number is somewhat less than in the honey-locust, but they are otherwise closely similar.

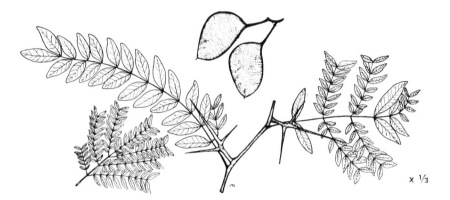

Fig. 116.   *Gleditsia aquatica*

The fruits are short, often asymmetrical, elliptic, ovate, or suborbicular, mostly 1-seeded, occasionally 2- or 3-seeded, the seeds orbicular.

Thorny stems, even-pinnate or bipinnate leaves with numerous small leaflets, and short, 1 - 3-seeded legumes characterize this tree. The very marked difference between the fruits of this and the honey-locust represents the only striking character by which the two can be distinguished.   If no fruits are present on a given tree, old ones can sometimes be found in the litter under the tree.

### 2. **Gleditsia triacanthos** L.   Honey-locust

The honey-locust attains large size and has scaly bark beset by long, sharp, often much-branched thorns.

The leaflets are numerous, 14 - 28 on once-pinnate leaves and up to 260 on twice-pinnate leaves.   They are oblong to elliptic, elliptic-oblong, or oval, mostly up to about 1 inch long and ½ inch broad.   Their bases are slightly unequally rounded, the apices obtuse, rounded, or emarginate, often with a small mucro. The margins are minutely serrate or crenate, the surfaces glabrous.

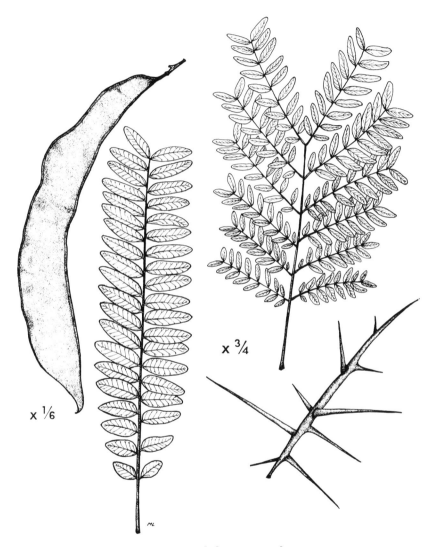

Fig. 117. *Gleditsia triacanthos*

The fruit is large, heavy, linear-oblong, 8 - 24 inches long, often twisted, with numerous oval seeds, and with a great deal of pulpy tissue between the seeds.

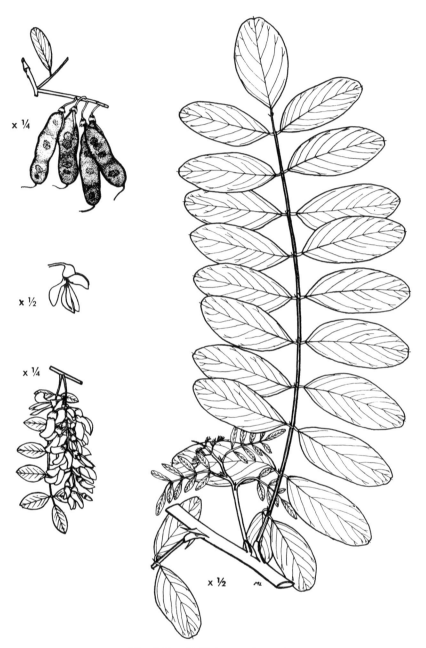

x ¼

x ½

x ¼

x ½

Fig. 118. *Robinia pseudoacacia*

The honey-locust occurs occasionally in moist, drained river bottom-lands and moist, flatland hammocks in western Florida.

Thorny stems, even-pinnate or bipinnate leaves with numerous leaflets, and long, numerous-seeded, heavy legumes distinguish the honey-locust. It is difficult, if not impossible, to distinguish it from the water-locust except by its fruits. See *Gleditsia aquatica.*

## ROBINIA

### 1. Robinia pseudoacacia L.   Black locust

A small tree, the black locust is not native to our range but is occasionally used as an ornamental and becomes naturalized in the vicinity of plantings. The bark is rough, dark brown or blackish, and is ridged and furrowed.

The leaves are deciduous, alternate, once-odd-pinnately compound, the over-all length of the leaf 8 - 14 inches, and with 7 - 19 leaflets. The leaflets are oblong-elliptic, elliptic, or oval, mostly ½ - 2 inches long and ¼ - ¾ inch broad. They are mostly cuneate at their bases, obtuse to rounded or emarginate and with a short mucro at their summits. Their margins are entire or shallowly and irregularly wavy, the upper and lower surfaces glabrous, the lower whitish. Pulvini are present at the bases of the petioles and at the bases of the leaflet stalks, and the leaflets fold with certain changing environmental conditions. The twigs bear 2 persistent, sharp, stipular spines at each node.

The flowers are white or creamy-white, delightfully fragrant, and are borne in dangling, compact racemes 4 - 6 inches long. They are papilionaceous, about ¾ - 1 inch long.

The fruits are linear-oblong flat legumes, up to about 4 inches long.

In northern Florida, *Robinia pseudoacacia* is occasionally naturalized in the vicinity of plantings.

The once-odd-pinnately compound leaves together with pairs of sharp stipular spines at the nodes distinguish the black locust from other trees in our range.

## RUTACEAE.   RUE FAMILY

1. Leaves mostly 3-foliolate; stems and leaves not prickly; fruit a nearly circular samara................................................................................................PTELEA
1. Leaves 7 - 9 pinnate; stems and leaves prickly; fruit a fleshy follicle..............
   ................................................................................................ZANTHOXYLUM

## Ptelea

### 1. **Ptelea trifoliata** L.   Common hop-tree; wafer-ash

This is a shrub or small tree with alternate, deciduous, 3-foliolate (rarely 5-foliolate), long-petioled leaves. The leaflets are sessile, broadly elliptic, oval, or obovate, the lateral ones often somewhat asymmetrical, their bases cuneate or rounded, the apices rounded to acuminate,

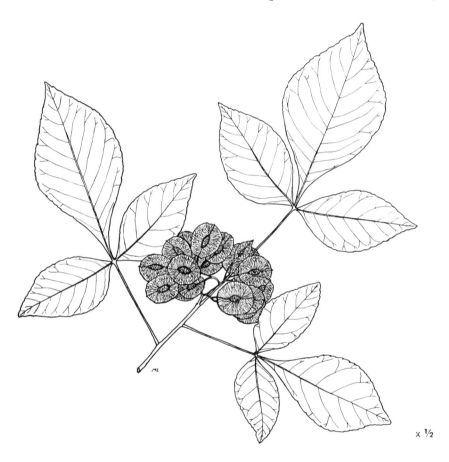

x ½

Fig. 119. *Ptelea trifoliata*

punctate, and with entire or irregularly crenate-serrate margins. The upper surfaces of the leaflets are green and glabrous, the lower pale, and glabrous to softly and uniformly pubescent. The crushed foliage has a mildly orange-like aroma.

The flowers are small, greenish-yellow, and are borne in delicate terminal cymes. The flowers are functionally unisexual, some plants, at least, dioecious. The fruits are nearly orbicular samaras, the seeds centrally located in winglike disks. They persist on the plants until late autumn.

The common hop-tree inhabits rich woodlands of slopes and bluffs and limestone woods in scattered localities throughout northern Florida.

This plant is readily recognized by the musky-aromatic, 3-foliolate leaves and wafer-like winged fruits. The latter scarcely suggest the Rue family to which citrus fruits belong. The trifoliolate leaf, however, is suggestive of that of the shrubby *Poncirus trifoliata* (L.) Raf.

## ZANTHOXYLUM

1. **Zanthoxylum clava-herculis** L. Hercules-club; prickly-ash

This is a small tree, or sometimes a shrub, which is armed with stout, sharp prickles ("thorns") on the trunks, branches, twigs, and foliage. The bark is gray and warty with corky, domelike growths. Each of these is at first armed with a sharp prickle. This is ultimately sloughed, leaving a smooth dome. The elongated bases of the prickles parallel the longitudinal axis of the young twigs. As the stems grow, the corky bases widen horizontally, apace with increase in girth, so that on older stems and trunks the corky domes are elongated transversely. They are prominent until the trunks are about 6 inches in diameter.

The leaves are alternate, deciduous, once-pinnately compound, with 5 - 19 (commonly 7 - 9) leaflets. The leaf rachi are often prickly. The leaflets are ovate to lanceolate, oblique or falcate, punctate, their margins crenate-serrate or serrulate and with button-like glands inset from the notches of the teeth. The upper surfaces of the leaflets are glossy-green, the lower dull and paler, glabrous or with a few scattered hairs. The crushed herbage has an orange-like fragrance.

The flowers are small, greenish-yellow, and are borne in terminal cymes. They are unisexual or bisexual, the plants dioecious or polygamous.

The fruits are small 2-valved follicles. Before ripening they resemble tiny green oranges. The dehisced follicles expose 1 - 5 shiny black seeds.

This plant inhabits dunes, sandy hammocks, and roadsides, mostly near the east and Gulf coasts but in scattered localities elsewhere.

Hercules-club may be recognized by its prickly 1-pinnate leaves which have peculiar button-like glands inset from the notches of the teeth of the leaflets. To taste, the inner bark has a sharp astringent quality.

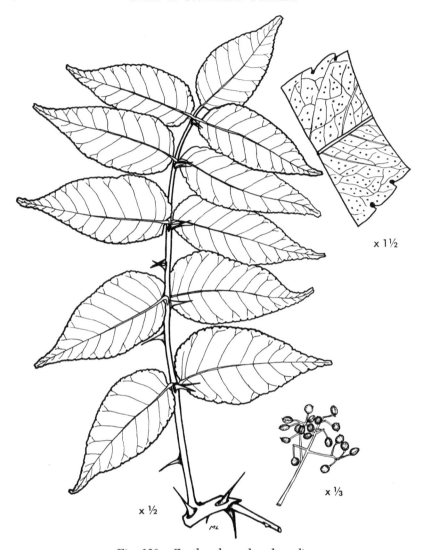

Fig. 120. *Zanthoxylum clava-herculis*

## SIMAROUBACEAE. QUASSIA FAMILY

### AILANTHUS

1. **Ailanthus altissima** (Mill.) Swingle.  Ailanthus; tree-of-heaven

This is the "tree-of-heaven" of the book *A Tree Grows in Brooklyn,* by Betty Smith (New York: Harper & Bros., 1943).  It is a rapidly growing tree which spreads extensively by underground runners. Although rare in northern Florida, it is picturesque and easily recognized.

The leaves are alternate, deciduous, 1-pinnately compound, up to 3½ feet in length. The leaflets number 11 - 39, are oblong, lanceolate, or

Fig. 121. *Ailanthus altissima*

ovate-lanceolate, asymmetrically rounded at their bases, the tips long-acuminate. Their margins are large-toothed near the base of the blades, each tooth bearing a broad gland on the lower side of its tip. The bruised foliage has a strong, disagreeable musky odor. The bark is tan and relatively smooth.

The flowers are unisexual, the trees dioecious. The staminate flowers emit a strong, disagreeable odor. The fruit is an oblong samara, the seed borne at its middle. The wings taper toward both tips which at maturity are twisted.

An introduced Asiatic tree, it is rarely planted in northern Florida and hence infrequently becomes naturalized. We know it in only two localities, a vacant lot in Tallahassee, Leon County, where there are several trees reaching 45 feet in height and about a foot in diameter, and a single tree in the woods at Camp O'Leno, on the Santa Fe River in Columbia County.

The large pinnate and ladder-like leaves, the leaflets glandular-toothed near their bases and long-acuminate at their apices, and the strong, musky or skunklike, odor of the crushed herbage characterize this tree.

## MELIACEAE.  MAHOGANY  FAMILY

### MELIA

#### 1. Melia azedarach L.  Chinaberry

This introduced, fast-growing, commonly naturalized tree is considered a doubtful blessing.  Its large, handsome, pinnately decompound leaves provide abundant shade and its large panicles of lavender flowers appeal equally to the senses of sight and smell.  On the other hand, its abundant fruits are both messy and toxic.  The toxicity of the fruits is not to be taken too lightly.

The leaves are alternate, deciduous, 2 - 3-pinnately compound, and 12 - 30 inches long by 6 - 12 inches wide.  The lowermost leaflets of a leaf segment tend to be ovate, the more distal ones passing from oblong-elliptical to elliptical, lanceolate-elliptic, to the terminal one obovate, their respective bases rounded or truncate varying to cuneate, all inequilateral, the apices mostly acuminate, but varying to obtuse or rounded.  Their margins are coarsely and irregularly serrate, to irregularly incised or lobed.  They are dark green above, medium-green below, and glabrous.

The twig bark has conspicuous transverse lenticels.  The trunk bark becomes shallowly fissured between broad, smoothish ridges.

The flowers are lavender, fragrant, and are borne in attractive panicles 6 - 9 inches long.   The panicles are axillary on the lower parts of
stem segments of the season.   Flowers have 5 - 6 sepals, 5 - 6 spreading-
recurved petals, many stamens whose filaments form a tube, and a 5 - 6-
locular ovulary.

The fruits are yellow, globose, 1 - 6-seeded drupes, the stones with
5 - 8 prominent ridges.

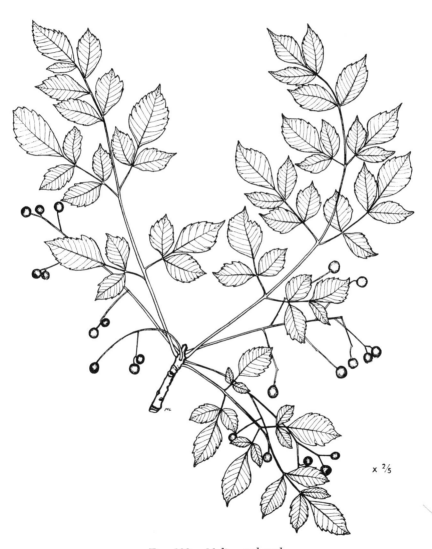

x ⅖

Fig. 122.   *Melia azedarach*

An introduction from Asia, reproducing abundantly, this tree is common about dwellings, vacant lots, borders of woods, in clearings, and is frequently to be found in well-developed forests. We have seen it in the interior fastnesses of the floodplain forests along the Chattahoochee and Apalachicola rivers.

The chinaberry, having 2 - 3-pinnately compound leaves with irregularly serrate, incised, or lobed leaflets, and lacking thorns, spines, or prickles, is distinctive amongst our kinds of trees. The ornamentally ridged stones of the fruits, easily pierced, have been popular in making beads, especially with children. The poisonous properties of the fruits are to be noted, however, and caution should be exercised in permitting children to play with them.

An umbrella-like form of this tree, called *Melia azedarach* var. *umbraculiformis* Berckmans, has a compact, dense foliage, is popularly known as umbrella-tree, and is an especially efficient provider of shade.


# EUPHORBIACEAE.  SPURGE FAMILY

## ALEURITES

### 1. **Aleurites fordii** Hemsl.  Tung-tree

The tung-tree, native in China, is a small tree extensively cultivated in northern Florida and near the coast in other Gulf states. Its seeds yield an oil used in the manufacture of paints and varnishes. The trees produce a profusion of large terminal clusters of showy flowers so that in the spring the groves lend striking beauty to the countryside wherever it is grown. The plant reproduces voluntarily in the general vicinity of plantings and is thus sporadically naturalized. This, together with the general interest provoked by its striking appearance when in bloom, leads us to include it here.

The leaves are simple, alternate, and deciduous. Those of larger plants, or their normal branches, are differently shaped than those of vigorous sucker sprouts, seedlings, or saplings. All are long-petioled, the blades broad and palmately-veined, having 5 principal veins arising from the leaf base. A pair of hemispheric, bright red glands is present on the upper surface of the very summit of the petiole. The blades are dark green above, paler below, and both surfaces clothed with a sparse, appressed pubescence, or glabrate in age. Leaves of the larger plants, or their mature branches, are broadly ovate, their bases barely subcordate or nearly truncate, the apices abruptly short-acuminate. The margins are entire. Leaves of vigorous sucker shoots, seedlings, and saplings differ in that they are distinctly cordate at the base and the broad apex has 3 broad lobes, each abruptly short-acuminate. Commonly in the angles of each sinus between the lobes there is a reddish gland terminating a vein which ends at the sinus.

Fig. 123. *Aleurites fordii*

The flowers are borne in large cymes from the ends of shoots of the previous season. Flowering occurs before and during the developing of the leaves. The flowers are unisexual, the plants monoecious. Usually a single central flower of a given cyme is pistillate and all the others are staminate, or a given cyme may have all staminate flowers. Cymes occasionally may bear more than one pistillate flower.

Each flower is usually about 1½ inches across although the range of size is from 1⅛ to 2¾ inches. The calyx consists of 2 short, oblong-ovate sepals, fused only at their bases.  Five oblong-obovate, spreading, rolled-recurved, separate petals usually comprise the corolla.  Sometimes 6, 7, or 8 petals are present in a flower, the variable number more characteristic of pistillate flowers.  Each petal is essentially white on the back or outside; the inner petal surface is prominently and closely red-veined near the base, the reddish veins spreading upward, the color gradually becoming fainter.  The staminate flowers have 2 series of fertile stamens, the outer shorter than the inner.  The total number of stamens varies from 8 to 16.  The pistillate flowers have a single pistil with an ovate ovulary below which is a thick, stipelike base, and above which is a triangular style bearing 3 - 5 stigmas.

The fruits are ovoid to globose, depressed-globose, or obovoid thick-fibrous capsules, 1½ - 3 inches in diameter.  They are 3 - 5-valved and bear 3 - 7, mostly 5, large seeds each with 2 flat and 1 round face.

In common cultivation in large groves and sporadically naturalized more or less throughout our range.

The tung-tree is the only tree in our area having long-petioled, broadly ovate, palmately-veined leaves with a pair of prominent red glands on the upper side of the summit of the petiole just below the base of the leaf blade.

# ANACARDIACEAE.  CASHEW FAMILY

## RHUS.  SUMACS

Sumacs are shrubs or small trees with alternate, deciduous, 1-pinnately compound leaves.  Their stems and leaves have copious watery or milky sap.  The flowers are unisexual or bisexual, the plants dioecious or polygamous.  The flowers are small, greenish-cream, 5-merous, but with 1 pistil, the ovulary of which is 1-celled and 1-seeded, and with 3 styles and stigmas.  Inflorescences are terminal or axillary panicles.  The fruits are dry drupes.

Sumacs multiply prolifically by vegetative, underground runners.  Since they are dioecious or polygamous, one may see large clones or thickets of male or of polygamous plants.

Beware the poison sumac!  (See *Rhus vernix*.)

1.  Leaflets entire, rachis and petioles maroon; flowers and fruits in axillary panicles; fruits white; swamp tree................................................................3. *R. vernix*

1.  Leaflets entire or serrate, rachis and petioles not red; flowers and fruits red, crowded in terminal panicles; upland trees.
    2.  Rachis winged; leaflets somewhat hairy below....................1. *R. copallina*
    2.  Rachis not winged; leaflets whitish, glabrous and glaucous below...........
    ................................................................................................2. *R. glabra*

1. **Rhus copallina** L.   Shining sumac; winged sumac

This is usually a shrub, occasionally a small tree, often occurring in thickets.   The twigs are closely pubescent and have conspicuous wart-like reddish lenticels.   The sap is clear and watery.

x ⅓

x 1

Fig. 124.   *Rhus copallina*

The compound leaf is 8 - 12 inches long, the leaflets number 9 - 19. They are oblong-lanceolate, tapering-acute to rounded at their asymmetric bases, the apices acute or acuminate (rarely obtuse), the margins entire, or occasionally remotely few-toothed.   The upper surfaces of the leaflets are shiny, the lower sparsely pubescent.   The leaf rachis is pubescent and has green, marginal wings which are interrupted where the leaflets join the rachis.   The foliage turns an attractive red in autumn.

The inflorescence is a compact, broadly ovate, terminal panicle, the flowers small, greenish-cream in color.

Fruits are in compact clusters which are often rigidly nodding. They are fuzzy-red, ovoid or depressed globose, about ⅛ inch in diameter. The fruiting clusters persist into the winter.

The winged sumac occurs in a variety of situations: roadsides, old fields, upland open woodlands, shady hammocks, or drained river bottoms. It is common throughout the area.

The characteristic most peculiar to this sumac is the winged leaf rachis.

## 2. Rhus glabra L.  Smooth sumac

The smooth sumac is commonly a shrub; rarely it attains the stature of a small tree. A milky sap is yielded by the twigs and leaves. The young twigs are glabrous and glaucous.

The compound leaf is 8 - 14 inches long, the leaflets number up to 21 or more. The blades of the leaflets are lanceolate to oblong-lanceolate, their bases rounded or somewhat cuneate, the apices acuminate, the margins serrate. The lower surfaces of the leaflets and the rachi are glabrous, but they have a copious, easily removable waxy bloom, as do the twigs.

The plants are mostly dioecious. The flowers are borne in terminal, erect panicles, the staminate panicles larger and more open than the pistillate or polygamous ones.

The drupes are brilliant red and are densely covered with minute, appressed hairs.

In our area, the smooth sumac is rare, known to us only in the Tallahassee Red Hills, on a natural levee of the Apalachicola River in Liberty County, and on moist roadsides bordering woods in Jackson County.

Distinguishing features of *Rhus glabra* are the alternate, pinnately compound leaves whose lower surfaces and rachi (as well as the twigs) are copiously covered with a waxy white bloom, and whose twigs and leaves have a milky sap. The base of the petiole encloses the axillary bud, a characteristic common to this, the American sycamore, and the boxelder.

## 3. Rhus vernix L.  Poison sumac

*Toxicodendron vernix* (L.) Kuntze

This very poisonous sumac, often a shrub, but frequently having the dimensions of a small weak tree, should be known, so as to be avoided, by everyone who has occasion to traverse swampy woodlands and thickets.

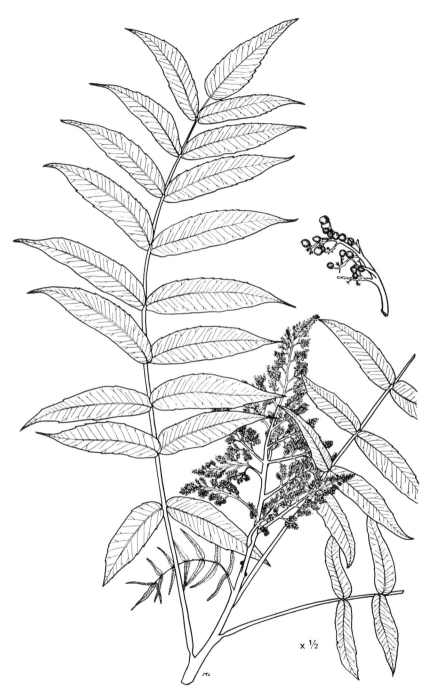

Fig. 125. *Rhus glabra*

The compound leaf is 8 - 13 inches long, the leaflets number 7 - 15. The blades of the leaflets are glabrous, oblong, elliptic, or ovate, their bases wedge-shaped to rounded, the apices acuminate or acute, the margins entire. The petioles and rachi are glabrous, reddish or maroon in color. The foliage turns a brilliant red in autumn.

The young twigs are reddish, also, and glabrous, the sap copious and clear.

Flowers are unisexual or bisexual, the plants dioecious or polygamous.

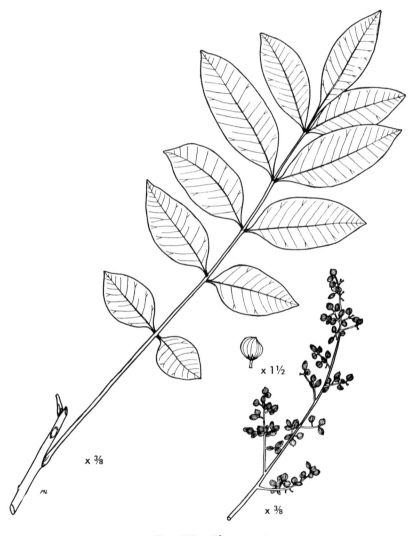

x 1½

x ⅜

x ⅜

Fig. 126. *Rhus vernix*

The inflorescence is a loose drooping axillary panicle of small, greenish-yellow flowers.

The fruits are ovoid or depressed-globose, somewhat asymmetric, and apiculate, ¼ inch in diameter, smooth, yellowish-white, or stained-ivory, with purple streaks on them. They persist on the leafless plants into the winter.

The poison sumac occurs in flatwoods depressions, bays, branch-bays or swamps, and in nonalluvial swamps in general, from Marion County northward and westward in Florida.

Like its relatives, poison-ivy and poison-oak, this shrub may poison a person upon contact. Some persons appear not to be susceptible and the degree of sensitiveness varies from person to person. Authorities hold, however, that no one who is not susceptible has assurance of constant or continued immunity to the poisons of any of these three. It is apparently possible to be resistant for years, then, suddenly and unexpectedly, one may become susceptible. Because of its restricted habitats and because such places are not often frequented by most people, the poison sumac is less frequently encountered than the others, hence less well known. Nonetheless, it can "sneak up on the unwary." It is well, if one must enter a bay, branch-bay, or swamp, or any non-alluvial swamp, to guard against contact with a shrub or small tree having leaves resembling a hickory, or having whitish, open panicles of fruits. Hickory leaves are serrate, the poison sumac's are not, and they can thus easily be distinguished. In winter, when these plants are leafless, and when the male plants, at least, have no fruits to "give them away," touch only those plants known to be innocuous.

## CYRILLACEAE.  TITI  FAMILY

1. Flowering in early spring, prior to new shoot growth, the flowers borne in terminal racemes; sepals unequal; petals obtuse; stamens 10; fruit 2 - 4-winged........
................................................................................................CLIFTONIA

1. Flowering in summer subsequent to new shoot growth, the flowers borne mostly in clustered racemes at the summit of the previous season's growth and below the twigs of the season; sepals equal; petals acute; stamens 5; fruits terete, not winged................................................................................................CYRILLA

### CLIFTONIA

1. **Cliftonia monophylla** (Lam.) Britton.   Buckwheat-tree; black titi

A small evergreen tree or shrub, often with crooked trunks, the branches ascending. It nearly always occurs in dense stands; rarely are individual isolated trees encountered.

The leaves are simple, alternate, persistent, leathery, oblanceolate, elliptic, or elliptic-oblanceolate, mostly 1 - 2 inches long by ½ - ¾ inch broad. They taper from their middles or above their middles to sessile bases, the apices being short-cuneate and acute to obtuse, the tips not sharp-pointed, sometimes inconspicuously emarginate. The margins are entire, both surfaces glabrous, the lower surfaces often bluish-whitish. The lateral veins tend to anastamose near the leaf margins, forming a fairly well-pronounced vein which runs parallel to the leaf margin. The twigs are numerous, thin, stiff, and clustered, reddish but with a grayish bloom more or less obscuring the red color.

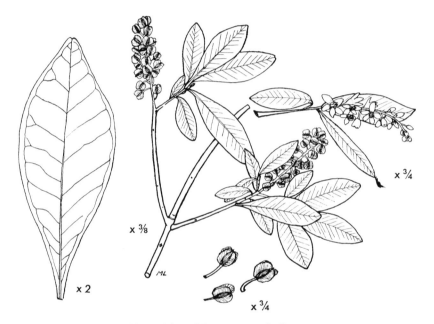

Fig. 127.  *Cliftonia monophylla*

The flowers are small, white, and are produced in terminal racemes in early spring before the new twig growth begins. The racemes resemble somewhat those of laurelcherry or the black cherry.

The fruits are 2 - 4-winged, indehiscent, ovate to ovoid in outline, about ¼ inch long, deep yellow and shining, conspicuous in summer. The browned old fruits often persist through the winter and into the second season.

The buckwheat-tree is a conspicuous inhabitant of bays, bayheads, and nonalluvial, acid swamps from Jefferson County westward in Florida.

This plant is readily distinguished by its winged buckwheat-like fruits. Since it grows in profusion where it does occur and new or old fruits may be found on some plants at almost any season, the fruit character is particularly helpful in identification. The leathery, evergreen leaves having fairly well-pronounced marginal veins are helpful, also.

## CYRILLA. CYRILLA; TITI

The cyrillas, commonly called titi, or he-huckleberry, are shrubs or small trees, commonly with crooked trunks and branches. They are often associated with the buckwheat-tree, which they resemble somewhat in growth habit and foliar characteristics, but from which they differ markedly in time of flowering and appearance of the fruits.

The leaves are simple, alternate, deciduous, semipersistent, or persistent.

The flowers are small, white, and are borne in clustered stiffish racemes in summer. The inflorescences are produced near the summit of the previous year's branchlets but below the twigs of the season.

The fruits are small beadlike drupes, becoming straw-colored then deep yellow.

1. Leaves oblanceolate to linear-oblanceolate, mostly ¾ - 1½ inches long and ¼ - ½ inch broad at their broadest points; inflorescences mostly 1½ - 3¼ inches long; fruits subglobose, as broad as or slightly broader than long............1. *C. parvifolia*

2. Leaves oblanceolate to narrowly obovate, or elliptic-oblanceolate, mostly 2 - 4 inches long and ½ - 1 inch broad at their broadest points; inflorescences mostly 4 - 6 inches long; fruits ovoid, longer than broad....................2. *C. racemiflora*

### 1. **Cyrilla parvifolia** Raf. Little-leaf cyrilla; little-leaf titi

This is a shrub or small tree; deciduous or semievergreen. Specimens are known to us which attain 20 - 25 feet in height and diameters of 5 - 7 inches.

The leaves are short, petiolate or sessile, oblanceolate or linear-oblanceolate, mostly ¾ to 1½ inches long and ¼ - ½ inch broad at their broadest points. Their bases are long-cuneate, their apices acute or rarely rounded. The leaf margins are entire and revolute, and both surfaces are glabrous.

The inflorescences are mostly 1½ to 3¼ inches long.

The fruits are beadlike drupes, subglobose, as broad as or slightly broader than long, about ⅒ inch in length. The two sutures of the fruit are prominently furrowed.

The little-leaf cyrilla is common in flatwoods depressions from at least Taylor County westward in northern Florida.

The clustered racemes of small white flowers or beadlike fruits borne below the twigs of the season and at the summits of the previous year's twigs make the cyrilla distinctive. The little-leaf cyrilla is distinguishable from the swamp cyrilla chiefly by its smaller leaves, shorter in-

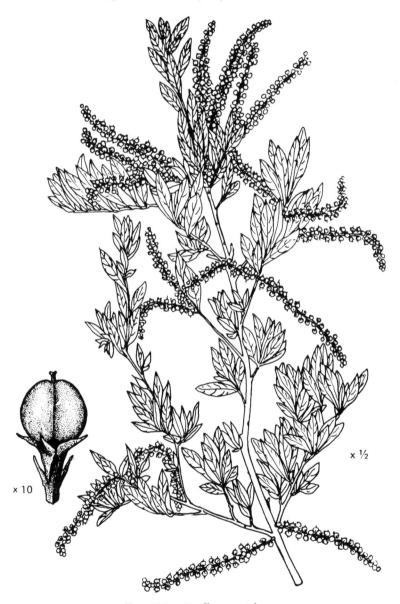

x ½

x 10

Fig. 128. *Cyrilla parvifolia*

florescences, and more nearly globose fruits.   Thomas (Contrib. Gray
Herb. of Harvard University, CLXXXVI, 1960) considers that the popu-
lations of *Cyrilla* comprise a single polymorphic species, *C. racemiflora*.
Although the north Florida populations, in particular, include forms not

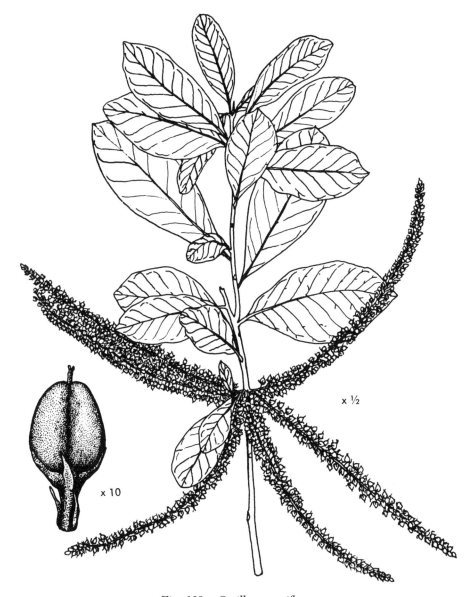

Fig. 129.   *Cyrilla racemiflora*

clearly distinguishable as either one or the other species here treated, we are inclined to the view that lumping the two is an oversimplification.

### 2. Cyrilla racemiflora L.   Swamp cyrilla; titi; he-huckleberry

The swamp cyrilla is a shrub or small tree having deciduous or semi-persistent leaves.

The leaves are short-petioled, oblanceolate to narrowly obovate, or elliptic-oblanceolate, mostly 2 - 4 inches long and ½ - 1 inch broad at their broadest points.   Their bases are cuneate, the apices obtuse to rounded or emarginate, or more rarely short-acuminate or acute.   The leaf margins are entire and revolute, both surfaces glabrous.

The inflorescences are mostly 4 - 6 inches long.

The fruits are ovoid drupes, slightly longer than broad, nearly ⅜₆ inch long, ⅟₁₆ inch broad.   The two sutures of the fruit are inconspicuously furrowed.

The swamp cyrilla inhabits river banks, alluvial and nonalluvial swamps and bays throughout northern Florida.

For the characteristics by which it differs from *C. parvifolia*, see that species.

## AQUIFOLIACEAE.  HOLLY  FAMILY

### ILEX.  HOLLIES

The hollies are, for the most part, small trees or shrubs, some of which are deciduous and some evergreen.   The leaves are simple and alternate.   Their small, greenish-white flowers are borne in the leaf axils, solitary or in clusters, and are unisexual or bisexual, the plants dioecious (or very rarely polygamous).

The flowers are hypogynous, the calyx 4 - 8 ( - 9) lobed, the petals 4 - 6 ( - 9), stamens as many as the petals, pistil 1, 4 - 8 ( - 9) celled (in male flowers minute and rudimentary).

The fruits are berry-like drupes with 1 nutlet ("stone") in each cell and at maturity are red, reddish-orange, black, or rarely yellow, and have the calyces persistent at their bases.   In some hollies the fruits persist into the winter, or even spring, and in female or polygamous plants, at least, offer helpful means of identification.

The mature fruits of flowering dogwood and the immature fruits of some viburnums are somewhat similar, but these can be distinguished readily in that the remnants of their calyces persist at the summits of the fruits rather than at their bases.  Moreover, these have opposite leaves whereas those of the hollies are alternate.

The deciduous hollies of our area are difficult to interpret and it is particularly difficult to construct satisfactory keys.  In part this reflects our meager knowledge and the relative paucity of specimens of these plants collected in the region.  The dilemma relative to making a key arises from the fact that there is so much similarity in leaf characters; yet flowers or fruits, which are more distinctive, may not be found on the living specimens except at certain times.  This is further complicated by the dioecious nature of most holly plants.  Male plants exhibit reproductive structures only during the short period of flowering.

1. Leaves membranous to firm but not leathery; deciduous.
    2. The leaves oblanceolate, narrowly obovate, or spatulate, decidedly broadest above their middles, crenate-serrate................................................4. *I. decidua*
    2. The leaves oval, elliptical, oblong, or broadly obovate.
        3. Calyx glabrous; flower or fruit stalks much exceeding the flowers or fruit in length................................................5. *I. longipes*
        3. Calyx pubescent, or at least ciliate on the margins of the lobes; flower or fruit stalks exceeding the flowers or fruits little if at all in length.
            4. Plants occurring in wet habitats; nutlets smooth; leaves firm, veins embedded in upper leaf surfaces; flowers 5 - 8-merous........................ ................................................................................10. *I. verticillata*
            4. Plants occurring on well-drained sites; nutlets ridged; leaves membranous, veins not embedded in upper leaf surfaces; flowers 4 - 5-merous.
                5. Fruits ⅜ - ½ inch in diameter; larger leaves mostly exceeding 2 inches long................................................6. *I. montana*
                5. Fruits not exceeding ¼ inch in diameter; larger leaves mostly not exceeding 1 - 1½ inches long................................................1. *I. ambigua*
1. Leaves leathery; evergreen.
    6. Margins of the leaves dentate, the dentations and tips of the leaves with stiff, sharp spines.
        7. Leaves 2½ - 6 inches long and 1½ - 2 inches broad, broadly elliptic to ovate, or obovate, slightly revolute, the blades flat, dark green....8. *I. opaca*
        7. Leaves 1½ - 2 inches long and ½ - ¾ inches broad, cuneate-spatulate to elliptic, prominently revolute and the sides of the leaves markedly rolled downward, yellowish-green................................9. *I. opaca* var. *arenicola*
    6. Margins of the leaves entire to variously toothed but the teeth not in the form of stiff sharp spines.
        8. Largest leaves not over 1½ inches long.
            9. Leaves oblong or elliptic, the apices rounded, margins crenate with appressed teeth................................................11. *I. vomitoria*
            9. Leaves linear to linear-oblong, the apices mostly acute, often with a few sharp, bristly teeth near the apices........................7. *I. myrtifolia*
        8. Largest leaves over 2 inches long.
            10. Leaves mostly not more than twice as long as broad, entire, or with

a few appressed-spinescent teeth above the middle; fruits black
....................................................................................................3. *I. coriacea*
10. Leaves mostly more than twice as long as broad, entire; fruits red
....................................................................................................2. *I. cassine*

## 1. **Ilex ambigua** (Michx.) Torr.    Carolina holly

The Carolina holly is, in general, a shrub; but it occasionally attains tree stature.  It is deciduous, has slender, glabrous branches which are commonly dark reddish-brown and bear prominent lenticels.

The leaves are flat, elliptic to oval, or obovate, the bases obtuse to acute, the apices mostly short-acuminate, more rarely obtuse or acute. The leaf margins vary from nearly entire to appressed-crenate-serrulate. The leaf blades, variable in size, usually do not exceed 1 - 1½ inches long and ¾ - 1 inch broad.  They are glabrous to very sparsely pubescent on both surfaces.

x ⅔

R. K.

Fig. 130.  *Ilex ambigua*

The flowers are small, scarcely ¼ inch across, 4 - 5-merous, mostly 4. The calyx tube is sparsely pubescent, the lobes ciliate.  Flowers are borne in the leaf axils of new growth, the staminate in pairs or clusters of up to 6 or 8, the pistillate mostly in pairs or singly.

The fruits are red at maturity, subglobose, or more often ellipsoid, about ¼ inch in diameter, and they mature in late summer. They are not held long after maturing.

The Carolina holly occurs in well-drained hammocks, and in sand pine-evergreen oak scrub more or less throughout northern Florida.

In our area the Carolina holly and the mountain winterberry, both plants of well-drained habitats, are similar. In general, the larger leaves of the former do not exceed 1 - 1½ inches in length and ¾ - 1 inch in breadth whereas those of the latter are larger and broader. The size ranges do, however, overlap and they are much alike in leaf shape and pubescence. The mature fruits of the mountain winterberry are considerably larger and pulpier, being mostly ½ inch in diameter and globose; those of the Carolina holly do not exceed ¼ inch in diameter, are less pulpy, and are more often ellipsoid.

## 2. Ilex cassine L.   Dahoon

The dahoon is a small to medium-sized tree with a variously shaped crown.

The leaves are stiff, leathery, and evergreen. Their blades are elliptic, oblanceolate or obovate, 1 - 6 inches long. The margins are mostly entire and revolute, but occasionally have one or more teeth above their mid-points. The leaf tips are bristle-tipped. They are glabrous except along the midrib below.

The fruits are globose or ovoid, about ¼ inch in diameter, bright red, reddish-orange, or yellowish-red (rarely almost yellow). They are borne in axillary clusters of several to many (up to 100 in one count!). Each fruit has 4 rounded calyx lobes at its base.

The dahoon occurs in low hammocks and flatwoods depressions near the Gulf Coast, on stream banks, and in nonalluvial swamps and floodplains, from west Florida eastward and southward.

The evergreen leaves of *Ilex cassine* sometimes resemble those of *I. opaca* in size, but are not dentate-spiny. The fruits of the two are often very similar in color and size. In general, the dahoon is a tree of essentially wet habitats while the American holly occurs on well-drained sites.

## 3. Ilex coriacea (Pursh) Chapm.   Large or sweet gallberry

The large or sweet gallberry is not commonly a tree, although we have seen a few individuals the stature of which is of tree dimensions.

The leaves are leathery and evergreen, short-petioled, their blades elliptic, oval, oblanceolate, or obovate, 1½ - 3 inches long. Their bases are cuneate, the tips acute or abruptly acuminate. The leaf margins are entire, or they may have a few irregularly and remotely spaced, small, bristle-tipped teeth above the middle. They are punctate on the lower surfaces.

x ½

Fig. 131. *Ilex cassine*

The fruits are globose, black, juicy and sweet, about ¼ inch in diameter, contain 6 - 8 nutlets, and have 6 - 8-lobed persistent calyces appearing like miniature stars at their bases.

This shrub or tree occurs in flatwoods, depressions, branch-swamps, and bays from middle northern to western Florida.

The large or sweet gallberry is more often seen as a shrub than a tree. It is not uncommonly associated with the shrubby, bitter gallberry, *Ilex glabra* (L.) Gray. The two are similar, but can be distinguished as follows: The leaves of *I. glabra* are mostly blunt-tipped, have crenate-serrate margins above the middle of the blades, the teeth closely appressed. Its fruits are black, but dryish, bitter, and persistent through the winter. The leaves of *I. coriacea* are mostly acute-tipped, entire,

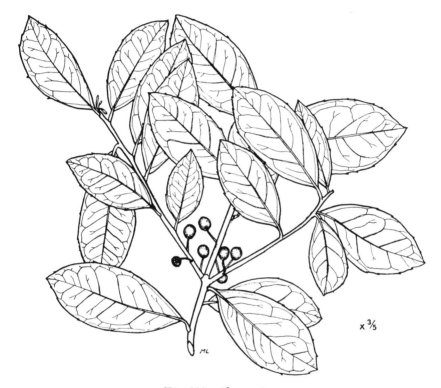

Fig. 132. *Ilex coriacea*

or with bristly, salient teeth above the middle of the blades. Its fruits are soft, pulpy and sweet, and drop soon after maturing in late summer or autumn.

### 4. **Ilex decidua** Walt. Possum-haw

The possum-haw is a small, deciduous tree or shrub.

The leaves are broadest above the middle, spatulate, oblong-spatulate, oblong-lanceolate, or elliptic, 1 - 3½ inches long. The leaf margins are appressed-crenate, the undersides of the blades more or less pubes-

cent with curly hairs, conspicuously so on the veins.  The twigs are
spurred, leaves appearing widely spaced on fast-growing twigs, but
closely spaced or clustered on the spurs.  The flower clusters (and fruits)
are often more abundant in the cluster of leaves at the spur tips than
elsewhere on the twigs.

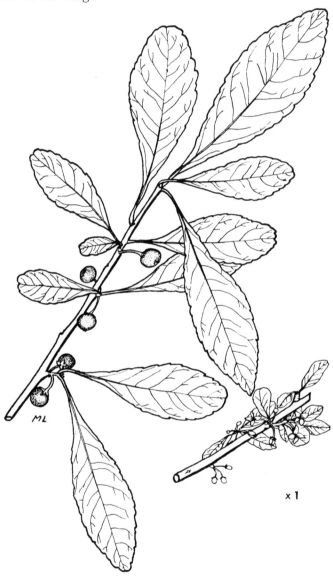

x 1

Fig. 133.  *Ilex decidua*

The fruits are small, red, globose, about ¼ inch in diameter, and persist on the leafless trees late into or through the winter.

The possum-haw occurs along low hammock sloughs and is common on river floodplains and in Gulf hammocks, from the Suwannee River westward in Florida.

Amongst our deciduous hollies, this one has leaves of distinctive shape. In vegetative condition it resembles *Viburnum obovatum*, the small-leaved *Viburnum*, but this has opposite leaves while those of *Ilex* are alternate. *Ilex curtissii* (Small) Fern. is apparently closely similar and has been treated as a variety of *I. decidua*.

### 5. Ilex longipes Chapm. ex Trel.   Georgia holly

The Georgia holly usually occurs as a shrub but may reach small-tree stature. It has spreading branches and glabrous twigs.

The leaves are elliptic-oblong to narrowly obovate, usually broadest above their mid-points. The leaf bases are acute to cuneate, the tips usually short-acuminate or obtuse. The leaf blades are glabrous above, glabrous or sparsely hairy below, the margins crenate-serrulate. The blades are thickish and rough-veiny, the veins embedded in the upper surfaces.

The flowers are small, about ¼ inch across. The perianth is 4 - 5-merous, usually 4, the calyx glabrous. The flower and fruit stalks are relatively long, ½ - ¾ inch long and exceeding the flowers and fruits in length.

The mature fruits are red, subglobose, and about ¼ - ⅜ inch in diameter. The nutlets are ribbed.

The Georgia holly occurs in swampy places. It is apparently rare in our area, in Florida known only from the western counties.

*Ilex longipes* is similar to *I. verticillata* and occupies a similar habitat. The flowers of the former are 4 - 5-merous, usually 4, and those of the latter are 5 - 8-merous. The calyx of *I. longipes* is glabrous, that of *I. verticillata* pubescent. The flower and fruit stalks of the former are longer, up to ¾ inch in length. Those of the latter usually do not exceed ⅜ inch in length.

### 6. Ilex montana T. & G.   Mountain winterberry

This is a small deciduous tree, or a shrub, with slender, glabrous branchlets.

The leaves are elliptic, oblong-lanceolate, ovate, or obovate, 1 - 3 inches long. Their bases are rounded to cuneate, the apices acute to acuminate. The margins are appressed-serrate, tending to double-ser-

R.K.

x⁴/₅

Fig. 134.  *Ilex longipes*

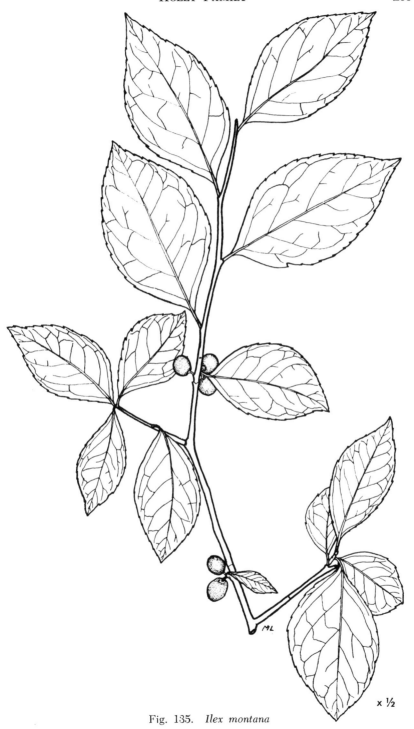

Fig. 135. *Ilex montana*

x ½

rate, the teeth short-bristle-tipped. The leaf surfaces are glabrous to finely pubescent, often pubescent only on the nerves beneath.

The flowers are small, white, and 4 - 5 (rarely 6)-merous.

The fruits are red, spherical or oval, small-plum-like, ⅜ - ½ inch in diameter.

This plant occurs in open, dry, sandy, mixed hardwood forests, from about Tallahassee westward in Florida.

*Ilex montana* resembles *I. verticillata*. The leaves of the former are membranous, those of the latter firm and with the veins appearing sunken on the upper leaf surfaces. The fruits of the former are from ⅜ - ½ inch in diameter, those of the latter ¼ inch in diameter. *I. montana* grows in well-drained upland woods, *I. verticillata* in swamps. For a comparison to *I. ambigua*, see that species.

7. **Ilex myrtifolia** Walt.   Myrtle-leaved holly; myrtle dahoon

The myrtle-leaved holly is a small tree or shrub with a compact crown of rigid, crooked limbs.

x 1

Fig. 136.   *Ilex myrtifolia*

The leaves are evergreen, usually glabrous, the blades rigid, linear, linear-elliptic, linear-oblong, elliptic, or oblanceolate. The veins are obscure except for the midrib below. The blades are ½ - 1 inch long, or slightly longer, by ⅕ inch wide or slightly wider, the bases rounded or cuneate. The margins are entire and revolute, occasionally with a few spiny-tipped teeth toward the apices. The leaf apex is blunt or rounded, but bristle-tipped.

The drupes are globose, or broader than long, red (rarely orange or yellow), about ¼ inch in diameter. At the base of the fruit, 4 pointed persistent calyx lobes form a square.

The myrtle-leaved holly occurs around the edges of sandy ponds, in sandy pinelands, or sand-loam-clay cypress or gum depressions, from middle northern to western Florida. Its frequent associates are *Taxodium ascendens, Pinus elliottii, Nyssa biflora*, and *Magnolia virginiana*.

*Ilex myrtifolia* may be distinguished from *I. cassine* by its much smaller, much narrower, and very revolute leaves which seldom exceed 2 inches long (usually about an inch long) and ⅕ inch broad. The smallest leaves of the latter species are not so short and narrow. As to habitat, the former occurs mostly in poor or acid sandy sites, most often in depressions, whereas the latter occurs in rich, mucky sites, often along streams, and near the coast even grows in brackish situations.

## 8. **Ilex opaca** Ait., var. **opaca**.  American holly

This is a common and generally well-known tree, which may have a trunk up to 2 or 3 feet in diameter. Growing under favorable (not crowded) conditions, it forms a symmetrical, conical to cylindrical crown whose rigid branches extend more or less at right angles from the central trunk.

The American holly has handsome dark green foliage which makes even the male plants very attractive. In fruiting plants, this foliage characteristic combined with heavy clusters of rich-red drupes ("berries") yields a subject popular both as a cultivated ornamental and as a victim of mutilation for Christmas decorations.

The leaves are evergreen, stiff and leathery, glabrous, have broadly elliptic, ovate, obovate, or oblong blades 2½ - 6 inches long and 1½ - 2 inches broad. The margins of the blades are wavy to dentate, the dentations tipped by stiff and sharp spiny teeth (rarely entire). The petioles are short and rigid, about ¼ inch long.

The flower parts are in fours. The fruits are dull, rich-red or (rarely) orange drupes which are globose or ovoid. They occur solitary or in clusters in the axils of the leaves, and have persistent calyces of 4 lobes forming squares at their bases.

The habitats of the American holly are well-drained rich woods, hammocks, wooded ravines, hills and valleys, and it is widely distributed throughout northern Florida.

The leathery, dark green, spine-margined leaves of the American holly are distinctive.

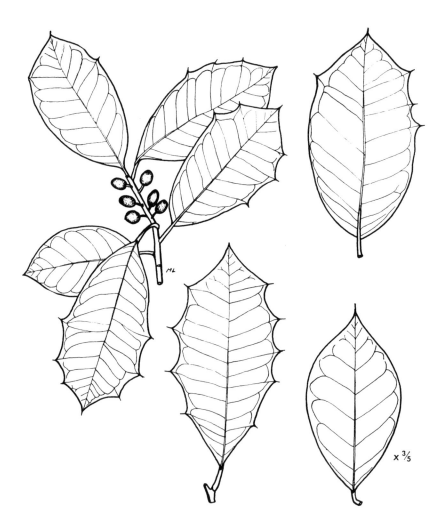

Fig. 137.   *Ilex opaca*, var. *opaca*

9. **Ilex opaca** L., var. **arenicola** (Ashe) Ashe.  Scrub holly; hummock holly

*I. cumulicola* Small

A shrub or a small tree, the scrub holly is here considered a variant of the wider-ranging American holly.  From the latter it differs in its ecological requirements.  It occurs on much drier and more open sandy

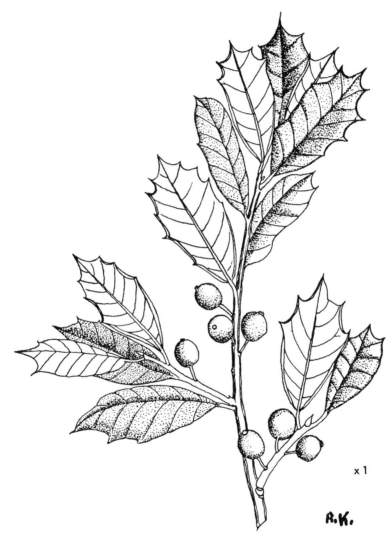

Fig. 138.  *Ilex opaca,* var. *arenicola*

sites, namely the sand pine-evergreen oak scrub. This is in contrast to the moist, rich, mixed woodlands inhabited by *Ilex opaca*. In habit, the branching of the scrub holly is more rigid-ascending, the crowns more dense, than those of the American holly.

The leaves of the scrub holly are yellowish-green in contrast to the dark green ones of the American holly. They are much smaller than those of the latter, mostly not exceeding 1½ - 2 inches in length and ½ - ¾ inch in breadth. They are much more stiff-leathery, the teeth stiffer and sharper. The leaf margins are strongly revolute and in gen-

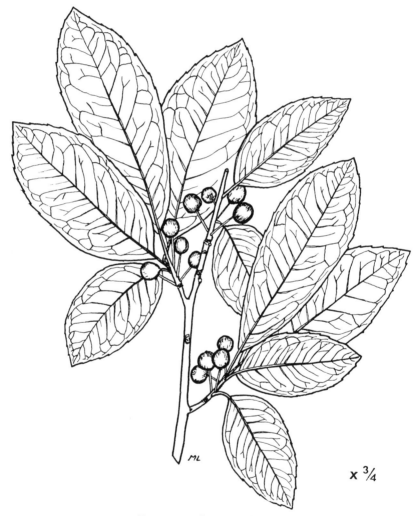

x ¾

Fig. 139.  *Ilex verticillata*

eral the sides of the leaves roll downward making them somewhat inverted boatlike. In leaf outline, they vary from cuneate-spatulate to
elliptic.

The scrub holly is most common in the scrub vegetation of the southern part of the Florida lake region southward of our range. However,
it is said to occur in a few sand pine-evergreen oak scrub areas of northeastern Florida.

### 10. **Ilex verticillata** (L.) A. Gray. Common winterberry

The common winterberry, a deciduous holly, does not commonly attain tree stature.

The leaves are oval, round-obovate, elliptic, or oblong, 1½ - 3½ inches
long, the blades cuneate at base, acute to acuminate at the tip, the margins sharply serrate, the lower surfaces pubescent. The leaf venation
is prominent, particularly on the undersides where it is often rugose-
reticulate. The petioles are about ½ inch long.

The drupes are globose, red, about ¼ inch in diameter, the pedicels
about as long or longer, and the nutlets are smooth.

The common winterberry occurs in swamps and low woods; it is
rare in our area, known to us only in Jackson County. For comparisons
see *Ilex montana* and *I. longipes.*

### 11. **Ilex vomitoria** Ait. Yaupon

In nature infrequently a tree, the yaupon does attain tree stature
under favorable conditions. It not uncommonly forms shrub thickets,
particularly on dunes along the coast. There it often is a component
of the slanting, salt-spray-pruned dense masses of shrubs so characteristic of seashore communities. The leathery, dark green foliage is attractive in itself, but in female plants this, combined with the bright
scarlet or dark red fruits, makes it an attractive decorative subject.
Moreover, it responds favorably to pruning and is widely used for
hedges.

The leaves are evergreen, thick and leathery, their blades oblong,
oblong-elliptic, or oval, 1 - 2¼ inches long. The leaf tips are blunt or
rounded, the margins crenate-serrate, the teeth appressed.

Yaupon fruits are uncommonly handsome, scarlet or dark red, globose, about ¼ inch in diameter, and produced in profusion on short,
stubby spurs.

Besides its seaside dune habitats, the yaupon occurs on sandy roadsides, along fence rows, woods' margins, open upland woods, and in
hammocks, throughout northern Florida.

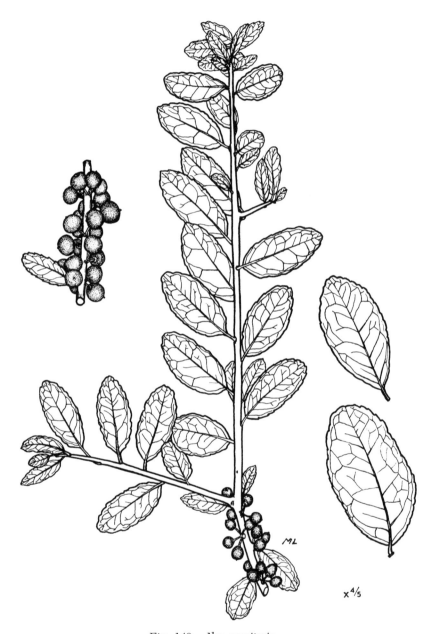

Fig. 140.　*Ilex vomitoria*

The myrtle-leaved holly and the yaupon, both having small, ever-green leaves, are somewhat similar, but are easily distinguished by leaf characters. Those of the former are, in general, much longer than broad, mostly approaching linear. They are revolute, either entire or with a few bristle-tipped teeth, the apices bristle-tipped. The latter are not over twice as long as broad, are flat, crenate-serrate, the tips blunt.

## ACERACEAE. MAPLE FAMILY

### ACER. MAPLES; BOX-ELDER

*Acer* is a genus of deciduous trees, including the maples and box-elder. The maples are easily recognized by their palmately 3 - 5-lobed, opposite leaves. No other native trees exhibit these two characteristics. Both the maples and box-elder have fruits peculiar to the group (2-winged, the double-fruit bodies joined, Siamese-twin fashion, each with a wing). The plants are polygamous or dioecious, however, so not all individuals bear fruit. In some cases, an individual may bear mostly male flowers, but few female ones, and bear fruit sparsely, therefore. Box-elder differs from the maples in having pinnately compound leaves with 3 - 9 leaflets.

1. Leaves simple, palmately-veined and (with rare exceptions) palmately-lobed.
    2. Primary lobes of the leaf ½ or more the length of the entire blade................
    ....................................................................................................5. *A. saccharinum*
    2. Primary lobes of the leaf less than ½ the length of the entire blade.
        3. Leaves whitish or silvery on their lower surfaces.
            4. Terminal and upper lateral lobes of the leaf with straight or concave sides, the lobes squarish................................................1. *A. barbatum*
            4. Terminal, and/or at least the upper lateral lobes of the leaf with tapering sides, the lobes triangular......................................4. *A. rubrum*
        3. Leaves yellowish-green on their lower surfaces................2. *A. leucoderme*
1. Leaves compound, with 3 - 9 pinnately-veined leaflets..................3. *A. negundo*

#### 1. **Acer barbatum** Michx. Florida maple; southern sugar maple

##### *A. floridanum* (Chapm.) Pax

This is a tree of medium height with rather a dense foliage. In winter, the dead and brown foliage tends to persist on the trees. The bark is gray, smoothish on younger stems, shallowly ridged and furrowed on older trunks.

The leaves are palmately 3 - 5-lobed, truncate or slightly cordate at their bases, the lobes short-acuminate with few-toothed margins. On leaves of fertile twigs, the tips of the lobes are often blunted or rounded and cupped; on leaves of vigorous shoots of sterile twigs (and on saplings), the teeth are numerous and acuminate. In general, the tips of the leaf lobes are angular-rounded. The lower surfaces of the leaf blades are whitish, pubescent or glabrate.

Fig. 141. *Acer barbatum*

Flowers of the Florida maple appear as the leaves develop. They are small, clustered, greenish-yellow, and are borne on slender stalks.

The fruits mature in midsummer, their wings brownish, tinged with red.

The Florida maple occurs in rich woodlands having clay or limestone soils, and in sandy or limestone hammocks, from central Florida northward and westward to the higher floodplains of the Choctawhatchee River, and in sandy hammocks of the Choctawhatchee Bay area.

*Acer barbatum* is most nearly like *A. leucoderme*. Distinguishing features of the former are its gray bark, whitish lower leaf surfaces, and the blunted tips of the lobes of leaves of its fertile branches. In contrast, the latter has chalky-white bark, yellowish-green lower leaf surfaces, and the lobes of leaves on both fertile and sterile branches have acute or acuminate tips.

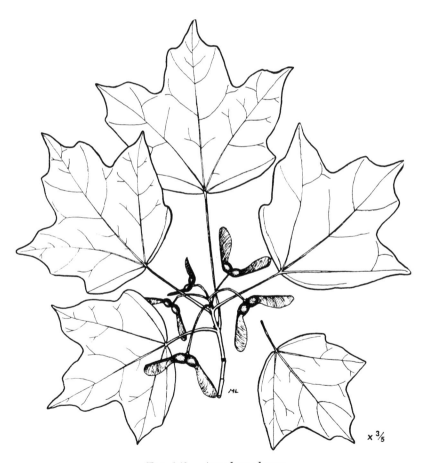

Fig. 142. *Acer leucoderme*

## 2. Acer leucoderme Small.   Chalk maple

The chalk maple is a small tree with chalky or whitish bark.   It is most nearly like the southern sugar or Florida maple (which see).

The leaves are 3 - 5-lobed, frequently only 3, the lobes acute to acuminate.   The lobes of leaves on sterile branches tend to have the sides rolled downward, the lobes thus being cupped; those of the fertile branches generally are not cupped.   The lower surfaces of the leaf blades are yellowish-green (*not* whitish), and are hairy or glabrate.

The chalk maple blooms as the leaves appear.   The fruits are brick-red or tan tinged with red, and they mature in midsummer.

In our area *Acer leucoderme* is restricted to the slopes of bluffs along the Apalachicola River in Liberty and Gadsden counties.

## 3.  Acer negundo L.   Box-elder

The box-elder is a small to medium-sized, fast-growing tree, which has brittle wood.   Short trunks from which several spreading more or less equal branches arise are characteristic.

The leaves are pinnately compound, the leaflets number 3 - 5 (commonly 3, more rarely 7 - 9).   The blades of the leaflets may be nearly entire, but are characteristically coarsely and irregularly toothed from about their mid-points upward, those of sprouts often lobed and not otherwise toothed.   The lateral buds are enclosed by the petiole bases. The twigs are smooth and bright green.

Box-elder flowers are unisexual, the plants dioecious, the flowers appearing before or as the leaves develop.   They are small, greenish, the male borne in long-stalked pendant clusters, the female in long-stalked pendant racemes.   From the latter develop graceful, pendant racemes of greenish-winged fruits.

Floodplain woodlands and low hammocks are the usual habitats of the box-elder.   It is known to occur in such places from middle Florida to the Apalachicola River.

Notable distinguishing characteristics of the box-elder are its green, often glaucous, twigs, and buds covered by the petiole bases.   The only other native trees exhibiting the latter characteristic are the American sycamore, which has large, simple, palmately-veined alternate leaves, and the smooth sumac, which has alternate, pinnately compound leaves and a milky sap.   The box-elder may be mistaken for an ash since the ashes also have opposite, pinnately compound leaves.   The lateral buds of the ashes, however, are borne in the axils of the petioles.

Fig. 143. *Acer negundo*

#### 4. **Acer rubrum** L.   Red maple

A small to large tree, the red maple is conspicuous in winter because of its clusters of small red flowers which appear long before the leaves develop. Fruiting trees become even more conspicuous since their prominent, winged fruits are red and they develop practically to maturity prior to the appearance of the leaves.

The leaves of red maple, variable in size and shape, range from lanceolate (rarely) to ovate and are palmately 3 - 5-lobed. They are from 2 to 5½ inches long, sometimes as broad, rarely broader. Their bases vary from U-shaped to truncate, or semicordate. Leaf and lobe margins have teeth of various sizes. The blades are whitish underneath, sometimes silvery, occasionally tinged with blue or lavender, and may be glabrous or pubescent, even soft-tomentose.

The twigs have lateral accessory flower buds, one on either side of the axillary bud, and the branchlets are usually reddish.

Staminate flowers are borne in capitate clusters, the bisexual or pistillate ones in sessile umbels, the pedicels elongating as the fruits develop. Flowers are red to scarlet. Many individual trees are male.

The winged fruits are usually scarlet, but may be brownish-red, or even straw-colored. The wings spread from each other at various angles.

The red maple is widely distributed throughout northern Florida, occurring in woodlands on moist to very wet sites.

Variation in size, form, lobing, and pubescence of the leaves of red maple is inordinate (see illustration). Variations occur from leaf to leaf of the same tree, or from tree to tree in the same habitat. Environment influences the size of trees and leaves as well as the type of leaves. In a number of localities in northern Florida sandy soils with little humus content produce small trees with dwarfed, slightly lobed, hairy leaves. On the other hand, in the same general vicinity there may be richer soils that support larger trees which bear larger, more deeply lobed, and less hairy leaves. Transition sites display intermediate types. Some of the extremes in variation have been treated as species, varieties, or forms by authors. It appears best to consider the red maple a variable and inclusive species.

#### 5. **Acer saccharinum** L.   Silver maple

The silver maple is a tall, fast-growing, slender open tree, typically with several nearly equal, upright, secondary trunks from the principal one. The bark is smooth on the smaller branches, becoming reddish-brown and ridged and furrowed on old trunks.

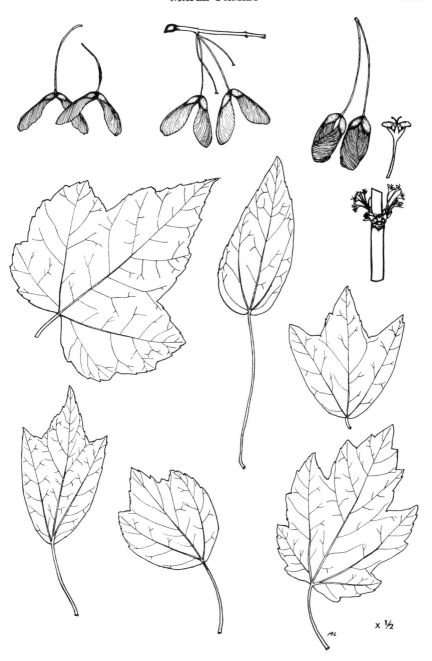

Fig. 144.   *Acer rubrum*

x ½

The leaves are palmately 3 - 5-lobed (usually 5), and are up to 6 - 7 inches long. The primary lobes are ½ or more the length of the entire blade (¾ in most cultivated trees). The bases of the lobes are curved so

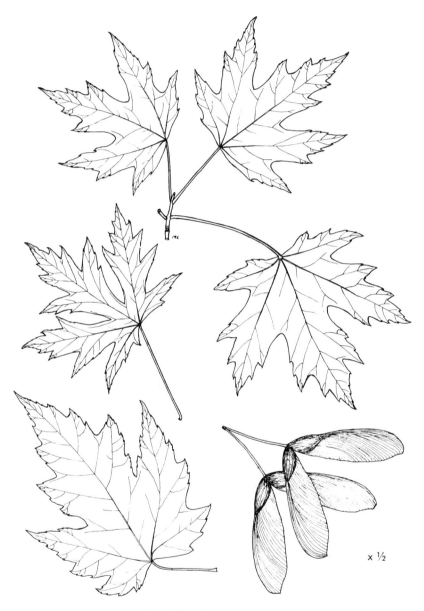

x ½

Fig. 145. *Acer saccharinum*

that the sinuses between are more or less lens-shaped. The teeth of the margin and lobes are prominent and sharp. The lower surfaces of the leaves are white or silvery.

A notable characteristic of the twigs is the presence of a lateral accessory flower bud on either side of the axillary bud, a character shared by the red maple.

The flowers are small, greenish-yellow, and are borne in many-flowered fascicles; they appear before the leaves develop, for the most part.

The fruits are straw-colored, 2 - 3 inches long, the largest of our maples (those of the other species do not exceed 1¼ inch), and they mature in the early spring.

This tree is known in our range only on banks and natural levees of the Apalachicola River. It is infrequently cultivated in our area.

The leaves of the silver maple are distinctive in that their lower surfaces are white or silvery and the primary lobes are ½ or more the length of the entire blades. Those of the red maple are whitish or silvery below but the primary lobes are much shorter.

## HIPPOCASTANACEAE.   BUCKEYE   FAMILY

### AESCULUS

### 1.  **Aesculus pavia** L.   Red buckeye

The red buckeye is a small tree or a shrub. The bark of older trunks is grayish-brown and irregularly flaky.

The leaves are deciduous, opposite, palmately compound, long-petioled, and with 5 - 7 leaflets (usually 5). The leaflets are elliptic-oblong to elliptic-obovate, mostly about 6 - 7 inches long and 2 - 2½ inches broad at their broadest places. Their bases are long-cuneate, the tips acute to acuminate, the margins finely and irregularly toothed. They are pinnately-veined, dark green and glabrous above and with tufts of hairs in the principal vein axils below.

The flowers are red, about 1 - 1½ inches long, and are borne in an oblong panicle terminating the new growth in early spring. The calyces are cylindric-tubular, 5-lobed, red, the petals 4 - 5, unequal, separate, exserted from the calyx tube and ascending, the stamens usually 7 and extending beyond the corolla.

The fruit is a leathery, 3-valved capsule, globose to obovate, 1 - 2 inches in diameter, and bears 1 - 3 large seeds.

The red buckeye inhabits rich deciduous woodlands, low mixed hammocks, and river banks throughout northern Florida.

No other tree of our range has opposite, palmately compound leaves with 5 - 7 pinnately-veined leaflets. These, being distinctive, make its identification easy.

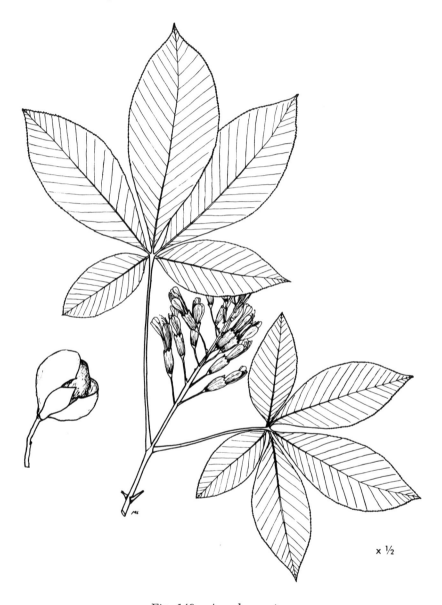

x ½

Fig. 146. *Aesculus pavia*

# SAPINDACEAE.  SOAPBERRY FAMILY

## SAPINDUS

1. **Sapindus marginatus** Willd.  Florida soapberry; wildchina-tree

This small tree of infrequent occurrence has alternate, deciduous, pinnately compound leaves which may be up to 15 inches long.  The leaflets, numbering 7 - 13, are lanceolate, oblique or scythe-shaped, and entire.  The tips are acuminate, the surfaces glabrous except sometimes on the midribs below, and the leaflets are from 3 to 6 inches long.

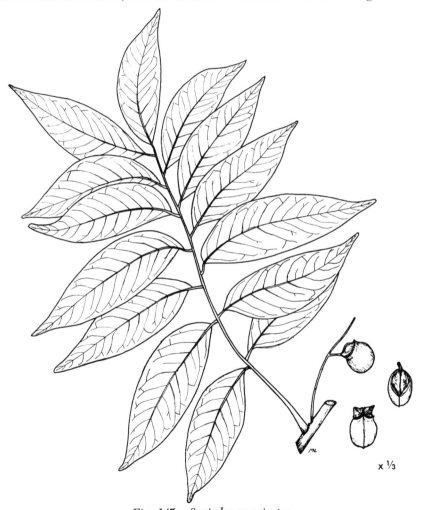

x ⅓

Fig. 147.  *Sapindus marginatus*

The flowers are small, greenish, sometimes tinged with red, and are borne in broad, pointed, pubescent panicles. The ovulary is 3-celled but 2 of the cells usually abort. One cell enlarges and bears 1 large seed. The mature fruit is a peculiar, very lopsided drupelike structure with a nearly globose fertile half to one side and 2 dried-up, aborted, humped ovulary remains on the other. The fruit is about ¾ inch in diameter.

The Florida soapberry occurs in dry hammocks from Marion County northward (West and Arnold, 1956).

In fruit, this tree is readily distinguishable by the peculiarly lopsided, nearly globose, hard and tough drupes. Its 1-pinnate foliage resembles that of several other trees, but no other of our trees has pinnately compound leaves which are at the same time alternate, have entire leaflets, and do not have a prominently winged rachis.

# RHAMNACEAE.  BUCKTHORN FAMILY

## RHAMNUS

### 1. **Rhamnus caroliniana** Walt.   Carolina buckthorn

A small, unarmed tree somewhat resembling a holly when in fruit.

The leaves are simple, alternate, petioled, and deciduous, dark green and shining above, prominently veined, and 4 - 6 inches long. Their blades are oblong or oblong-elliptic, glabrous or slightly pubescent above, finely pubescent below and becoming glabrous except on the principal veins. The petioles and twigs are pubescent. The leaf bases are rounded to cuneate, the tips obtuse, short-acuminate, or rounded. Their margins are finely serrate.

The flowers are small, bisexual, 5-merous, solitary or in short-peduncled axillary clusters.

The fruits are globose drupes, about ⅓ inch in diameter, with 2 - 4 smooth nutlets. They are red in summer, becoming a shiny black at maturity.

In our range, this tree is not common. It occurs in deciduous woods on limestone in the vicinity of Marianna, Jackson County, and along the Apalachicola River in Gadsden and Liberty counties. Harper (1914) reports it for coquina rock areas on the east coast, and West and Arnold (1956) record it as growing commonly on limestone outcrops as far south as Orange County.

The leaves of the Carolina buckthorn are distinctive, being oblong or elliptic-oblong with prominent, nearly parallel lateral veins which curve gently forward and arch-anastomose near the margins. Although the fruits are holly-like, these plants can be distinguished from the deciduous-leaved hollies by the characteristic leaves. Moreover, their fruits become black at maturity while those of the deciduous hollies are red.

Fig. 148. *Rhamnus caroliniana*

## TILIACEAE. BASSWOOD FAMILY

### TILIA. BASSWOOD; LINDEN

Sargent (1933) recognized eight species or varieties of *Tilia* as occurring in Florida. Benjamin Franklin Bush, contributing *Tilia* for Small's manual (1933), included six species for Florida. Coker and Totten (1945), noncommittal on the validity of some species and varieties, include a total of fourteen that have been reported for this state. Brown (1945) reduced the seven species and varieties reported for Louisiana to one species, *Tilia americana*. He supports this drastic reduction with a report of a study of his own collections and of authentically named types and cotypes from larger herbaria. We quote in part from page 180 of Brown: "The reduction of seven species and varieties reported for Louisiana to one is not due to ultra-conservatism, but is the result of the study of a series of specimens, plus type or cotype material collections, and of authentically determined material. If there are more species of basswood in Louisiana, they must be differentiated by some character other than hairiness. This study indicates that the degree of hairiness has little or no value." The seven species or varieties that he places with *T. americana* include the following reported also for Florida: *T. caroliniana*, *T. floridana*, and *T. floridana*, var. *oblongifolia*.

Fernald (1950) treats four American species for the range of Gray's manual and indicates that his treatment is wholly tentative, indicating that the genus demands careful restudy.

The authors have made field observations of trees in 12 Florida counties from the central peninsular to the western part of the state. Material from more than 350 trees in this range was carefully studied, the analysis being concentrated on characteristics of the leaves, flowers, and inflorescence bracts. Moreover, both fresh and dried specimens from trees occurring in other states were represented in our analyses, including specimens from trees named *T. americana* on the University of Illinois campus at Urbana. It is of more than passing interest that our material was subsequently borrowed by a student of *Tilia* and that individual herbarium specimens taken from separate parts of a single tree were designated by him with more than one species name.

Flowers from a number of trees from different critical localities were so similar as to offer no criteria for species differentiation. An attempt was made to correlate style pubescence with other characters, but to no avail. One might expect the degree of hairiness of the styles to be correlated with the extent of pubescence of the leaves. In actual cases, some trees with pubescent leaves had flowers in which the styles were partially pubescent; in others with pubescent leaves, the styles were glabrous. Moreover, some trees with glabrous leaves had flowers with glabrous styles; others had flowers with pubescent styles. At Oviedo, Seminole County, where trees with glabrous leaves predominate, such trees had glabrous styles, too. The slight variation found in the form and size of the floral parts of flowers from trees otherwise differing as to leaf pubescence, bract size and shape, and other characteristics, were well within the range limits for a species.

The inflorescence bracts vary so greatly in shape, size, and relative dimensions even within a population with uniform character of leaf pubescence and floral characteristics that they are of no value for diagnostic purposes. In conference, Ernest J. Palmer, Arnold Arboretum, retired, stated that he found the bracts of little taxonomic value.

Leaf form and dimensions are so variable, even on a single tree, that they have no diagnostic significance. Almost any local population will have all the leaf forms and dimensions that may be found in Florida Tilias generally.

In some local populations, there is exhibited a constancy in degree of pubescence or glabrosity of the lower surfaces of the leaves, or of the twigs. In other local populations, individual trees with hairy or glabrous leaves and twigs stand side by side.

Similarly, consistency in the nature of the marginal teeth of the leaves prevails in some local populations and can be correlated with pubescence, but overlapping and intergradation occurs. Apparently, environmental differences can be correlated with the pattern of toothing of the leaves, and this necessitates the employment of extreme caution in the matter of using these characters taxonomically. The leaves of trees of open, sunny habitats tend to be smaller and to have smaller, sharper serrations than those of shady places. Likewise, the leaves of the exposed tops of trees, subject to full sunlight, tend to be smaller and have reduced, sharper teeth than those of the same tree lower down and shaded.

Granting the fact that local populations of *Tilia* in our range do exhibit, in general, degrees of difference in their over-all pattern of characteristics, we are inclined to recognize but one variable complex, *T. americana.* It seems futile to attempt segregation into more taxa, certainly not without studies applying techniques and employing values other than those traditionally used.

In northern Florida, *T. americana,* thus broadly interpreted, embraces a range of plants, some of which individually correspond to *T. heterophylla, T. floridana, T. crenoserrata,* and *T. georgiana.*

1. **Tilia americana** L. American basswood; American linden

The basswoods are small to large trees with broadly round-topped crowns, the branches often short and pendulous. Its inner bark yields distinctive long and tough fibers. When cut or injured, this tree sprouts and suckers freely from the base. The wood is light in color and soft, so that the basswoods are known as soft-hardwoods. It is an altogether handsome tree, its foliage attractive, and with flowers having remarkably sweet and penetrating odors. When basswoods bloom, bees forsake other plants. Basswood honey is regarded as of high quality.

The leaves are alternate, 2-ranked, deciduous, and simple. Their blades are ovate, semiorbicular, or oblong-ovate, subpalmately-veined, 2 - 8 inches long by 2 - 5 inches broad. Their bases are commonly

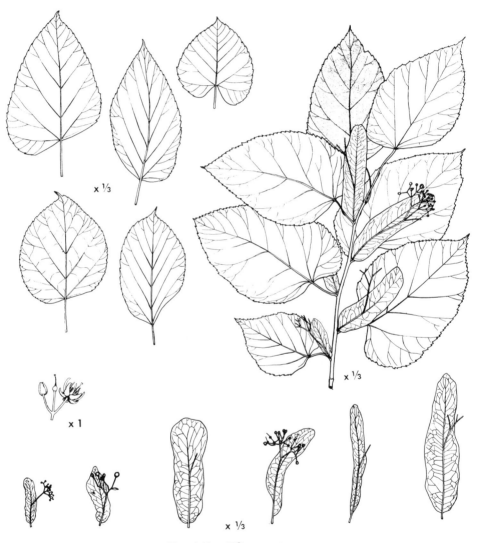

Fig. 149.  *Tilia americana*

oblique-cordate, truncate, or wide-angled to cuneate with concave sides, the tips abruptly acuminate. The leaf margins vary from serrate to crenate or dentate. The lower surfaces show varying degrees of pubescence, the hairs white to gray, tan, or brown, or they may be glabrous and green, or dark-bluish, or coated with a whitish or bluish bloom. The petioles vary from ¼ to ½ the length of the blades.

Cross-sectional views of the twigs disclose a toothed pattern of the phloem. This pattern resembles the teeth of a buzz saw.

The flowers are fragrant, small, borne several to numerous in axillary cymose clusters. They have 5 sepals, 5 oblong-spatulate, cream-colored petals, numerous stamens cohering at their bases in 5 groups, with a petal-like scale (staminode) opposite each true petal, and a single pistil. The ovularies are hairy, the styles more or less hairy to glabrous, the stigmas 5-parted. The ovularies are 5-locular. The flower pedicels are club-shaped. Each flower and each cyme branch is subtended by a bract, but these are shed by the time the flowers are fully open. The peduncles and cyme branches vary from pubescent to almost glabrous. The peduncles of the cymes are united part of the way to conspicuous straplike, spatulate or oblong bracts, the bracts themselves extending beyond the points of departure of the peduncles. The effect of these curious structures is that the inflorescences seem to arise from the blades of narrow leaves. The weight of the flowers and leverage twist the bracts so that the flower clusters seem to dangle from their lower sides. The bracts are 2 - 6½ inches long by ¼ - 1½ inches broad.

The fruits are dry, woody, indehiscent, elongate-globose to depressed-globose in shape and ¼ - ⅓ inch in diameter.

The basswoods inhabit mesic, fertile, sandy, clayey, or limestone woodland sites from Seminole to Okaloosa counties.

The 2-ranked leaves of basswoods are somewhat similar to some mulberry leaves. The mulberries have a milky sap, however, and their leaves and buds are not 2-ranked (except on vigorous shoots), so they can thus be easily distinguished. The basswoods' curiously and conspicuously bracted flowers and fruit clusters are unique among our trees.

## NYSSACEAE. SOURGUM FAMILY

### Nyssa. Tupelo; sourgum

Four species of *Nyssa* inhabit our range, three in low grounds, one in upland well-drained woods.

Leaves are deciduous, alternate, simple, pinnately-veined, and entire, or some with a few irregular dentations or teeth.

The flowers are unisexual or bisexual, the plants dioecious or polygamous. They are small, green, inconspicuous, the staminate in a stalked capitate cluster, umbel, or raceme, the pistillate or bisexual solitary or few at the ends of bracted stalks. The staminate flowers have 5 minute sepals or none, 5 petals, and 5 - 12 stamens. Pistillate flowers have 5 small sepals, 5 small petals (or none), 5 - 10 stamens or staminodes, and 1 pistil. The ovulary is 1-celled and 1-seeded. The fruit is a drupe.

A significant characteristic for which to look when trying to locate a *Nyssa* is a tree whose leaves are mostly entire but with some leaves having one or more irregularly spaced teeth.

1. Trees with a single, erect trunk; mature fruits black, or bluish-black, the stones ribbed.
   2. Fruits usually 1 to a stalk; leaves 6 inches or more long........1. *N. aquatica*
   2. Fruits usually 2 or 3 - 5 to a stalk; leaves 2 - 5 inches long.
      3. The fruits generally 2 to a stalk; leaves mostly 2 - 5 inches long............
      .........................................................................................2. *N. biflora*
      3. The fruits usually 3 - 5 to a stalk; leaves mostly 2 - 6 inches long............
      .........................................................................................4. *N. sylvatica*
1. Trees usually with several crooked trunks; mature fruits red, the stones papery-winged.........................................................................3. *N. ogeche*

### 1. Nyssa aquatica L.   Water tupelo

The water tupelo is a large tree with erect, buttressed trunks.

The leaf blades are large, ovate to oblong-ovate, cuneate to sub-cordate at their bases, acuminate at the tips. They range from 5 - 7 ( - 12) inches long. Their margins vary from entire to coarsely and irregularly dentate-serrate. They are glabrous above, paler below, the lower surfaces downy-pubescent when young, becoming glabrate. The twigs are glabrous or nearly so.

Staminate flowers are crowded at the end of a peduncle, the pistillate solitary on a peduncle.

The drupes are about 1 inch long, dark blue or purple at maturity, borne on drooping stalks which are longer than the fruits. The stones have about 10 ridges.

The water tupelo inhabits clayey or muddy soils. of sloughs, river swamps, and pond and lake margins, mainly from the Tallahassee Red Hills region to western Florida. We have one record from Duval County in eastern Florida.

Although the water and Ogeechee tupelos have similar leaves, those of the former are usually long-pointed and glabrous or glabrate. Those of the latter are generally blunt or round at their tips, are densely pubescent on their lower surfaces and petioles and have pubescent twigs. The fruit stalks of the water tupelo exceed the fruits in length. Those of the Ogeechee tupelo are no longer than or are commonly shorter than the fruits.

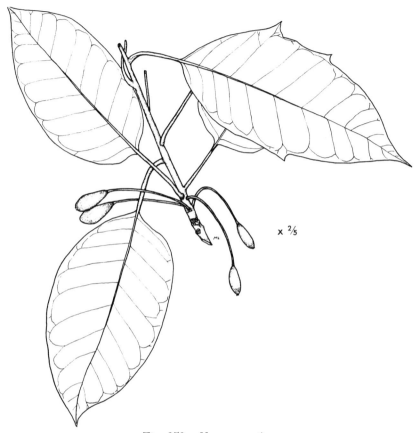

Fig. 150. *Nyssa aquatica*

2. **Nyssa biflora** Walt. Swamp tupelo; blackgum

This is a tall, gregarious tree of swamps or low grounds, or a scrubby tree in habitats subject to periodic burning. The trunks are buttressed when growing in inundated areas. The bark is light gray and roughened with interlacing fissures and ridges.

The leaves are coriaceous or subcoriaceous, lustrous above, paler and duller below, glabrous or glabrate, varying from oblanceolate to narrowly oblong-lanceolate, or narrowly obovate. They taper at their bases and have rounded to obtuse or subacute tips.

Staminate flowers occur crowded on the tips of peduncles. The pistillate are borne in pairs on peduncles.

The drupes are blue-black, ⅓ - ½ inch long, usually paired, on stalks of variable lengths. The stones are prominently ribbed.

The swamp tupelo occurs in nonalluvial swamps and flatwoods, shallow ponds, and bays, throughout northern Florida.

Fig. 151. *Nyssa biflora*

From Vilas to Sumatra, along Florida Highway 65, and from Wewa-
hitchka to Port St. Joe, along Florida Highway 71, are situations in
which the habit of *Nyssa biflora* is strikingly different. Sizes and growth
forms from scraggly shrubs to large, single trees inhabit areas grading
from pine flatwoods proper to interior swamp, respectively. Fruits of
these plants are essentially similar in size, shape, and number per peduncle, whether on the scrubby, scraggly shrubs, on the trees, or on
intermediate forms. The fruiting peduncles range from almost sessile
to 1¼ inches long on the scrubby forms. In the scrubby form, the internodes of the twigs are short and the fruiting peduncles are approximate, giving the effect of more fruits together in a cluster. However,
there are still only 1 - 2 fruits per peduncle. It is thought that this has
been misinterpreted. Occurring with the *Nyssa biflora* in the flatwoods
were forms, also shrubby and scrubby, of sweetbay (*Magnolia virginiana*), red maple (*Acer rubrum*), and sometimes pond-cypress (*Taxodium
ascendens*). The habitats here, grading from flatwoods proper to interior swamps, are subject to periodic burning, the burning more severe
in the flatwoods and progressively less so toward the interior swamps.
The scrubby habit of *Nyssa biflora* found in these flatwoods is evidently
related to fire injury. (See also *Magnolia virginiana*.)

It is likely that Small, in describing *Nyssa ursina* from the Apalachicola River delta, was dealing with this scrubby form of *Nyssa biflora*.

*Nyssa biflora* and *Nyssa sylvatica* are the most nearly similar of the
tupelos. The former has 1 - 2 (mostly 2) fruits per stalk and grows in
poorly-drained situations; the latter typically has 3 or more fruits per
stalk and inhabits well-drained upland woodlands.

3. **Nyssa ogeche** Bartram ex Marsh.    Ogeechee tupelo; ogeechee-lime

This is a small to medium-sized tree. Often it leans outward over the
water from river banks and has numerous upright branches from the
leaning trunks; more frequently, it is characterized by several upright
trunks from near the base. The trunks are crooked and the trees commonly appear stunted or injured. Not infrequently it is a many-
stemmed shrub and even this form bears fruits.

The leaves vary from oblong, oblong-obovate, or oblanceolate, to
broadly elliptic. Their bases vary from rounded to cuneate, the apices
from rounded to acuminate. The leaf margins are entire, or some leaves
may have a few irregularly spaced teeth. Leaves are thickish at maturity, green above, paler beneath, the lower surfaces velvety-pubescent to hairy only along the veins. The young twigs are velvety to
sparsely pubescent.

The male flowers occur in globular-capitate clusters; the female are borne singly on short stalks. The plants are male or polygamous.

The drupes are oblong to obovate, 1 - 1½ inches long, and are borne on short, stiff stalks, ½ inch long or less, which extend outward from the twigs. At maturity they are rose-red. The stones are attached by papery wings to the skin of the fruit.

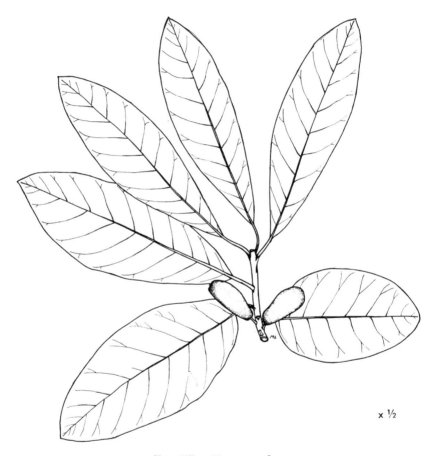

x ½

Fig. 152. *Nyssa ogeche*

The Ogeechee tupelo is common throughout our area in sloughs, bayous, on river banks, in swamps, and on pond and lake shores.

Distinguishing characters of this species are the usually blunt-tipped leaves, velvety pubescence of twigs and lower leaf surfaces, and the red fruits whose stalks do not exceed the fruit in length.

### 4. Nyssa sylvatica Marsh.   Black tupelo; sourgum

This is an upland forest tree which occurs generally solitary in the forest and does not form a tupelo community as do the other species of *Nyssa*.   The branches tend to be stiffly horizontal, the lower very often descending.   The bark is very rough and blocky with interlacing ridges and fissures.

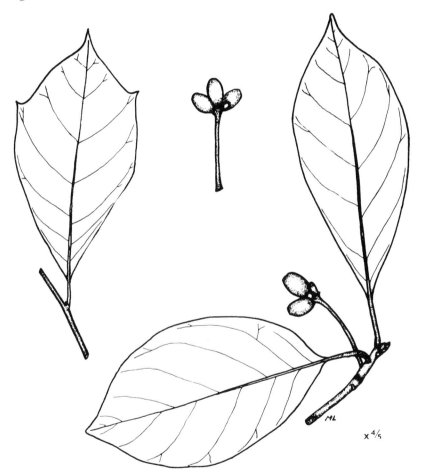

Fig. 153.   *Nyssa sylvatica*

The leaves are broadly lanceolate, broadly oblanceolate, narrowly obovate, or elliptic, their blades 2 - 6 inches long by 1 - 3 inches broad. The leaf bases are cuneate to rounded, the tips obtuse to acute or acuminate.   Their margins are entire, irregularly wavy, or with a few irregularly spaced teeth. They are lustrous above, glabrous below. The foliage turns a brilliant crimson early in autumn, or even in summer on individual twigs or branches.

Staminate flowers are borne in close umbels or umbel-like racemes at the ends of stalks, the pistillate 3 - 5, sessile at the ends of stalks.

The mature drupes are dark blue, ¼ - ½ inch long, and are borne 1 - 5 per stalk (frequently 3). The stones are indistinctly ribbed.

This tree occurs in open or dense upland forest, or on slopes, usually where the soil is clayey, from the Tallahassee Red Hills region westward in Florida.

Two upland trees which are often distinguished with difficulty when only leaves are available are the black tupelo and the persimmon. Critical characters by which they may be separated are as follows:

Black tupelo (*Nyssa sylvatica*)

Margins of leaves on vigorous shoots sometimes few-toothed; leaf blades frequently marked by dark maroon spots or blemishes, pale green underneath; growth in length from terminal buds.

Persimmon (*Diospyros virginiana*)

Margins of leaves never toothed; leaf blades marked by black spots, whitish underneath; the growth in length from axillary buds, owing to abortion of the terminal buds.

## STERCULIACEAE. STERCULIA FAMILY

### FIRMIANA

1. **Firmiana platanifolia** (L.f.) Schott. & Endl.   Chinese parasol-tree; Japanese varnish-tree

*Sterculia platanifolia* L.f.

An ornamental, introduced from China and Japan, this small tree has a notably smooth, green to greenish-gray bark and very large lobed leaves.

The leaves are simple, alternate, deciduous, palmately 3 - 5-lobed with 5 - 9 principal veins, and with petioles up to 20 inches in length. The blades are cordate-orbicular in over-all outline, up to 15 inches long or broad. The margins, aside from the lobing, are entire or have large, shallow teeth. They are green and glabrous above and vary from glabrous to whitish-tomentose below. The twigs are bright green, have a large pith, and bear velvety-brown buds. The older bark is gray-green, the grayness due to a waxy bloom.

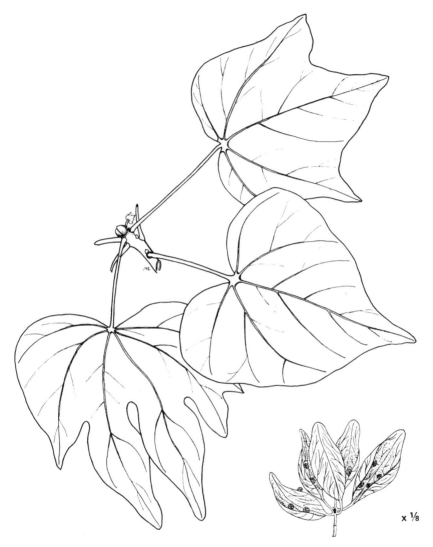

x ⅛

Fig. 154. *Firmiana platanifolia*

The flowers are small, greenish, unisexual or bisexual, the plants polygamous. They are borne in large terminal panicles 15 - 24 inches long. The carpels are 3 - 5, distinct, borne in a whorl. They are at first closed and bottle-shaped, but open well before maturity, becoming spoonlike and bearing exposed seeds on the edges. The whole fruiting panicle is large, distinctive, and conspicuous even subsequent to fruit-fall, its skeletal framework remaining on the tree for a considerable period.

Mostly seen as an ornamental in cultivation, this tree is to some extent naturalized in city lots, on roadsides, and in thickets not too far removed from human habitations.

The Chinese parasol-tree is notable for its large palmately 3 - 5 lobed, 5 - 9-veined leaves (the veins arising from kidney-shaped areas at the bases of the blades), by its smoothish greenish-gray bark, green twigs, and conspicuous panicles of open spoonlike fruits bearing exposed seeds on their margins.

## THEACEAE.   TEA   FAMILY

1.  Plants evergreen, leaves leathery, their marginal teeth blunt and appressed, the lower surfaces glabrous; stamens yellow.................................................GORDONIA
1.  Plants deciduous, leaves thin, their marginal teeth sharp, the lower surfaces pubescent; stamens purple.................................................................STEWARTIA

### GORDONIA

#### 1.  Gordonia lasianthus (L.) Ellis.   Loblolly-bay

This is a small to medium-sized, stiffly erect tree with a conical or cylindrical crown.

The dark green leaves are simple, alternate, leathery, and evergreen. The blades are oblong, long-elliptic, or ovate-elliptic, 2½ - 6½ inches long. The leaf bases are tapering, the tips acute or obtuse, often notched. The margins have blunt, appressed teeth, and the surfaces are glabrous. The young twigs are reddish and smooth.

The flowers of the loblolly-bay are exquisitely beautiful. The general effect is rendered by a pure white corolla, about 3 inches across, its petals crinkly-fringed and their broadly rounded tips turned up; in the middle of the flower is a cluster of golden-yellow stamens. There are 5 sepals and 5 petals (the back of each of which is clothed by silky hairs), numerous stamens, their filaments united at the base into a 5-lobed cup, and a pistil with a 5-locular ovulary.

The fruit is an ovoid capsule, about ⅔ inch long, clothed with silky hairs. It splits into 5 parts at maturity, liberating numerous winged seeds.

This tree occurs in flatwoods depressions, bays, branch-bays, and low hammocks, from northeastern Florida to Liberty and Franklin counties.

*Gordonia lasianthus* and *Stewartia malacodendron,* although closely related, are easily distinguished. The former has leathery, dark green, glabrous, and persistent foliage, its white flowers with yellow stamens. The latter has membranous, light green leaves which are hairy below, its white flowers with purplish stamens. The symmetrical crown, glabrous, glossy, dark green, leathery evergreen leaves with blunt appressed teeth, and showy white flowers distinguish the loblolly-bay.

x ²⁄₃

Fig. 155. *Gordonia lasianthus*

## STEWARTIA

1. **Stewartia malacodendron** L. Virginia stewartia; silky camellia

This shrub or small tree is inconspicuous except during its early summer flowering period. It is then a plant of great beauty.

The leaves are simple, alternate, deciduous, 2 - 3½ inches long by 1 - 2 inches wide. The blades are membranous, oblong-ovate, elliptic, or oval. Their bases are rounded or cuneate, the apices acute or acuminate, the margins serrate, the teeth sometimes bristle-tipped, and they are softly pubescent below.

The young twigs and the buds are silky-pubescent with straight hairs.

The flowers of the silky camellia are uncommonly beautiful. They are large, about 2½ inches across, are borne singly in the leaf axils but with the peduncles turned so that they all extend in one plane above the leaves, the branches, then, appearing like floral sprays. They have 5 large, spreading, creamy-white crinkled petals, numerous stamens with purple filaments and bluish anthers making a highly decorative center, and a pistil with a 5-locular ovulary, and 5 united styles.

The fruits are depressed-globular, pubescent capsules, about ⅔ inch across, splitting into 5 parts at maturity.

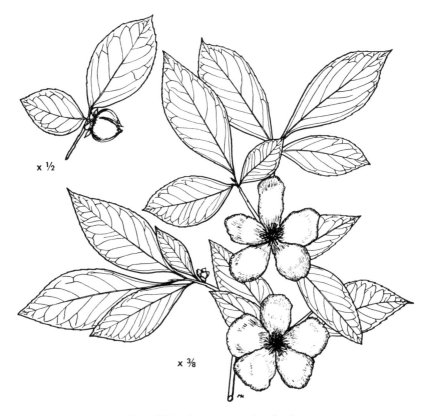

x ½

x ⅜

Fig. 156. *Stewartia malacodendron*

This plant occurs as an understory shrub or tree in rich, acid woodlands. It is known to us in the following counties of western Florida: northwest of Lake Talquin in Gadsden County; Laurel Hill, Okaloosa County; southeast of DeFuniak Springs, Walton County; and eastern slopes of the Escambia River in Santa Rosa County. Coker and Totten (1945) report it for Round Lake, Jackson County.

In bloom, *Stewartia malacodendron,* with its sprays of large, creamy-white flowers with purplish centers, is unmistakable. Without flowers, it is not easily recognized by the casual observer. This and the loblolly-bay (*Gordonia lasianthus*) are our native representatives of the plant family to which the Asiatic camellias of commerce belong. See *Gordonia.*

# ARALIACEAE. GINSENG FAMILY

## ARALIA

### 1. **Aralia spinosa** L. Devils-walkingstick

The devils-walkingstick is a shrub or small tree whose stems and leaves are prickly or coarsely spiny. Specimens are usually unbranched, sometimes with a few short, upright branches, and the huge, compound leaves on growth of the season form an umbrella-like crown. Spreading by long underground runners, clones are often formed which have the appearance of umbrellas on prickly canes.

The leaves are alternate, 2 - 3-pinnately compound, and up to 4 feet long. Leaflets are ovate, 1 - 4 inches long, with acute to rounded bases and acute to acuminate apices, the margins sharply serrate, their upper surfaces with scattered, erect-spinescent hairs. The rachi and petioles are beset with spines. The petioles are greatly enlarged at their bases, clasping and nearly encircling the stems. Frequently there are accessory leaflets in pairs, one on either side of the primary rachis where the two opposite secondary rachi arise.

The canelike stems are marked by persistent, almost completely circular leaf scars accompanied by a ring of strong prickles, even on old trunks. Eventually, the prickles are sloughed off.

The inflorescence is a very large, terminal, compound panicle 2 - 4 feet long, the ultimate division of which are umbels of small, greenish-white, unisexual and bisexual flowers. These are visited by bees and other insects in very large numbers.

Fruits are juicy, black, globose drupes, about ⅛ inch in diameter; these are crowned with the persistent style bases.

The devils-walkingstick occurs in low hammocks, moist thickets along streams, low ground of rich woods, and frequently even in well-drained sites, throughout northern Florida. It serves as a picturesque ornamental, but spreads freely and is thus hard to confine.

The characteristic prickly, canelike stems marked by ring-scars and crowned by an umbrella-like canopy of very large 2 - 3-pinnately compound leaves make this tree easily identifiable.

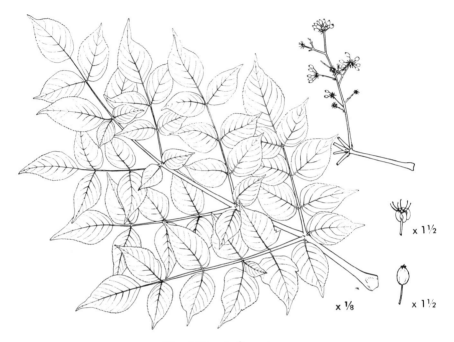

x 1½

x ⅛            x 1½

Fig. 157.   *Aralia spinosa*

# CORNACEAE.  DOGWOOD FAMILY

## CORNUS.  DOGWOODS

The dogwoods are small trees or shrubs with opposite leaves (alternate in one species). The leaves are simple, deciduous, pinnately veined, the lateral veins arch-ascending, their upper extremities more or less paralleling the margins. A significant characteristic of a dogwood leaf is that when it is torn apart crosswise the veins pull out as fine cobweb-like strands. Flowers are bisexual, epigynous, small, white or yellowish-green, have perianth parts in 4's, 4 stamens, a 2-celled ovulary. Each locule of the ovulary bears an ovule but the fruit is often 1-seeded. The fruit is a berry-like drupe.

1. Leaves alternate..............................................................................1. *C. alternifolia*
1. Leaves opposite.
    2. Flowers yellowish-green, in a compact cluster surrounded by four large, white, petal-like bracts (the whole cluster with its bracts popularly known as a flower); fruits red, in a tight cluster..........................................2. *C. florida*
    2. Flowers creamy-white, in open cymes (without showy bracts); fruits blue ..........................................................................................................3. *C. foemina*

### 1. **Cornus alternifolia** L. f.   Alternate-leaf dogwood

This is a small tree with bark which is smooth, greenish, or olive-brown and streaked with gray; the bark of the twigs is dark maroon.

x ½

Fig. 158.   *Cornus alternifolia*

The leaves are alternate, elliptic to oval, 3 - 5 inches long, their bases broadly cuneate or rounded, the apices abruptly contracted to acuminate tips. They are entire or slightly wavy, the lower surfaces whitish-glabrous or with sparse, stubby hairs. The petioles are slender, up to 2½ inches long, about ½ the length of the blades.

The flowers are small, cream-colored, borne in flat-topped or rounded, showy cymes.

Fruits are dark blue, subglobose, about ⅓ inch in diameter.

In our range, this dogwood is known to occur only in deep ravines just east of the Apalachicola River in Gadsden County.

The alternate arrangement of leaves in this species is unique for dogwood. This alternate arrangement is obvious on elongate branches, but where the leaves are crowded at the ends of twigs, it is obscure. Since basic leaf arrangement is reflected in branch arrangement, the alternate branching helps to determine this characteristic. Another distinctive feature of this tree, as compared to other dogwoods, is its slender, long petioles.

## 2. **Cornus florida** L.   Flowering dogwood

The flowering dogwood is a small, graceful, very leafy tree, most conspicuous in flower, popularly used as an ornamental, and contributing greatly to man's springtime pleasure of the countryside.

The leaves are ovate to broadly elliptic, 3 - 6 inches long by 1½ - 2½

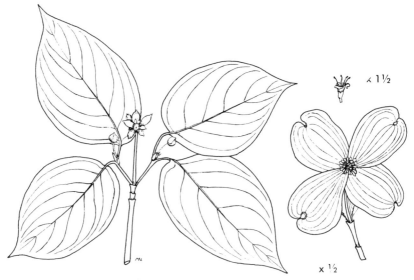

Fig. 159.   *Cornus florida*

inches broad, their bases broadly cuneate to rounded, the apices abruptly acuminate or acute. They are glabrous, or have some short appressed hairs on the lower surfaces. The petioles are short, about ¼ the length of the blades or less.

Young twigs are green, turning greenish-gray, and have a waxy bloom. The opposite leaf scars frequently encircle the stem.

Individual flowers are yellowish-green, in tight clusters surrounded by 4 large, showy white petal-like bracts. This inflorescence resembles a flower, is popularly known as such, and gives the plant its familiar name. The Latin specific name "florida," literally translated, means "flowering."

The fruits are scarlet, shiny, ovoid or oblong, about ⅓ - ½ inch in diameter, and are crowned by 4 persistent calyx lobes.

The flowering dogwood occurs naturally throughout northern Florida. Best developed in mesic woodlands, it grows in a variety of situations, relatively open pine woods, clearings, and along fence rows. Cherished by man as an ornamental, it is almost universally used as a garden tree. As such, it has a dual season attraction, in the spring season covered with garlands of white bloom and in autumn its foliage and fruits turned brilliantly red.

The wood of this beautiful tree is very hard and is highly prized for making certain small utilitarian items, not the least among which are shuttles used in the textile industry. Throughout much of its range, where not protected by law, it is harvested for these purposes. It is said that the commercially valuable trees are being cut far in excess of the annual growth rate.

The flowering dogwood is easily distinguished from other dogwoods by its tight clusters of flowers surrounded by 4 large, white bracts, or later by its tight clusters of red fruits.

### 3. **Cornus foemina** Mill. Stiffcornel dogwood

*C. stricta* Lam.

This plant is usually a shrub, but may become a small tree. We have a record of one individual in Calhoun County which is 5 inches d.b.h. and about 25 feet high.

The leaves are broadly lanceolate to ovate-elliptic or oval, up to 3½ inches long and 2 inches broad. The petioles are short, about ¼ the length of the blades, or less. The leaf bases are broadly tapering to rounded, the apices abruptly acuminate or acute. The upper leaf surfaces are smooth, glabrous, and green, the lower mostly whitish-green, glabrous, or more often with a sparse appressed pubescence. The young twigs are reddish and smooth or nearly so.

The flowers are small, creamy-white, and are borne in flat-topped or rounded cymes.

The drupes are blue, globose, about ¼ inch in diameter.

The stiffcornel dogwood is of general occurrence in northern Florida in swamps, low wet woodlands, and on river and stream banks.

*Cornus foemina* can be readily distinguished from *C. florida* by its loose, open cymes of flowers (which are not surrounded by showy white bracts), and by its loose cymes of blue fruits. Its leaf arrangement is opposite whereas that of *C. alternifolia* is alternate. In our range there is a closely related dogwood, *C. microcarpa* Nash, of fairly common occurrence in upland woodlands and mixed deciduous flatwoods. This is shrubby, rarely if ever attaining tree stature. Its twigs are hairy, the upper leaf surfaces sparsely hairy and roughish, the lower pubescent with long, spreading hairs. This is in contrast to the smooth twigs, smooth upper leaf surfaces, and glabrous or sparsely appressed pubescent lower leaf surfaces of *C. foemina*.

x ⅜

Fig. 160. *Cornus foemina*

## ERICACEAE. HEATH FAMILY

1. Leaves oval, elliptical, or oblanceolate, mostly exceeding 2 inches in length.
  2. Leaves glabrous and green.
    3. Leaf margins entire; leaves leathery and persistent; flowers borne in showy, terminal, panicled corymbs..........................................KALMIA

3. Leaf margins serrulate; leaves membranous, deciduous, sour to taste; flowers small, borne in bractless racemes which diverge more or less in one plane from a central axis, the whole inflorescence spraylike..............................................................................................OXYDENDRUM

2. Leaves rusty-scurfy...................................................................................LYONIA

1. Leaves short-elliptical, short-oval, or suborbicular, not exceeding ½ - 1¾ inches in length.........................................................................................VACCINIUM

## KALMIA

### 1. Kalmia latifolia L. Mountain-laurel

The mountain-laurel is mostly shrubby with multiple trunks; single-trunked specimens rarely attain tree stature. Along the Escambia River, west of Jay, individual plants are 20 feet high and 3½ inches in diameter. The trunks and branches are characteristically crooked and contorted and have a compact foliage system near the summits of the ultimate branches.

The leaves are simple, leathery, and evergreen, alternate or opposite, the blades 2½ - 4 inches long, 1 - 1½ inches broad, elliptic, elliptic-lanceolate, or oblanceolate, tapering to both ends, the apices sometimes acuminate. They are entire, glabrous, and have whitish calluses at their extreme tips.

The young twigs are reddish-green. Leaf scars are deeply impressed and rimmed. Above the scars and the axillary buds are visor-like scars. The bark is reddish-brown, with long shallow furrows and narrow ridges, shredding into narrow strips.

The flowers are borne in showy, terminal, panicled corymbs. The flowers are exquisite, both in bud and when fully expanded. The buds are pointed-ovoid, ridged and pebbled, and a deep rose-pink. The expanded corollas are angled-saucer-shaped, appearing like inverted starched calico skirts. They are rose-pink, delicate pink, or almost white, frequently varying thus as they age. The corollas are marked with a wavy, pink band just inside the throat, and each segment has twin pouches at base in which the anthers are at first locked and from which they later spring when the filaments are tripped by visiting bees. As the anthers spring from the pockets the pollen is catapulted out and dusts the bodies of the insects.

The fruits are dry, depressed-globose capsules, 5-celled, opening opposite the partitions separating the cells.

Much more common northward, this plant is locally abundant as an understory shrub or tree in woods on ravine slopes, along some small streams, and on wooded bluffs along the larger rivers, from Leon County westward, in the interior of western Florida.

In blossom, the mountain-laurel has no rival amongst our evergreen woody plants.  Its angled-saucer-shaped, calico-like flowers are unmistakable.  The whitish calluses on the leaf tips and visored leaf scars establish its identity otherwise.

x ⅓

Fig. 161.  *Kalmia latifolia*

## LYONIA

### 1. **Lyonia ferruginea** (Walt.) Nutt.  Staggerbush

The staggerbush is an inelegant, arborescent shrub or small tree with crooked trunks, rusty-scurfy twigs and foliage, and corky bark.

The leaves are simple, alternate, persistent, 1 - 3½ inches long by ½ - 2 inches broad.  The blades are elliptic, oval, obovate, or oblance-olate, their bases and apices rounded to acute, the tips with a blunt cartilaginous tip (mucro).  The margins are entire and revolute, but the blades ruffled or wavy.  The twigs and lower leaf surfaces are coated with grayish or rusty-scurfy scales.

The flowers are small, have a 5-lobed calyx, a subglobose-ureceolate, pinkish corolla about ⅛ inch across.  They are borne in small clusters in the axils of old leaves.

The fruit is a dry ovoid capsule about ¼ inch long.  Prior to opening, the sutures of the valves of the capsule are visible as longitudinal bands; when the capsule opens, it splits into 10 parts.

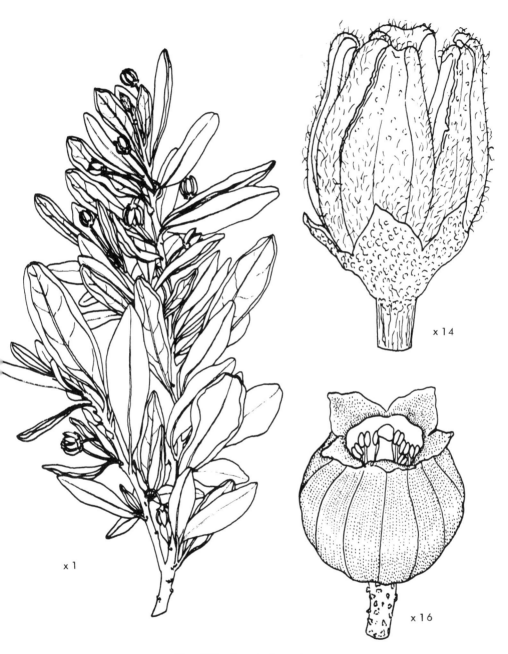

x 14

x 1

x 16

Fig. 162.  *Lyonia ferruginea*

This plant inhabits well-drained to fairly well-drained sites: dunes, sand pine-evergreen oak scrub, dry hammocks, and local slight rises in flatwoods.

In its shrubby form *Lyonia ferruginea* is easily mistaken for the closely related and similar, strictly shrubby *L. fruticosa* (Michx.) G. S. Torrey. The latter grows in wetter, poorly drained situations, and seldom attains a height of as much as 9 feet. A notable characteristic is a gradual diminution of the size of its leaves upward on stiffly ascending twigs. *L. ferruginea,* on the other hand, is commonly a small tree which inhabits drained sites, and its upper leaves do not gradually diminish in size. Its ultimate branchlets are not rigidly ascending. *Bumelia lanuginosa* and *B. tenax* also have brownish-rusty lower leaf surfaces, but this appearance is rendered by hairs, not scales. Moreover, these plants are thorny.

Bearing these points in mind, the staggerbush can be recognized by its scurfy twigs, ruffled or wavy leaves, and by the 10-parted capsules, some of which are almost always present on the older twigs.

## OXYDENDRUM

### 1. **Oxydendrum arboreum** (L.) DC.   Sourwood

This is a small, slender tree whose flowers appear in midsummer long after the leaves have completed their growth. The trunk bark is gray tinged with red and is divided by longitudinal furrows into broad, scaly ridges.

The leaves are simple, alternate, deciduous, up to 7 inches long. The blades are membranous, finely serrate (rarely entire), oblong or long-elliptical. Their bases are rounded or acute, the tips pointed. They are shining, bright yellowish-green above, paler below. The leaves have a distinctly sour taste. They become scarlet or crimson in autumn, the trees then being wondrously attractive.

The flowers are individually small and are borne on an unusual type of inflorescence. It consists of a branched raceme bearing bractless flowers, the raceme branches elongate and subequal, diverging more or less in one plane, spraylike or plumelike, from a common central axis, the spray drooping downward from the tips of branches of the tree. The flower buds and flowers hang vertically from the raceme stalks, then shortly after anthesis the stalks of the developing fruits begin to turn upward. Ultimately the mature capsules extend approximately vertically regardless of the droop of the axis. Each flower has five small, nearly distinct sepals, an ovoid-urceolate, 5-lobed white corolla about ⅓ inch long, 10 stamens, and a pistil with a 5-locular ovulary.

The fruits are small, elongate to subcylindric, angled, pubescent capsules which split into 5 parts, the splits occurring between the septae. The capsules persist into the autumn, even after leaf fall.

Fig. 163. *Oxydendrum arboreum*

This tree is sparsely scattered in woods on slopes of ravines and river bluffs of middle northern and western Florida.

The elongate, bright yellowish-green, membranous leaves of the sourwood are distinctive as are its sprays of drooping flowers or sprays of vertically oriented capsular fruits.

## VACCINIUM

### 1. Vaccinium arboreum Marsh. Tree sparkleberry

A small tree with handsome, glossy foliage and bearing a lavish supply of white bell-shaped flowers in spring.

The leaves are simple, alternate, evergreen or semievergreen, elliptic, oval, suborbicular, or obovate, ½ - 1¾ inches long. Their bases are rounded to cuneate, the tips obtuse or acute and mucronate. They are glabrous and lustrous above, glabrous below, or hairy only on the veins, and with a vein network which is prominent on both surfaces. The twigs are slender, stiff, and crooked.

The white flowers are borne in profusion on bracted or leafy-bracted racemes resembling sprays of lilies-of-the-valley. Each is bell-shaped, about ½ inch across, with a 5-lobed calyx and corolla, usually 10 stamens, and a pistil with a 10-celled ovulary. The flowers develop slowly, earlier on some trees than others; thus the season of bloom extends over several weeks.

The fruits are black berries, about ¼ inch in diameter, with a scant but pleasant-tasting pulp surrounding 8 - 10 seeds. They persist on the trees even into winter.

This tree inhabits open, sandy woods and hammocks, is apparently tolerant of a wide range of moisture conditions. It is common in our range.

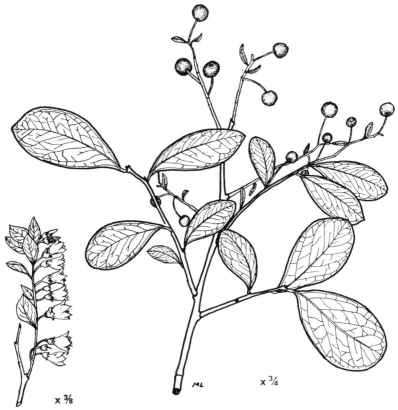

ML     x ¾

x ⅜

Fig. 164.  *Vaccinium arboreum*

The tree sparkleberry is a small tree with irregular and crooked branches, variable-shaped, small, glossy, veiny leaves. In early summer its great abundance of lily-of-the-valley-like sprays of flowers set amidst the glossy foliage renders it altogether enchanting and distinctive.

# SAPOTACEAE. SAPODILLA FAMILY

## BUMELIA

The bumelias are among the few trees of our range that have a milky juice or latex in their herbage. In this group the latex is not especially abundant. It is particularly noticeable in lush shoots or in the leaf stalks. Otherwise the parts may be squeezed to force out some of the milky juice.

Thorns are often present on bumelias and are of two kinds. Some are naked, others are leafy or are terminal leafy branch thorns. The unrelated osage-orange also has thorns and milky juice but its thorns are always naked.

On the elongated shoots resulting from rapid growth the leaves are obviously alternate. However, short, slow-growing, stubby spur-shoots are characteristic in the group and on these the leaves are approximate and appear fascicled or in false whorls. Flowers and fruits are borne mostly on the spur-shoots. After several years of flower and fruit production, the slow-growing spurs may take a spurt of rapid growth producing a branch segment with widely spaced leaves. These in turn give rise to lateral spurs. The alternating and irregularly occurring periods of accelerated and retarded growth engender a distinctive crooked and rough branch system. The short, stubby, rough spur segments provide a favorable habitat for lichens, liverworts, and mosses.

The flowers are small and pedicellate and are borne in fascicled clusters on the spurs. The sepals and pedicels are brownish, which gives the clusters a marked rusty-brownish cast. The fruit is a 1-seeded, black berry with scanty flesh. The seeds have 2 distinctive openings or scars at their bases.

1. Leaves glabrous or only sparsely hairy beneath; pedicels glabrous; plants of rich woodlands or river bottoms..................................................2. *B. lycioides*
1. Leaves tomentose beneath; pedicels tomentose; plants of dry, sandy woods or dunes.
    2. Pubescence on the lower surfaces of the leaves rusty-woolly and lusterless
    ........................................................................................1. *B. lanuginosa*
    2. Pubescence on the lower surfaces of the leaves lustrous, silvery, golden, or coppery..................................................................................3. *B. tenax*

1. **Bumelia lanuginosa** (Michx.) Pers.    Gum bumelia; false buckthorn

The gum bumelia is an irregularly shaped shrub or small tree.

The leaves are simple, alternate, and partially persistent, falling irregularly in winter. They are narrowly obovate, oblong, elliptic, or oval, 2 - 3 inches long by ½ - 1 inch broad. Their tips are rounded, obtuse, or rarely acute, sometimes mucronate, the bases cuneate. The leaf margins are entire, the upper surfaces green and shiny, the lower tomentose, becoming dull rusty-brown or tan, the short petioles and young twigs similarly pubescent.

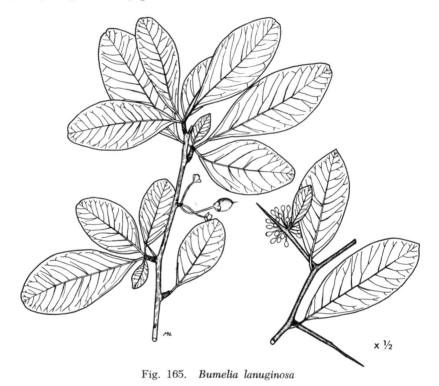

x ½

Fig. 165.   *Bumelia lanuginosa*

The flowers are small, pedicellate, and are borne in many-flowered (up to 70) clusters from leaf axils or from leafless nodes of the previous year or on the spur-shoots. The sepals and pedicels bear a conspicuous dull, rusty-brown, heavy pubescence. The petals are whitish.

The fruit is an oblong-ellipsoid or subglobose, blackish, 1-seeded berry about ⅓ inch long.

This plant inhabits dry, sandy woods, often open woods or old field thickets, throughout northern Florida.

The gum bumelia is characterized by its thorns, or thorn-branchlets, its spur-shoots, dull, rusty-brown tomentum on lower leaf surfaces, petioles, young twigs, pedicels, and calyces, and by the fascicles of numerous small flowers. *Bumelia tenax,* which is very similar, has a lustrous tomentum.

2. **Bumelia lycioides** (L.) Pers. Buckthorn bumelia; ironwood

This is a small tree with an irregular growth habit, and a flaky, brownish-red bark which is gummy and exudes a disagreeable, rancid odor when peeled.

Fig. 166. *Bumelia lycioides*

The leaves are simple, alternate, partially persistent. They are long-oval or elliptical, broadly oblanceolate, or lanceolate, commonly 5 inches long by 1 - 1½ inches broad. Their bases are long-cuneate; the apices mostly taper to an acute tip. Some leaves may be obtuse or rounded at the apex. The blades are relatively thin and the vein network is conspicuous, especially below.  The upper surface is light green, the lower pale, and both are glabrous at maturity.

The floral and inflorescence features are similar to those of *Bumelia lanuginosa* except that they are essentially glabrous.

The berries are shiny black, ovoid or obovoid, abruptly contracted into an elongated persistent style, about ¾ inch long.

The buckthorn bumelia is rare in our area.  We know it from bluffs and natural levees on the east side of the Apalachicola River in Liberty County, a swamp along the St. Mark's River in Wakulla County, and rich woods at Lake Miccosukee in Jefferson County.  At the latter station, trees reach a height of 50 feet and a diameter of 7 inches.

The thorns, or thorn-branchlets, spur-shoots, and fascicles of numerous pedicellate flowers or fruits on the twigs help to identify this tree as a bumelia.  It can be distinguished from the other two species herein treated by its glabrous, reticulate-veined leaves.

### 3. **Bumelia tenax** (L.) Willd.    Tough bumelia

The tough bumelia is a small, scrubby tree.  It appears not to differ greatly from *Bumelia lanuginosa* except that its pubescence is more appressed and conspicuously lustrous.  The pubescence is shiny pale gold, coppery, or rusty-brown.  The leaves tend to be smaller and narrower.  They are mostly about 1 - 2 inches long by ½ inch broad.

This plant occurs on the east coast dunes and in the sand pine-evergreen oak scrub of the interior.

## EBENACEAE.  EBONY FAMILY

### DIOSPYROS

### 1. **Diospyros virginiana** L.    Common persimmon

This is a medium-sized tree which in open areas sometimes spreads by underground parts and forms thickets.  The crowns are usually bushy because of their numerous ultimate branchlets.  The bark is brown to blackish, its surface rough, broken into many small blocks by longitudinal and cross fissures.

The leaves are simple, alternate, entire, deciduous, petioled, the blades oval or elliptic, 2 - 6 inches long.  The bases of the blades are cuneate to rounded (or rarely slightly cordate), the apices acute to acuminate.  The leaf surfaces are glabrous, the upper dark green and often with blackish blemishes, the lower paler and whitish.

The terminal buds not infrequently abort, following which upper axillary buds become the leaders. This results in a characteristic bushy and spraylike foliage pattern.

The flowers are unisexual or bisexual. Staminate flowers and bisexual ones occur on different plants. The bisexual ones have sterile stamens so the plants are functionally dioecious. The male flowers

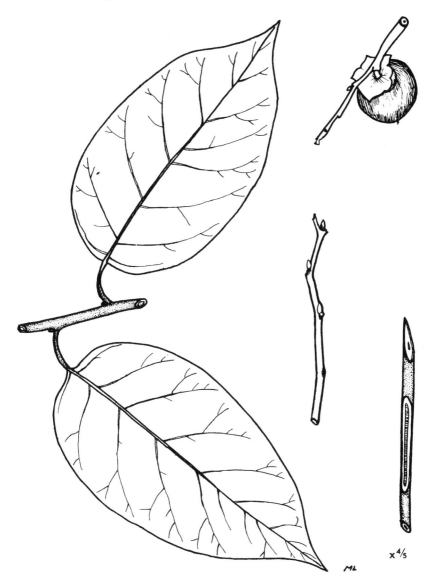

Fig. 167. *Diospyros virginiana*

are smaller and are borne in few-flowered clusters, the female larger and solitary in leaf axils. The calyx is 4 - 6-lobed, the corolla pale yellow, tubular, urn- or bell-shaped. Male flowers commonly have up to 16 fertile stamens, the female 8 sterile ones. The pistil has 4 styles, each of which is 2-lobed at the summit. The ovulary is 8-locular. The thick sepals enlarge and persist at the base of the mature fruit.

The fruit is a several-seeded, globose to depressed-globose berry, up to 1½ inches in diameter. In ripening, it changes from green to yellow, then orange, finally often becoming purplish- or brownish-black, its surface glaucous. The fruit contains several fairly large, flattened seeds. The pulp is exceedingly astringent during maturation, but becomes sweet when fully ripe and has a subtly delicious flavor. The palatability of the fruits of different trees varies widely, however, fruits of some having much more highly desirable flavors than others.

The environmental adaptability of the persimmon is extraordinary and exceeds that of any other tree in our range. It is common and grows on a wide variety of sites and is a component of many communities from seaside dunes to inland forest. It grows in open, relatively sterile, sandy woods and fields and through just about the gamut of possible places to river bottomlands.

Female trees are readily identifiable by the fleshy fruits which have persistent sepals at their bases. Male or sterile trees, however, may present difficulty to the beginner, particularly in relation to nonfruiting black tupelos. The leaves of persimmon characteristically have black blemishes on their upper surfaces and are whitish underneath. Moreover, the abortion of the terminal buds with resultant bushy twig growth is peculiar to it. (See *Nyssa sylvatica*.)

## STYRACACEAE.　STYRAX　FAMILY

1. Lateral, accessory buds superimposed, the upper two contiguous, the uppermost triangular in outline; petals 4, not at all or little spreading; fruit indehiscent, 2 - 4-winged................................................................................................*Halesia*
1. Lateral, accessory buds superimposed, the upper 2 spaced apart, the uppermost thumblike in shape; petals usually 5, occasionally 4 or more than 5, spreading or recurved; fruit globose, about half enclosed in the floral tube, dehiscent by 2 - 4 valves................................................................................................*Styrax*

### HALESIA.　SILVERBELLS

The silverbells are small trees which, in early spring as the leaves unfold, bear from the axils of the leaf scars umbels or racemes of dangling white flowers. The leaves are simple, alternate, and deciduous. The flowers have a floral tube completely surrounding and fused to the ovulary. Borne at its summit are 4 small sepals and 4 much larger showy petals which are essentially separate or partially fused into a bell-like corolla. There are 8 - 16 stamens whose filaments are in part fused into a tube which is barely inserted on the corolla. There is a single, unbranched, persistent style.

The fruits are longitudinally 2- or 4-winged, dry, indehiscent, and 1-seeded. The summit of the fruit bears the 4 small, hairy, persistent sepals, and the awl-like persistent style remains. Like the flowers, they dangle from the branches.

1. Larger leaves broadly oval, obovate, or suborbicular, rounded to broadly cuneate at their bases, abruptly short-acuminate at their tips; petals scarcely if at all fused; fruit with 2 broad wings and 2 low ridges.
   2. Flowers ⅜ - ⅝ inch long.............................................1. *H. diptera* var. *diptera*
   2. Flowers ¾ - 1¼ inch long.........................................2. *H. diptera* var. *magniflora*
1. Larger leaves elliptical, oval, or oblong, cuneate to rounded at base, gradually tapering at their summits to a prominently acuminate tip; petals fused more than half their length; fruit 4-winged...................................................3. *H. tetraptera*

### 1. **Halesia diptera** Ellis, var. **diptera.** Two-wing silverbell

A small tree with showy white, pendant flowers, the two-wing silverbell is a worthy garden ornamental. The bark is finely furrowed and ridged and sloughs in narrow plates. With the removal of the petioles, close observation reveals that the twigs bear superimposed lateral buds, the upper two of which are contiguous, the uppermost triangular in outline.

The leaf blades are broadly oval, obovate, or suborbicular, 3 - 6½ inches long and up to 4½ inches broad. Their bases are broadly cuneate or rounded, the tips abruptly short-acuminate. The leaf margins are irregularly serrate-dentate. The upper and lower leaf surfaces are both sparsely stellate-pubescent, the lower paler green than the upper.

The flowers are white, pendant, the petals essentially separate. Flowers are borne from the axils of the leaf scars in umbels of 2 - 3 or in racemes with up to 6 - 7 flowers. The corollas are ⅜ - ⅝ inch long. Flowering occurs prior to or as the leaves unfold.

The fruits vary from oblanceolate to elliptic or oblong, or more rarely they are broadly oval or suborbicular. They are from 1 to 2 inches long and are broadly 2-winged, the wings extending well below the fruit body.

In Florida this variety of the two-wing silverbell occurs in the floodplain woodlands of the Choctawhatchee and Escambia rivers.

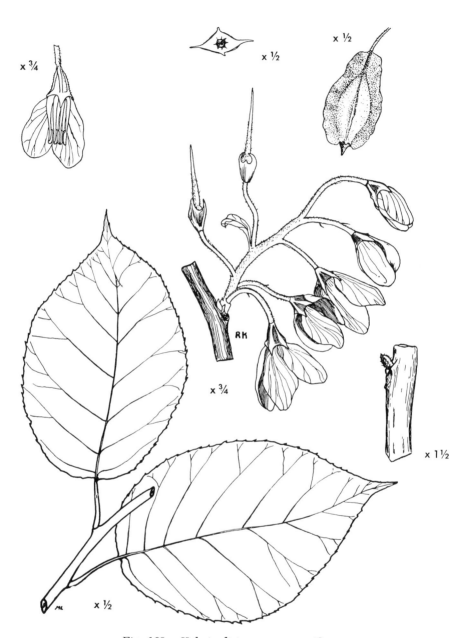

Fig. 168. *Halesia diptera,* var. *magniflora*

## 2. **Halesia diptera** Ellis, var. **magniflora** Godfrey

This variety of the two-wing silverbell grows in rich deciduous woodlands of upland or ravine slopes in the Tallahassee Red Hills, on slopes of bluffs and ravines along the Apalachicola and Chipola rivers, and in upland limestone woodlands in the vicinity of Marianna. So far as we know at present it grows elsewhere only in restricted localities of eastern Alabama. It is to be noted that its habitats are upland in contrast to the floodplain woodland habitat of the variety *diptera*. The latter ranges more widely; it occurs westward to Texas and northeastward to the Savannah River.

Aside from its distinctive habitat and restricted geographic range, the variety *magniflora* appears to differ from the variety *diptera* only in the considerably larger size of the flowers. They are from ¾ to 1¼ inches long and in fact are on the order of twice as large as those of variety *diptera* in all their proportions.

The two-wing silverbells are easily distinguished from the little silverbell by characteristics of the flowers or fruits. The former have petals which are essentially separate and a broadly 2-winged fruit. The latter has petals which are fused well over half their length and the fruits are narrowly 4-winged. The leaf characters by which they can be separated are as follows: those of the two-wing silverbell are broader, in outline broadly oval, obovate, or suborbicular, the tips short-acuminate; those of the little silverbell are narrower, more uniformly elliptic to oval, the tips tapering more gradually into acuminate apices. The lower leaf surfaces are more distinctly paler green or glaucous than the upper.

Without flowers or fruits the two-wing silverbell is very difficult to distinguish from the big-leaf snowbell, *Styrax grandifolia*. We rely on lateral bud characters to separate them. Both have superimposed buds, but the upper two of the silverbell are contiguous, the uppermost triangular in outline; the upper two of the big-leaf snowbell are spaced apart from each other and the uppermost is thumblike.

### 3. **Halesia tetraptera** Ellis. Little silverbell

*H. parviflora* Michx.

The little silverbell is a small tree with a rather tight striated bark. The twigs bear 3 superimposed, contiguous, lateral buds, the uppermost triangular in outline.

The leaf blades are elliptic, oval, or oblong, up to 4 inches long and up to about 2 inches broad. Their bases are cuneate to rounded and they gradually taper into acuminate apices. The leaf margins vary from irregularly wavy to finely serrate. Both surfaces are stellate-pubescent when young. In age the upper surfaces may be very sparsely stellate-pubescent or glabrate, the lower sparsely stellate-pubescent at least on the principal veins. The lower surfaces are distinctly paler green than the upper, or often they are whitish.

The flowers occur mostly in umbels of 2 - 3 in the axils of leaf scars. They are about ½ inch long, the petals fused for over half their length and bell-like. Since they are small and are borne in small clusters as the leaves emerge, the trees are not very showy during the flowering period as are the other Halesias.

The fruit is 4-winged, oblanceolate or obovoid in outline, the base

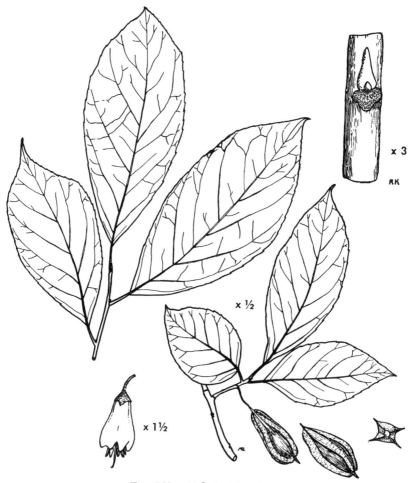

Fig. 169. *Halesia tetraptera*

narrowed and stalklike.    The fruit is about 1 inch long, exclusive of the persistent style.

In northern Florida, the little silverbell occurs on rich wooded slopes and in floodplain woods, chiefly near the major rivers, from Columbia County westward.

For distinctive features of *Halesia parviflora* and *H. diptera,* see the latter.

## STYRAX.   SNOWBELLS; STORAXES

The snowbells are shrubs or small trees which, in early spring, bear on the new shoots terminal or axillary racemes of handsome white flowers.    The twigs bear superimposed lateral buds, the upper 2 spaced apart, the uppermost thumblike.    The leaves are simple, alternate, and deciduous.    In the flowers, a floral tube is adherent to the base of the ovulary and bears a 5-lobed calyx.    The corollas consist of 4 - 8 (usually 5) white, spreading or recurved petals which are united only at base. There are 4 - 10 stamens whose filaments are fused into a short tube at base and inserted on the base of the corolla tube, and a pistil with 1 style.    The fruit is globular, dry, 3 - 4-valved and usually 1-seeded. The floral tube is persistent around the lower half of the fruit.

1.  Leaves elliptic, oval, or obovate, or the smaller ones lanceolate, up to 3 inches long and 1½ inches broad; racemes not exceeding 2 inches long......1. *S. americana*
1.  Leaves broadly oval or broadly obovate to nearly orbicular, 3 - 6 inches long; racemes 2 - 6 inches long................................................................2. *S. grandifolia*

### 1.  **Styrax americana** Lam.   American snowbell; storax

Commonly a shrub, occasionally reaching small-tree stature, the American snowbell is, at time of flowering, an ornamental plant, although not so conspicuous as the big-leaf snowbell.

The leaf blades are elliptic, oval, obovate, or the smaller ones lance-olate, up to 3 inches long and up to 1½ inches broad.    Their bases are cuneate, the tips obtuse, acute, or short-acuminate.    The leaf margins vary from entire to shallowly and irregularly dentate or serrate.    The upper leaf surfaces are dark green, usually sparsely stellate-pubescent when young and glabrate in age; the lower, pale green or grayish and vary from sparsely to copiously stellate-pubescent.

The flowers are white, about ½ inch long, the petals spreading or recurved and usually 5 in number.    Flowers are borne in terminal and axillary racemes as the leaves develop, usually with 2 - 5 flowers to a raceme, the latter not exceeding 2 inches in length.

The fruits are globose, densely short-hairy, little exceeding ¼ inch in diameter.

The American snowbell is of common occurrence in our area, generally in moist to wet situations—bottomland woods, swamps, and floodplains.

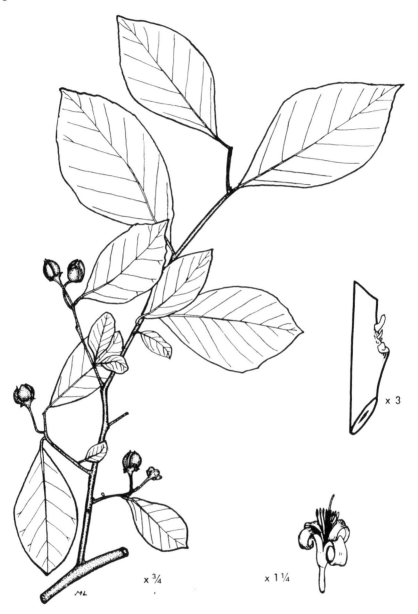

Fig. 170.  *Styrax americana*

*Styrax americana* is distinguished by its elliptic, oval, or obovate, stellate-pubescent leaves, superimposed lateral buds, the upper 2 of which are separated from each other, the uppermost thumblike. Other distinctive features are its racemes of white, mostly 5-parted flowers with spreading or recurved petals, and its globose, densely short-hairy fruits with persistent floral tubes enveloping their lower halves. Its leaves are smaller than those of S. *grandifolia*, and the racemes shorter and fewer flowered.

### 2. **Styrax grandifolia** Ait.   Big-leaf snowbell

Usually a shrub, but occasionally with the dimensions of a small tree, the big-leaf snowbell is conspicuous and pretty when in bloom.

The leaf blades are broadly oval, obovate, or nearly orbicular, 3 - 6 inches long, and up to 5 inches broad. Their bases are broadly cuneate or rounded, the tips mostly abruptly short-acuminate. The leaf margins vary from nearly entire to irregularly dentate. The upper leaf surfaces are dark green and glabrous, the lower pale green and stellate-pubescent, copiously so when young, sparsely so at maturity.

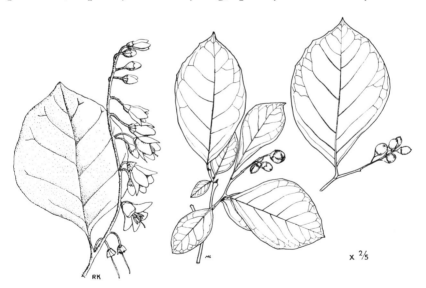

Fig. 171.  *Styrax grandifolia*

The foliage is very similar to that of *Halesia diptera*, and without flowers or fruits the two are difficult to distinguish. There is a difference in position and shape of the 2 - 3 superimposed lateral buds. In *Halesia diptera* they are contiguous; in *Styrax grandifolia* there is a definite space between the upper two. The uppermost of the buds in *Halesia diptera* is triangular in outline; that of *Styrax grandifolia* is thumblike in shape.

The flowers are white, about ¾ inch long, the petals spreading or recurved and usually 5 in number. Flowers are borne in terminal and axillary racemes as the leaves develop, up to 12 flowers on each raceme, the latter 2 - 6 inches long.

The fruits are globose, densely short-hairy, about ½ inch in diameter.

The big-leaf snowbell is not abundant anywhere in our range and is of limited distribution. It occurs in well-drained, rich woodlands of ravines and river bluffs in the Tallahassee Red Hills area, the Apalachicola River hills, and southeast of DeFuniak Springs in the lower Choctawhatchee River area.

*Styrax grandifolia* is distinguished by its broadly oval, obovate, or nearly orbicular, short-acuminate, stellate-pubescent leaves, and superimposed lateral buds, the upper 2 of which are separated from each other, the uppermost thumblike, and by its racemes of white, mostly 5-parted flowers with spreading or recurved petals, or by its densely short-hairy, globose fruits with persistent floral tubes enveloping their lower halves. The leaves are larger than those of *S. americana*, and the racemes are longer and have more and larger flowers.

## SYMPLOCACEAE.  SWEETLEAF  FAMILY

### SYMPLOCOS

1. **Symplocos tinctoria** (L.) L'Her.   Common  sweetleaf; horse-sugar

This is a shrub or a small tree with ascending branches and a spreading crown.

The leaves are simple, alternate, in our area persisting until just before (or through) the time of flowering in early spring. The leaf blades are oblong, elliptic, or oblanceolate, up to 6 inches long, tapering at base, their apices acute to short-acuminate. The margins are entire, slightly wavy, or with shallow serrations or dentations. The upper surfaces have remote, very short hairs, the lower a more pronounced pubescence of slightly longer and more abundant hair. In summer the leaves are bright green; they gradually become yellowish-green through the winter, especially along the midribs. Tissues of the old leaves, especially tissues near the midribs, are sweet to the taste. The twigs are reddish, but clothed with a sparse gray pubescence which often makes them appear ashy. An ash-colored bloom may also be present on the twigs.

The flowers are bright yellow to creamy-yellow, relatively small, and are borne in conspicuous clusters either in the leaf axils or at the leafless nodes. If the leaves, or most of them, happen to have fallen prior to flowering, the clusters of flowers make the plants fairly showy in early spring.

x 5

x 1¼

x ⅔

x ⅔

Fig. 172. *Symplocos tinctoria*

The fruits are drupelike, becoming dry at maturity. They are short-pedunculate, cylindric-ellipsoid, reddish-brown, about ⅓ inch long, and are clustered on the stems.

This plant inhabits rich, open woodlands of slopes, bluffs, hammocks, and old wooded dunes throughout northern Florida. In closed woodlands it is more distinctly evergreen, retaining most of its leaves through the flowering period and during the unfolding of the new leaves. In more open places, they may be essentially defoliated by the onset of the flowering period.

With or without foliage, the common sweetleaf is distinctive in spring because of its conspicuous, close-set axillary clusters of yellow or creamy-yellow flowers. At other times, the nearly cylindric clusters of short-pedunculate fruits, or the firm, sweet-tasting leaves, which usually have yellowish midribs, are distinctive.

## OLEACEAE. OLIVE FAMILY

1. Plants deciduous, the leaves membranous.
   2. Leaves once-pinnately compound; fruits dry, single-winged........3. FRAXINUS
   2. Leaves simple; fruits thin-fleshy, drupelike.
      3. Leaves entire, oblong-lanceolate or oval, mostly 4 - 6 inches long and 2 - 3 inches broad, their apices rounded to acute.........................1. CHIONANTHUS
      3. Leaves serrate from the middle upwards, ovate or rhombic-ovate, 1½ - 3 inches long and up to 1 inch broad, their apices strongly acuminate........
      ................................................................................................2. FORESTIERA
1. Plants evergreen, the leaves thick-leathery.............................................4. OSMANTHUS

### CHIONANTHUS

1. **Chionanthus virginica** L.   Fringe-tree; old-mans-beard

This is a small tree or shrub, inconspicuous when not in flower, but in spring as the leaves unfold, having abundant drooping panicles of airy, ethereal, white or creamy-white flowers. These make it a favorite subject for home gardens.

The leaves are simple, opposite, deciduous, their blades oblong, lanceolate or oval, up to 6 inches long, and 2 - 3 inches broad, their bases gradually narrowed into straight-sided or concave wedges. The leaf apices are acuminate, acute, or broadly rounded. Their margins are entire. The upper leaf surfaces are smooth, the lower sparsely hairy to copiously soft hairy when young and smooth in age. The petioles are commonly maroon or blackish-purple, as are the nodes. The twigs are glabrous but rough to the touch, due to warty, protruding lenticels.

Flowers are bisexual or functionally unisexual, the plants dioecious or polygamous. The flowers occur in clusters on conspicuous pendant, fringelike inflorescences. The fringelike quality is given by narrow, elongate white or creamy-white petals, 4 per flower. The inflorescences have numerous green leaflike bracts which, even after the corollas are shed, give the inflorescence the appearance of small, drooping foliar twigs.

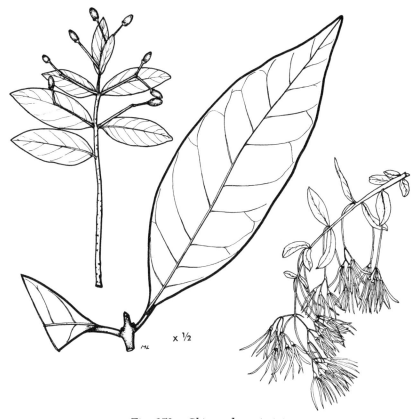

Fig. 173. *Chionanthus virginica*

The fruits are ovoid, bluish-black drupes, about ¾ inch long.

This plant is distributed generally throughout northern Florida in hammocks, rich woods, on river banks, dry bluffs, and even in low places of flatwoods.

In flower, the fringe-tree is easily recognized by its copious panicles of fringelike flowers. At other seasons, it may be recognized by its opposite, entire, deciduous leaves which have maroon or purplish petioles and nodes, and twigs with rough lenticels.   It may be confused with the American wild-olive, *Osmanthus americana*, but the former is deciduous; the latter has thick, leathery evergreen leaves.

### FORESTIERA

1. **Forestiera acuminata** (Michx.) Poir.   Swamp-privet

This is a weak, leaning shrub or a small tree.

The leaves are simple, opposite, and deciduous.   Their blades are oblong, ovate or rhombic (diamond-shape), 1½ - 3 inches long and up to 1 inch broad, tapering at both ends but with acuminate tips, the bases

x ½

x 2 ½

Fig. 174.   *Forestiera acuminata*

broadly wedge-shaped. The leaf blades are serrate from their middles upwards, their surfaces glabrous except along the midrib on the upper surface.

The flowers are bisexual or functionally unisexual, the plants dioecious or polygamous. Flowers are small and occur in clusters at the nodes along the twig, or in the leaf axils. They are greenish-yellow and have no petals.

The fruits are small, oval or ellipsoid drupes which look like soft, miniature, wrinkled sausages about ¼ inch long.

The swamp-privet is infrequent in our area. It occurs on stream banks, on bluffs, and in bottomlands from the Suwannee River westward to Jackson County.

This shrub or small tree may be recognized by its opposite, simple leaves which are more or less diamond-shaped and are serrate mostly from about the middle upward. In fruit, the tiny, wrinkled sausage-like drupes are distinctive.

## FRAXINUS. ASHES

Excepting the box-elder, *Acer negundo* (see description of this), the ashes are the only trees in our area having once-pinnately compound leaves with the opposite arrangement. Hickories, in the absence of fruits, may be mistaken for the ashes, but their once-pinnately compound leaves have an alternate arrangement. The flowers are borne in dense fascicles or in short, dense racemes or panicles on naked twigs of the previous season, prior to the development of the new leaves. They are mostly unisexual, rarely bisexual. The plants are, for the most part, dioecious. The fruit is a distinctive samara, usually with the wing in 1 plane and having 2 edges. However, in all species, occasional 3-winged samaras occur.

The taxonomy and nomenclature of *Fraxinus* has been jostled about considerably. Our field studies in northern Florida have led us to follow Little (1953) as to nomenclature, insofar as his treatment applies, with the exception of one species, namely *F. pauciflora* Nutt. Otherwise, intergradation of pubescence characteristics of leaves and fruit occurs in such haphazard fashion that we are unable to recognize the numerous varieties of the species herein treated which have been recognized by other authors.

1. Leaves whitish underneath.
    2. Trees of swamps, river banks, or low, wet places; leaflets usually 5; wing of the fruit decurrent on the seed body..................................3. *F. pauciflora*
    2. Trees of uplands; leaflets 5 - 9, usually 7; wing of the fruit not decurrent on the seed body..................................................1. *F. americana*

1. Leaves green or tawny underneath.

    3. Trees characteristically with several trunks; body of the fruit concave or flat ......................................................................................................2. *F. caroliniana*

    3. Trees characteristically with single trunks; body of the fruit round in cross-section.

        4. Stalks of the lateral leaflets ⅛ - ½ inch long, winged nearly throughout ......................................................................................................4. *F. pennsylvanica*

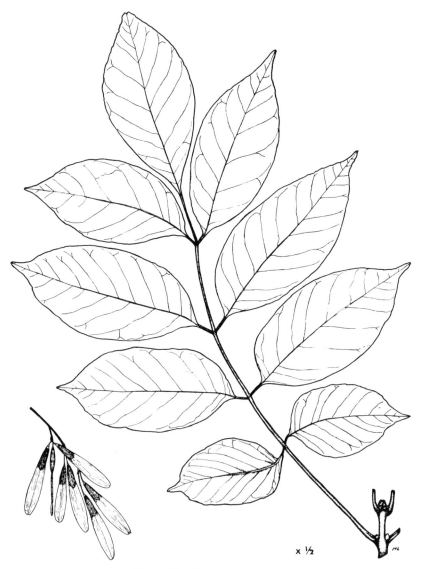

x ½

Fig. 175. *Fraxinus americana*

4. Stalks of the lateral leaflets ¼ - 1 inch long, wingless nearly throughout their entire length.................................................................5. *F. profunda*

### 1. Fraxinus americana L.   White ash

This is a large tree with rough gray bark whose ridges and furrows interlace to form a diamond pattern.

The leaves are up to 13 inches long, the leaflets 5 - 9 (usually 7), these 3 - 5 inches long, 1½ - 3 inches broad, glabrous above and below, or somewhat pubescent on and along the veins below, dark green above and conspicuously whitish below. The margins of the leaflets are entire or shallowly crenate-serrate, the bases rather abruptly narrowed and somewhat inequilateral, the apices mostly short-acuminate.

The fruit body is short and very plump and constitutes about ¼ the length of the samara. The wing is essentially terminal, not decurrent on the body of the samara, and is narrowly oblong, long-elliptical, or oblanceolate, the summit generally notched.

This is the only ash in our area which is confined to well-drained sites. It inhabits rich woodlands on upland clay or limestone, or floodplains which are never more than temporarily inundated. It is known to us from Alachua to Jackson counties.

The white ash is clearly distinguished by its short, plump fruit bodies which have terminal wings, the whitish lower surfaces of the leaflets, and the well-drained habitat.

### 2. Fraxinus caroliniana Mill.   Carolina ash; pop ash

This is a small or medium-sized tree, characteristically with several trunks which are commonly crooked or leaning.

The leaves vary greatly, being from 5 - 17 inches long, each having from 5 - 9 leaflets. The leaflets are variable in size and shape. They may be lanceolate, ovate, oblong, oval, elliptical, or obovate. The leaflets are rather abruptly narrowed and often somewhat asymmetrical at their bases, and their apices are broadly rounded, or obtuse to acuminate. Their margins are entire, remotely and irregularly crenate-serrate, to serrate. The upper surfaces are glabrous, the lower glabrous to sparsely short-hairy. Both surfaces are green, the lower somewhat paler than the upper but definitely not whitish.

The samaras are extremely variable in size and shape, perhaps more so than those of any other ash. The fruit bodies are flat or concave, usually more than ½ as long as the whole samaras, sometimes ¾ - ⅘ as long. The wings are broadly decurrent along the sides of the fruit bodies to or below their bases. The over-all shapes of the samaras vary from narrowly to broadly spatulate, linear-elliptical, broadly oblong-elliptical, broadly oval, ovate, or suborbicular.

This tree inhabits wet sites which may be inundated for long periods of time. These include river swamps, branch-swamp, flatwoods depressions, and pond margins, from Baker County westward to Escambia County.

Samaras with broadly decurrent wings to or below the bases of the fruit bodies, leaflets with green undersurfaces, and several trunks per individual plant are characteristics common to *Fraxinus caroliniana*.

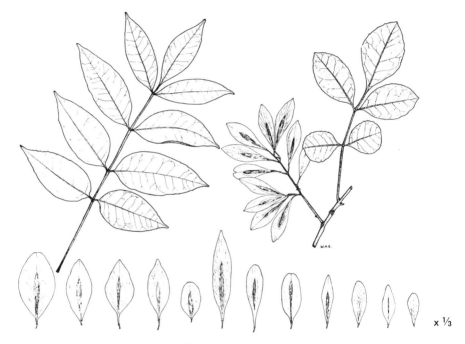

Fig. 176.   *Fraxinus caroliniana*

### 3. **Fraxinus pauciflora** Nutt.   Florida ash; swamp ash

The Florida ash is a medium-sized tree, usually with a single trunk, which reaches at least 65 feet in height and 14 inches in diameter. It is often somewhat buttressed where the bases are inundated.

The leaves vary from 5 to 14 inches long, have 5 - 7 leaflets (usually 5, and rarely 3). The leaflets are glabrous above and below, or sometimes pubescent in bands along the midribs below; the lower are generally whitish. The leaflets are not nearly so variable in size and shape as in *Fraxinus caroliniana*. They are mostly broadly lanceolate-ovate, ovate, or oblong-elliptical, their bases abruptly narrowed, the apices long-tapering and acute or acuminate.

The samaras are much less variable, too, than those of *Fraxinus caro-liniana*. The fruit body is ½ or less than ½ the length of the whole sa-mara; it is flattish but not tending to be concave. The wings are decur-rent along the seed bodies to or below their bases. The over-all shape of the samaras is fairly uniform. They are lanceolate, oblong-spatulate to spatulate, and are generally notched at their apices.

This tree inhabits swamps and wet limestone hammocks from Duval to Okaloosa counties in northern Florida.

The distinguishing combination of characteristics of the Florida ash are the swamp or wet hammock habitat, the whitish lower surfaces of the leaflets (which are often obscured in drying), samaras which are winged to or below the bases of the fruit bodies and commonly notched at the tips, and single trunks (unless injured).

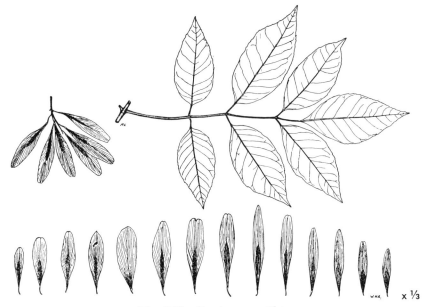

Fig. 177. *Fraxinus pauciflora*

## 4. **Fraxinus pennsylvanica** Marsh.   Green ash

The green ash becomes a large tree and has a single trunk which is buttressed when growing where inundated for long periods.

The leaves are 5 - 12 inches long and have 5 - 9 leaflets (usually 7). In shape, the leaflets are mostly oblong-elliptical, the basal and terminal ones sometimes ovate. They are mostly abruptly narrowed at their bases and acuminate at the tips. The margins are entire or irregularly and remotely toothed. Both surfaces are green, the upper somewhat darker, glabrous above and pubescent along the veins below. The leaflet stalks are short, ½ inch long or less.

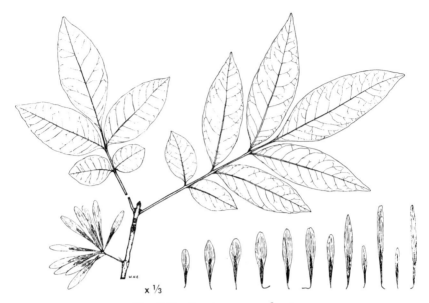

x ⅓

Fig. 178. *Fraxinus pennsylvanica*

The samaras are narrow, oblanceolate, or lanceolate to linear, rounded or notched at their apices. The fruit body, ⅓ - ½ as long as the whole samara, is long, slender and stalklike, but round in cross-section. The wing tapers upward and outward from about the middle or from just above the middle of the fruit body.

This tree occurs in river swamps and low hammocks from Columbia to Santa Rosa counties in northern Florida.

The characteristics which, taken together, help to identify the green ash are the slender, elongate fruit bodies of the samaras from about the middle of which the wings taper upward and outward, the wings themselves being mostly narrow, leaflets green above and below, and having short stalks, not over ½ inch long.

### 5. **Fraxinus profunda** (Bush) Bush.   Pumpkin ash

*F. tomentosa* Michx. f.

The pumpkin ash becomes a large tree, commonly has buttressed trunks, and has bark with interlacing ridges and furrows forming a diamond pattern.

The leaves vary from 5 - 16 inches long, the leaflets number 5 - 9 (usually 7) and are ovate, ovate-oblong, or oblong-elliptical. They are mostly abruptly narrowed, often rounded at their bases, their apices acute to acuminate. The upper surfaces of the leaflets are dark green and glabrous, the lower yellowish-green and pubescent in bands along their midribs or principal veins. The stalks of the leaflets are from ¼ to 1 inch long.

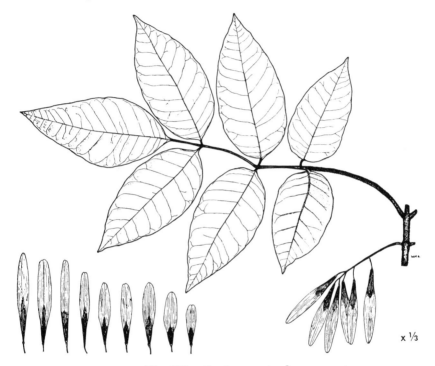

x ⅓

Fig. 179.   *Fraxinus profunda*

The samaras are narrowly oblong, oblong-elliptical, lance-oblong, or spatulate, usually notched at their apices, 1¾ - 3 inches long. The fruit body constitutes ⅓ - ¼ the length of the whole samara and is plump in cross-section. The wing of the samara extends as a narrow downward tapering edge to the base of the fruit body.

This tree inhabits muddy or mucky river swamps. It occurs in Duval County east of the St. Johns River and from Marion County in the northern part of the peninsula to Walton County in western Florida.

The pumpkin ash and Florida ash occupy similar habitats or the same habitat. The leaflets of the former are yellowish-green beneath and the bodies of the fruits are plump in cross-section. The leaflets of the latter are whitish below and the bodies of the fruit are flat.

## Osmanthus

**1. Osmanthus americana** (L.) Benth & Hook. f.   Devilwood; wild-olive

This is an evergreen shrub or small tree with pale bark.

The leaves are leathery, simple, opposite, and persistent, often persistent into the third year. The blades are elliptic, oblong-elliptic, lanceolate, or oblanceolate, variable in size, usually 4 - 5 inches long, but the larger leaves up to 9 inches in length, and up to 2 inches broad. They taper from about their middles to the bases and apices.   The

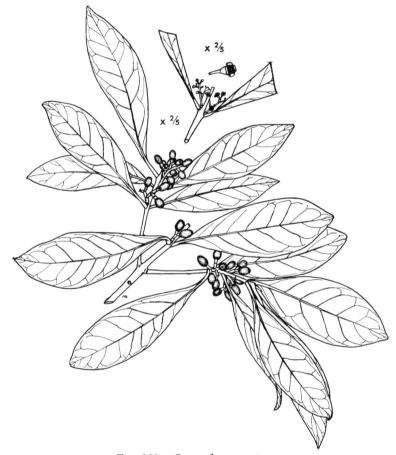

Fig. 180.   *Osmanthus americana*

apices are generally acute, more rarely short-acuminate, obtuse, or rounded, even notched. The margins are entire and revolute, the upper surfaces dark green and shiny, the lower somewhat paler and duller, glabrous.

The flowers are small, greenish- or creamy-white, and are borne in short axillary panicles, mostly on leafy twigs of the previous season. The immature flower clusters are evident in autumn and during winter. The flowers open in late winter and early spring. The calyx and corolla are 4-merous, the stamens 2.

The fruits are oval or elliptical dark blue drupes, ¼ inch or a little more in diameter. They are borne on small-bracted, jointed, thickish fruiting stalks. The fruits may persist on the plant into the year following the blooming period, and the old fruit stalks may be present even into the third year.

Although never abundant locally, the devilwood is widely distributed in northern Florida in a wide range of habitats—in sand, clay and limestone soils of rich woodlands, drained or low hammocks, upper banks of rivers, and on dunes along the Atlantic and Gulf coasts.

Distinguishing characteristics of the devilwood, which may be seen on most plants at any time, are the short, jointed, thickish flowering or fruiting panicles with small scaly bracts. Viburnums also have opposite, simple leaves, but their flowers are borne in terminal cymes and their buds are rusty-pubescent. The leaves of *Symplocos*, the sweetleaf, are similar to those of *Osmanthus*, but they are alternately arranged. The older leaves and the twigs of *Osmanthus* are generally clothed with a black sooty fungus which is an artificial, but a reliable, aid in identification.

## BIGNONIACEAE. BIGNONIA FAMILY

### CATALPA

#### 1. **Catalpa bignonioides** Walt. Catalpa; indian-bean

The catalpa usually is a small or medium-sized tree, occasionally reaching a diameter of 24 inches or more, and has a thin, scaly bark. It is locally known as caterpillar tree. Caterpillars commonly feed on its foliage and fishermen not infrequently plant the tree in the environs of their homes so that they may have a ready source of bait.

The leaves are simple, deciduous, in whorls of 3, or opposite. They are large, 5 - 11 inches long and 4 - 8 inches broad, ovate, heart-shaped, or elongate-triangular, with petioles about ½ the length of the blades. The leaf bases are slightly cordate to truncate, the apices acuminate.

Their margins are entire or wavy.　Both leaf surfaces are velvety-pubescent.

Catalpa flowers are large and showy, about 2 inches long, and are
borne in loose panicles.　Their corollas are tubular at base, bilaterally

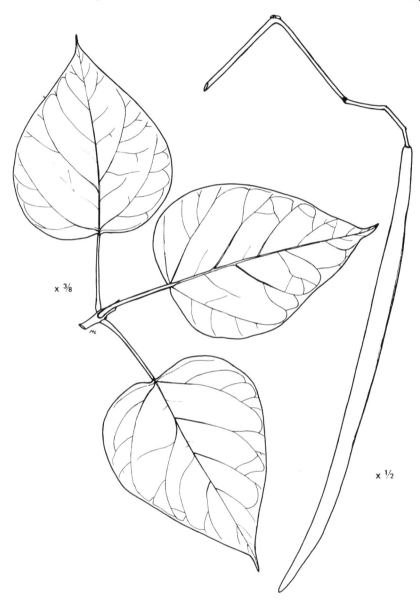

x ⅜

x ½

Fig. 181.　*Catalpa bignonioides*

symmetrical, white, marked within with yellow and brownish-purple streaks or spots.

The fruits are elongate, cylindrical, beanlike capsules which are pendant on the inflorescence branches. They are about ¼ inch broad and 12 or more inches in length. Seeds are 2-winged, the ends of the wings lacerated into fringes of long hairs. The winged seeds are about 1 inch long.

This tree is found on natural levees, banks, and on floodplains of the Apalachicola and other larger rivers in western Florida. Often it becomes naturalized in the vicinity of dwellings where it has been planted either for ornament or as a source of the caterpillars which feed upon it.

No other native tree in this area has the distinguishing features of large, ovate or heart-shaped, velvety, whorled or opposite leaves and long slender pods.

## RUBIACEAE. MADDER FAMILY

1. Flowers and fruits borne in dense globose heads; sepals minute and remaining so ............................................................................................CEPHALANTHUS

1. Flowers borne in cymose clusters; some of the sepals form greatly enlarged, conspicuous creamy to pink petal-like structures so that the inflorescence is strikingly showy; individual fruits are globose to ovoid capsules about ¾ inch in diameter ............................................................................................PINCKNEYA

### CEPHALANTHUS

1. **Cephalanthus occidentalis** L.   Common buttonbush

A scrubby shrub, or rarely a small tree, consistently confined to wet areas.

The leaves are opposite, or occasionally in whorls of 3 - 4, simple, and deciduous. Their blades are oblong-oval, broadly elliptical, or ovate, 3 - 7 inches long, entire, their bases from broadly rounded to cuneate, the apices acute to acuminate. They are glossy-green above, and the lower surfaces vary from sparsely stiff-hairy only on the veins to uniformly soft-pubescent. Triangular brown stipules occur between the petioles and these leave stipular lines on the younger twigs after being sloughed.

The buttonbush has a dishevelled, scrubby appearance owing to the dying of the leader-shoots leaving dead and dying stumps projecting. Often the subsequently developing lateral shoots are more prodigious on one side, making the plants conspicuously asymmetrical.

The twigs are reddish-brown, smooth or pubescent, and have elongate lenticels. The older bark is roughish ridged and furrowed, or bumpy. The axillary buds are deeply set and obscure; accessory buds sometimes are seen at some distance above the axillary ones.

Numerous small, tubular, white flowers with long protruding styles are closely compacted in globular heads about 1 - 1½ inches in diameter.

The individual fruits are small and angular, at maturity splitting upward into 2 - 4 nutlets. Like the flowers from which they are derived, they are borne in compact balls. These are rough-surfaced.

This plant occurs commonly throughout northern Florida in swamps, sloughs, river bottoms, on pond margins, and in wet places generally.

The buttonbush, a wet ground shrub or scrubby tree, is easily distinguishable by its opposite or whorled leaves and its white, pincushion-like balls of flowers, or by its rough balls of fruits.

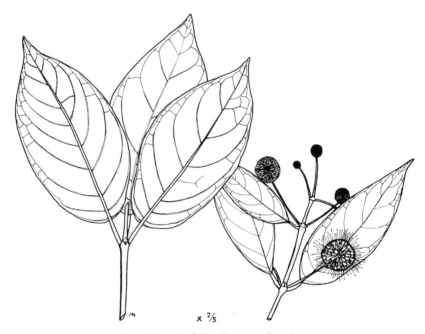

x ⅖

Fig. 182. *Cephalanthus occidentalis*

## PINCKNEYA

### 1. **Pinckneya pubens** Michx. Pinckneya; maidens blushes

This small tree or shrub is, during its flowering season, one of the most spectacularly beautiful ones occurring in northern Florida. The flower clusters are showy because of the remarkable enlargement and coloring of some of the sepals.

The leaves are opposite, simple, entire, and deciduous, their blades oval, elliptic or ovate, 4 - 8 inches long, mostly tapering toward both ends. The young twigs, petioles, and lower leaf surfaces are densely soft-pubescent, the upper leaf surfaces sparsely pubescent. Triangular stipules occur between the petioles. These fall early in the growing season, leaving stipular lines on each side of the twig between the petioles.

Flowers are borne in terminal cymose clusters. The calyx and corolla are 5-lobed, the stamens 5. The corollas are about an inch long, a dingy greenish-yellow. The pattern of growth of the sepals is extraordinary in that one on each flower expands greatly as the flowers develop, becoming creamy to rose-pink in color and thus petal-like. Since the flower clusters are relatively compact these showy sepals render the inflorescences conspicuously handsome. This effect lasts for a consid-

x ½

Fig. 183. *Pinckneya pubens*

erable period. Although deciduous, this plant has much to recommend it as an ornamental.

The fruit is a globose to ovoid, sparsely hairy capsule about ¾ inch in diameter. The surface is marked by lenticel-like whitish spots and the flattish summit is ringed by a circular perianth scar. It matures in late summer and persists on the tree into winter, at length splitting into 2 halves.

*Pinckneya* inhabits branch-bays, bays, and seepage swamps from middle northern Florida westward.

The plant is distinguished by its inflorescences, the flowers of which have showy rose-pink, petal-like sepals which last several weeks; by its 2-valved, circular-scarred capsules which persist into winter; and by its downy branchlets with stipular lines between the oppositely attached leaves.

## CAPRIFOLIACEAE. HONEYSUCKLE FAMILY

### VIBURNUM. VIBURNUM; ARROWWOOD; HAW

The viburnums are shrubs or small trees with simple, opposite leaves.

The flowers are small, white or cream-colored, 5-merous, inferior, and are borne in large numbers in terminal cymes. The fruits are drupes (ours dark blue to blue-black), each of which is crowned with 5 minute persistent sepals and the stubby remains of the styles.

Superficially, the viburnums resemble some dogwoods. However, the dogwood floral parts are in 4's, and the crown of sepals at the summit of the dogwood drupe consists of 4. Thus they may easily be distinguished in flower or fruit.

1. Leaves very lustrous (glistening-green) and smooth-surfaced above; twigs, petioles, and lower leaf surfaces densely scurfy (at least in patches) with a rusty, minute pubescence; inhabiting well-drained upland woods........4. *V. rufidulum*
1. Leaves not lustrous, dull, or if somewhat lustrous, then veiny above; twigs green or merely dotted; lower leaf surfaces glabrous, or if rusty-pubescent, then the leaves conspicuously veiny; inhabiting swamps or low grounds.
   2. The leaves small, averaging ½ - 2 inches long, mostly spatulate, narrowly obovate, or elliptic lanceolate.................................................3. *V. obovatum*
   2. The leaves much larger, averaging 2¼ - 5½ inches long, mostly long-elliptical, oval, or long-obovate to broadly oblanceolate.
      3. Leaves moderately lustrous above, veins raised below; margins conspicuously revolute; lateral veins extending outward, then abruptly forward; twigs, petioles, and lower leaf surfaces rusty-scurfy.................2. *V. nudum*
      3. Leaves dull-dark green above, veins not conspicuously raised below; margins slightly revolute; lateral veins extending gradually forward or gradually outward; twigs smooth and glabrous; lower surfaces of the leaves rusty-scurfy when young, becoming light green with scurfy dots in age.................................................................................1. *V. cassinoides*

### 1. **Viburnum cassinoides** L.  Witherod viburnum

This *Viburnum* is usually a shrub.  Occasionally it attains the dimensions of a small tree.

The leaves are long-elliptic, oblong, ovate-oblong, obovate, or broadly lanceolate, 1½ - 6 inches long by ½ - 1½ inches broad, the bases gradually tapering to rounded, the apices acute to short-acuminate.  Their margins are shallowly and irregularly crenate-undulate to entire, revolute, but not prominently so.  They are submembranous, dull-dark green above, rusty-scurfy below when young, becoming pale green with scurfy dots in age.  The principal lateral veins of the leaves extend gradually forward and outward from the midribs, or outward, but do not show, for the most part, pronounced curves.  The veins below are not conspicuously elevated.  The young twigs are smooth and glabrous.

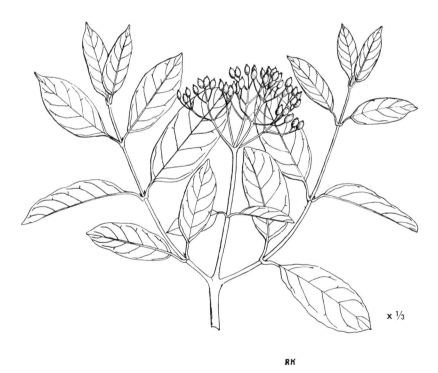

x ⅓

RK

Fig. 184.  *Viburnum cassinoides*

Cymes are peduncled, often short-peduncled, 1¼ - 4½ inches broad. Flowering occurs in spring.

The fruits vary from whitish-yellow, pink, to glaucous-blue-black during maturation.   They are globose to ellipsoid, sweet at maturity.

This shrub occurs in swamps, flatwoods, bays, and branch-bays, often
associated with *V. nudum*.   In Florida, we have seen it from Tallahassee
westward.

For comparative notes see *Viburnum nudum*.

### 2. **Viburnum nudum** L.   Possum-haw viburnum

This shrub or small tree is superficially similar to the witherod viburnum.

x ⅓

Fig. 185.   *Viburnum nudum*

The leaves are long-elliptic, oval, long-obovate, occasionally broadly
oblanceolate, 1½ - 5½ inches long by ½ - 2¾ inches broad.   Their bases
are mostly gradually cuneate, rarely rounded, the apices abruptly
acuminate to acute, rarely rounded.   Their margins are entire or slightly

wavy, rarely crenate-dentate, prominently revolute. They are thickish, conspicuously veiny, the principal veins elevated on the lower surfaces, the main veins strongly curved soon after branching from the midribs. The twigs, petioles, and lower surfaces of the leaves are more or less rusty-scurfy, especially when young. The upper surfaces are moderately lustrous.

Cymes peduncled, with 4 - 5 principal branches, 1½ - 5½ inches broad. Flowering occurs in spring.

The fruits vary from pink to red during maturation, finally becoming deep blue with a waxy bloom. They are globose to elliptical, about ½ inch long, bitter at maturity.

This shrub or small tree occurs in swamps, flatwoods, bays and branch-bays throughout northern Florida.

The stalked peduncles of the cymes and the usually entire leaves are common to *Viburnum nudum* and *V. cassinoides* and serve to distinguish them from the other viburnums. These two are much alike, often occur together, and are not infrequently misidentified. In general, the leaves of *V. nudum* are thickish, moderately lustrous above, rusty-scurfy below even in age. The principal lateral leaf veins curve outward from the midribs, then extend forward more or less at right angles and anastomose toward the leaf margins. Those of *V. cassinoides* are submembranous, or at least thinnish, dull above, somewhat rusty-scurfy when young but becoming pale green with scurfy dots below in age. The principal lateral veins extend gradually forward, then anastomose toward the leaf margin. The leaf margins are much less revolute than those of *V. nudum*.

### 3. Viburnum obovatum Walt.  Walter viburnum

This is a small tree, stiff-branched, and having stubby, spurred twigs.

The leaves are chiefly oblanceolate, obovate, or spatulate, varying to elliptic or suborbicular. They are 1 - 2½ inches long by ¼ - 1¼ inches broad, their margins revolute, entire or irregularly crenate-dentate from about the middle upward. The upper surfaces are glabrous, the lower with glistening scurfy-glandular dots.

The cymes are essentially sessile, with 2 - 5 (4) primary branches, 1½ - 2½ inches broad. Flowering occurs in early spring as the leaves develop.

The fruits are spherical, ovoid, or elliptic, about ¼ inch in diameter, passing from red to black in maturation.

This tree is common on floodplains, in low woods, and on stream banks throughout northern Florida.

The small, predominantly oblanceolate or obovate leaves, their bases narrowing imperceptibly into the petioles, and with crenate-dentate upper margins, mark this tree.   Its leaves resemble somewhat those of *Ilex decidua,* but the latter has alternate leaves whereas those of the viburnums are opposite.

x ⁴/₅

Fig. 186.   *Viburnum obovatum*

#### 4. **Viburnum rufidulum** Raf. Rusty black-haw

The rusty black-haw is a small tree or shrub having handsome glistening-lustrous foliage and bark which is peculiarly checkered into small blocks.

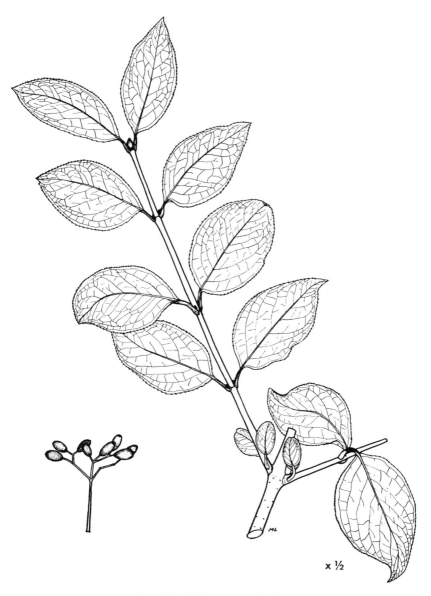

Fig. 187. *Viburnum rufidulum*

The leaves are mostly oval or broadly elliptical, varying to suborbicular, ovate, obovate, or lanceolate. The petioles, often broadly winged, are prominently rusty-red-satiny. Leaf bases are rounded to broadly cuneate, the apices mostly rounded or obtuse, often retuse, varying to acute or short-acuminate. The leaf margins are finely and sharply serrate. The upper leaf surfaces are glistening-lustrous; on the lower surfaces there is a loose, rusty-red tomentum most prominent on the veins, but with some of it between them. This sloughs off in age, yet some is nearly always present.

Young twigs and buds, as well as the petioles, etc., have the rusty-red pubescence. Twigs of the season characteristically have at their bases, in spring, at least, a pair of very small leaves which are orbicular or elliptic, notched at the apex.

The cymes are very attractive, essentially sessile, 2 - 4 inches broad, the primary branches 3 - 5 (4). The height of bloom occurs at about the time the leaves are fully expanded.

The fruits are dark blue to purple and glaucous when ripe, globose to ellipsoid, about ½ inch long, ripening in midsummer.

*Viburnum rufidulum* occurs in upland, well-drained woods. It is not anywhere abundant in our range, but occurs from the Suwannee River westward.

There is a considerable variation in size and shape of leaves; vigorous shoots or sprouts frequently have leaves so narrow they scarcely resemble those characteristic of mature branches. Their opposite arrangement, lustrous upper surfaces, fine serration, and rusty-red pubescence, taken together, make it easy to identify such shoots and sprouts with the typical adult.

Although deciduous, fine specimens of this small tree are so attractive that it is difficult to understand the reason for its not being used as an ornamental.

# Glossary

**Accessory buds.**—Buds which may be present in addition to the usual axillary bud. These may occur one on each side of the axillary bud or directly above it.

**Achene.**—A small, dry, indehiscent, 1-seeded fruit.

**Acuminate.**—An angled base or apex whose sides are somewhat concave and that tapers to a point.

**Acute.**—Terminating in a sharp or well-defined angle, usually less than 90 degrees. See obtuse.

**Alternate.**—As here used, an arrangement of leaves or branches such that one is borne at a given place on a stem, i.e., one at a node.

**Apetalous.**—Having no petals.

**Arborescent.**—Approaching the dimenmensions of a tree.

**Arcuate.**—Moderately curved or arching.

**Armed.**—Beset with spines, prickles, or thorns.

**Attenuate.**—Gradually tapering to a narrow tip or base.

**Axil.**—The upper angle formed by the juncture of two parts.

**Axillary bud.**—The bud occurring in the axil of a leaf or above a leaf scar.

**Bays.**—As here used, areas of predominantly evergreen shrubs, trees, and vines forming impenetrable thickets in depressions, on pond margins, and along small streams or branches.

**Berry.**—A fleshy fruit with the pulp surrounding the seeds; in popular usage any small fleshy fruit irrespective of structure (here called berry-like).

**Bilateral.**—Here referring to the symmetry of the flower. A bilaterally symmetrical flower can only be divided longitudinally in one plane to yield two identical halves. See radial.

**Bisexual.**—Flowers having both stamens and a pistil or pistils.

**Blade.**—The expanded part of a leaf or one of its subdivisions.

**Bloom.**—A whitish powdery or waxy covering of the surface; glaucousness.

**Bract.**—A much-reduced leaf or a leaf-like structure, generally subtending either a flower or fruit, a stalk of a flower or fruit, a primary branch of a flower or fruit cluster, or a head; a petal-like structure subtending a flower cluster.

**Branch-swamp or branch-bay.**—A swamp or bay associated with a brook or small stream.

**Branchlet.**—A terminal portion of a branch. Here used to designate the growth of the current year and one or two preceding years.

**Calcareous.**—Said of soils with obvious lime content as indicated by underlying or outcropping limestone.

**Calyx.**—The sepals of the flower, taken collectively, whatever their form.

**Capitate.**—Aggregated into a compact headlike cluster.

**Capsule.**—A dry dehiscent fruit which splits at maturity along two or more longitudinal sutures or along one transverse suture.

**Carpel.**—A structural unit of a pistil. A flower may have a pistil composed of a single carpel, several pistils each being a single carpel, or two or more carpels wholly or partially united.

**Carpellate.**—Possessing carpels, but not stamens, and producing fruits. Female.

**Catkin.**—A more or less compact spike of mostly unisexual and apetalous flowers. Referring generally to the peculiar inflorescences of trees such as the willows, oaks, poplars, walnuts, hickories, etc. Commonly the flowers in a given catkin are of but one sex.

**Climax forest.**—The ultimate forest

295

which develops on an area left undisturbed.

Clone.—A group of plants propagated by vegetative means and derived originally from a single plant.

Compound.—Composed of two or more similar parts forming one whole; here mostly used to refer to two or more similar leaflets which form a leaf blade.

Cordate.—Heart-shaped; with a sinus and rounded lobes on either side at the base.

Corolla.—The petals of the flower taken collectively, whatever their form.

Corymb.—A more or less flat-topped or rounded flower cluster in which the longer-stalked outer flowers open first.

Crenate.—Shallowly round-toothed or shallowly scalloped.

Cuneate.—Wedge-shaped.

Cuspidate.—Tipped with a sharp firm point or cusp.

Cyme.—A more or less flat-topped or rounded flower or fruit cluster in which the central flower blooms first, next the central flower of a primary branch (if any), etc.

Deciduous.—Falling off during or after the end of the growing season, in contrast with persistent or evergreen.

Decurrent.—Extending downward, as the blade of a leaf extending downward on either side of the petiole as wings or, in sessile leaves, down the stem.

Dehiscent.—Opening along a suture or sutures as in the case of a fruit.

Deltoid.—Triangular; delta-like.

Dentate. — Margined with saw-teeth pointing outward, in contrast to serrate in which the saw-teeth point forward.

Dioecious.—Flowers unisexual, the staminate and pistillate borne on separate plants of the same species.

Doubly serrate.—Having marginal forward-pointing teeth which in turn bear smaller teeth.

Drupe.—A stone fruit, with the inner portion or portions hard and the outer portion soft and fleshy, as a cherry. The several stony portions of a fleshy-stony fruit as in holly are called nutlets.

Ellipsoid.—A solid with an elliptical outline.

Elliptic, elliptical.—In outline, widest at the middle and curving similarly to either extremity.

Emarginate.—Having a shallow notch at the summit.

Epigynous.—Said of a flower the perianth parts and stamens of which arise from approximately the summit of the ovulary.

Evergreen.—Remaining green overwinter; sometimes shedding leaves all at once before new growth appears.

Falcate.—More or less sickle-shaped.

Fascicle.—A close cluster.

Floodplain.—More or less flat valley of a stream, subject to flooding.

Follicle.—A podlike fruit opening only along one side, longitudinally.

Glabrate.—Becoming glabrous, i.e., losing hairiness during maturation.

Glabrous.—Not pubescent or hairy.

Glandular.—Bearing secreting structures or glands. Often used to describe a surface on which resinous or sticky globules are exuded.

Glaucous.—Said of a surface covered with a whitish substance, commonly waxy, which easily rubs off.

Globose.—Spherical or nearly so.

Hypogynous.—Said of a flower the perianth parts and stamens of which arise from below the ovulary or ovularies.

Imbricated.—Overlapping, either vertically or spirally.

Incised.—More or less sharply, deeply, and irregularly cut or slashed, as if with scissors.

Indehiscent.—Not opening; remaining persistently closed.

Inferior.—Refers to the position of the ovulary with respect to the other floral parts, i.e., the other floral parts are above the ovulary.

Inflorescence.—Mode of flower-bearing; flower cluster.

Internode.—The portion of a stem between two nodes.

Involucre.—A series, often overlapping, or a whorl of small leaves or bracts standing close underneath a flower, a cluster of flowers, or a fruit.

Lanceolate.—In outline, several times longer than wide, the widest part toward the base and tapering toward the apex.

Lateral bud.—Any bud along the stem below the terminal bud; often used for axillary bud, but may include accessory buds.

Leaflet.—A single division of a compound leaf, or a primary division of a leaf which is more than once compound. In the case of a leaf which is twice or several times compound, the actual blade may be referred to as the "ultimate" leaflet.

Leaf scar.—A scar on the stem left by the fallen leaf.

Legume.—A fruit which dehisces longitudinally along two sutures, the product of a unicarpellate ovulary, and having one or more seeds borne longitudinally along one suture.

Lenticel.—Corky spots or openings on the bark of young twigs or branchlets.

Levee.—As here used, a ridge, formed naturally, paralleling a stream at its bank. It is built up by deposit of debris, sand, silt, etc., from overflow of the stream.

Linear.—In outline, long and narrow with approximately parallel sides.

Lobe.—Any part or segment of an organ, as a part of a sepal, a petal, a leaf, or a bract, that is significantly divided.

-locular.—Having locules, e.g., 3-locular.

Locule. — The cavity of an ovulary. Sometimes referred to as a cell.

Lustrous.—With a metallic gloss.

-merous.—In composition, having parts of a kind; as corolla 5-merous, having 5 petals.

Mesic.—Said of a habitat with medium moisture conditions.

Mesophytic.—A plant or community of plants living under moderate or medium moisture conditions.

Monoecious. — Flowers unisexual, both kinds borne on the same plant.

Mucro.—A short, narrow, abrupt tip.

Mucronate.—An apex with a short, narrow abrupt tip or mucro.

Nerve.—As here used, a prominent vein.

Node.—The position upon a stem which bears (or bore) a leaf.

Nut.—A 1-seeded hard and bony indehiscent fruit.

Nutlet.—A small, 1-seeded indehiscent fruit with a hard, bony covering (sometimes covered with fleshy tissue as in the hollies).

Oblanceolate.—In outline, several times longer than wide, the widest part toward the apex and tapering toward the base.

Oblique.—Unequal-sided.

Oblong.—In outline, two to several times longer than broad and with nearly parallel sides.

Obovate.—Egg-shaped in outline, with the broader portion toward the summit.

Obtuse.—Blunt-pointed or angled at the extremity, not acute.

Opposite.—As here used, an arrangement of leaves or branches such that two are borne on opposite sides of a stem, i.e., two at a node.

Orbicular.—Circular in outline.

Ovary.—See Ovulary.

Ovate.—Egg-shaped in outline, with the broader portion at the base.

Ovoid.—A solid with an ovate outline.

Ovulary.—The basal, usually enlarged, portion of the carpel or pistil bearing the ovules within it. The same as "ovary" as used with reference to plants.

Ovulate.—Bearing ovules. Here referring to the female cones of a Gymnosperm (which do not possess ovularies).

Ovule.—The structure or body within an ovulary which after fertilization and maturation is called the seed.

Oxbow.—Curved, more or less abandoned or cutoff stream channels which form basins of standing or fluctuating water.

**Palmate.**—Veined, lobed, or divided in a radiating fashion; equal veins, lobes or leaflets arising from approximately the same position.

**Panicle.**—A branching raceme; an inflorescence or flower cluster in which the branches or their subdivisions are racemes, the flowers stalked.

**Papillae.**—Minute nipple-shaped projections. A surface bearing them is said to be papillose.

**Papilionaceous.**—Literally, like a butterfly; usually applied to the corolla of a pea-type flower with the upper or odd petal (standard) larger than the others and enclosing them in the bud, two lateral ones (wings) oblique and exterior to the two lower which converge and are united along their lower edges forming the keel.

**Peduncle.**—The stalk of a flower (or fruit) borne singly or the primary stalk of a flower (or fruit) cluster.

**Perianth.**—The calyx and corolla of a flower, taken collectively, or one or the other if one is absent, whatever their form.

**Persistent.**—Said of leaves that remain overwinter (evergreen) and of flower parts and fruits that remain attached for protracted periods of time.

**Perigynous.**—Said of a flower in which there is a cuplike or urnlike structure surrounding the ovulary or ovularies (but not fused to them) and from which the perianth parts and stamens arise.

**Petal.**—A unit of the corolla or inner floral envelope, standing between the stamens and sepals. Usually said when the base of the corolla is not tubular; when it is tubular the free portions, if any, are spoken of as corolla lobes.

**Petiole.**—The leaf stalk, or the primary stalk of a compound leaf.

**Petiolule.**—The stalk of a leaflet.

**Pinnate.**—A type of leaf compounding or of vein arrangement in which the secondary components (leaflets or

lateral veins) arise from a common axis.

**Pistillate.**—Possessing pistils, but not stamens, and producing fruits. Female.

**Polygamous.**—Having bisexual and unisexual flowers on the same plant.

**Pome.**—A fruit having several tough papery-walled cavities each containing seed, the cavities surrounded by a thick flesh. Shrunken sepals and stamens may persist at the summit of the fruit. An apple is typical.

**Pubescence.**—Hairiness (as here used).

**Pubescent.**—Having hairs (as here used).

**Pulvinus.**—Swollen base of a petiole or petiolule, usually sharply defined and a different shade of green, of leaves of plants in the legume family.

**Punctate.**—With translucent or colored dots, depressions, or pits.

**Raceme.**—An elongated inflorescence in which the flowers are stalked and borne on a single axis.

**Rachis.**—The primary axis of a pinnately compound leaf, or of an inflorescence.

**Radial.**—Here referring to the symmetry of the flower. A radially symmetrical flower can be divided longitudinally in more than one plane and yield two identical halves.

**Ranked.**—Arranged in rows or series, as leaves 2-ranked, i.e., arranged in two rows on the stem.

**Reticulate.**—In the form of a network.

**Revolute.**—Rolled backward from the margin (margin of leaf rolled under).

**Rhombic.**—Shaped like a rhomboid, a parallelogram with equal sides, having two oblique angles and two acute angles.

**Rich woods or woodlands.**—As here used these are areas of mixed hardwoods with a good representation of understory trees. The habitat is characterized by a fertile, moist, but well-drained soil with a high humus content. In summer the shade is dense.

**Rugose.**—Wrinkled surface, usually as a consequence of the veins being elevated or depressed.

**Samara.**—An indehiscent fruit having a prominent wing or wings.

**Sapling.**—A young tree.

**Scabrous.**—Significantly rough to the touch.

**Sepal.**—A unit of the calyx or outer floral envelope. Usually said when the base of the calyx is not tubular; when it is tubular the free portions, if any, are spoken of as calyx lobes.

**Serrate.**—With the margin saw-toothed, the teeth pointing forward.

**Serrulate.**—Finely or minutely saw-toothed, with teeth pointing forward.

**Sessile.**—Without a stalk, as a leaf lacking a petiole, or a flower without a peduncle or pedicel.

**Sinuate.**—With the outline of the margin strongly wavy.

**Spatulate.**—Oblong, with the basal end attenuated and the summit rounded; like a spatula.

**Spike.**—An inflorescence or the division of an inflorescence in which the flowers are stalkless (sessile) or nearly so on a single axis.

**Spur.**—Here used to refer to a short, compact twig with close-set leaves, or leafscars, thus little internodal development.

**Stamen.**—A pollen-producing organ of a flower, typically composed of a threadlike filament supporting an anther at the summit.

**Staminate.**—Having stamens, but lacking pistils, and not producing fruits or seeds; male.

**Stellate.**—Starlike, having radiating arms.

**Stigma.**—The part of the carpel or pistil that receives the pollen. Generally it is somewhat sticky and of definite form at the summit of the style.

**Stipules.**—A pair of structures at the base of the petiole of certain leaves, or at the base of the blade of certain sessile leaves. Vary from minute bracts to foliaceous, sometimes form spines. Persistent with the leaves

or falling during leaf maturation.

**Style.**—The stalklike or columnar part of the carpel or pistil surmounting the ovulary and bearing the stigma or stigmas.

**Sub-.**—A Latin prefix, usually meaning "somewhat" or "slightly."

**Subulate.**—In outline, tapering from base to apex, two to several times longer than broad.

**Summer-green.**—Deciduous; with leaves only during the growing season.

**Swamps.**—Wooded wet areas associated with lakes, ponds, and streams, having fluctuating water level but with standing water present much of the time or over long periods of time.

**Syncarp.**—A fruit resulting from the ripening of several to many closely adjacent carpels or pistils of a single flower.

**Tawny.**—Brownish yellow.

**Terete.**—Having a cross-section which is circular in outline.

**Tomentose.**—Densely pubescent or hairy with matted wool-like hairs.

**Tomentum.**—A covering of dense wool-like hairs.

**Trifoliolate.**—A compound leaf having three leaflets.

**Truncate.**—Ending abruptly as if cut off transversely, as the base or apex of a leaf.

**Turbinate.**—Inversely conical like the outline of a top.

**Twig.**—A branchlet (which see), or sometimes used here more specifically as the terminal portion of the branch formed during the current year.

**Umbel.**—A flower or fruit cluster in which the flower stalks all arise at nearly the same point.

**Undulate.**—Wavy or wavy-margined.

**Unisexual.**—Flowers having stamens or a pistil (or pistils), but not both.

**Vascular bundle scars.**—The severed ends of the vascular strands in the scar left by the fallen leaf.

**Whorled.**—An arrangement of leaves or branches, or of flower parts, such that three or more are set in a circle about the axis.

# Bibliography

ARNOLD, Lillian E.
1937. Check list of native and naturalized trees in Florida. *Proc. Fla. Acad. Sci.* 2: 52-66.

BAILEY, L. H.
1949. Manual of cultivated plants, rev. ed. The Macmillan Company, New York.

BROWN, Clair A.
1945. Louisiana trees and shrubs. *Louisiana Forestry Commission Bulletin* No. 1. Baton Rouge.

CHAPMAN, A. W.
1885. *Torreya taxifolia* Arnott. A reminiscence. *Bot. Gaz.* 10: 251-254.

COKER, W. C., and H. R. TOTTEN
1937. Trees of the southeastern states, 2d ed. University of North Carolina Press, Chapel Hill.
1945. Trees of the southeastern states, 3d ed. University of North Carolina Press, Chapel Hill.

ELLIOTT, Charles N.
1931. Key to Georgia trees. *Georgia Forest Service Bulletin* 13. Atlanta.

FERNALD, M. L.
1950. Gray's manual of botany, 8th ed. American Book Company, New York.

GLEASON, Henry A.
1952. The new Britton and Brown illustrated flora of the northeastern United States and adjacent Canada, 3 vols. New York Botanical Garden, New York.

GREEN, Charlotte Hilton
1939. Trees of the south. University of North Carolina Press, Chapel Hill.

HARLOW, W. M., and E. S. HARRAR
1950. Textbook of dendrology. McGraw-Hill Book Company, New York.

HARPER, R. M.
1914. Geography and vegetation of northern Florida. *6th Ann. Rep. Fla. Geol. Surv.,* pp. 163-416, figs. 41-90, Tallahassee.

HARRAR, E. S., and J. G. HARRAR
1946. Guide to southern trees. Whittlesey House, McGraw-Hill Book Company, New York.

HUME, H. Harold
1953. Hollies. The Macmillan Company, New York.

KELSEY, Harlan P., and William A. DAYTON (eds.)
1942. Standardized plant names, 2d ed. J. Horace McFarland Company, Harrisburg, Pa.

KURZ, Herman
1927. A new and remarkable habitat for the endemic Florida yew. *Torreya* 27: 90-92.
1938. *Torreya* west of the Apalachicola River. Proc. Fla. Acad. Sci. 3: 66-67.

LITTLE, Elbert L., Jr.
1953. Check list of the native and naturalized trees of the United States (U. S.

D. A. Handbook No. 41). U. S. Government Printing Office, Washington, D. C.

MATTOON, Wilbur R.
1956. Common forest trees of Florida, 6th ed. Florida Board of Forestry, Tallahassee.

MICHAUX, Francois A.
1865. The North American silva, 3 vols. Rice, Rutter and Company, Philadelphia.

MÓWRY, Harold
1946. Ornamental trees. *Fla. Agr. Ext. Serv. Bull.*, 95, Rev. ed. Gainesville.
1955. Native and exotic palms of Florida. *Fla. Agr. Ext. Serv. Bull.* 152. Gainesville.

NUTTALL, Thomas
1865. The North American silva, 3 vols. in 2. Rice, Rutter and Company, Philadelphia.

PALMER, Ernest J.
1945. *Quercus durandii* and its allies. *Am. Midl. Nat.* 33: 514-519.
1948. Hybrid oaks of North America. *Jour. Arn. Arb.* 29: 1-48.

PEATTIE, Donald Culross
1950. A natural history of trees of eastern and central North America. Houghton Mifflin Company, Boston and New York.

SARGENT, Charles S.
1891-1902. The silva of North America, 14 vols. Houghton Mifflin Company, Boston and New York.
1933. Manual of the trees of North America, 2d ed. Houghton Mifflin Company, Boston and New York.

SMALL, John K.
1913. Florida trees. Published by the author, New York.
1933. Manual of the southeastern flora. University of North Carolina Press, Chapel Hill.

SNYDER, Ethel
1940. Florida trees. Geddes Printing House, Fort Myers, Florida.

TRELEASE, William
1924. The American oaks. *Mem. Nat. Acad. Sci.*, 20.

VINES, Robert A.
1960. Trees, shrubs and woody vines of the Southwest. University of Texas Press, Austin.

WEATHERBY, C.A.
1926. A new *Magnolia* from west Florida. *Rhodora* 28: 35-36.

WEST, Erdman, and Lillian E. ARNOLD
1956. The native trees of Florida, rev. ed. University of Florida Press, Gainesville.

# Index

134 camphor

186 Chinaberry

274 Forestiera Acuminata